Might Have Been Trams and Tramways

Tony Young

LRTA
Since 1937

Published by the Light Rail Transit Association
8 Berwick Place
Welwyn Garden City
AL7 4TU

www.lrta.org

Copyright © Light Rail Transit Association 2021

Designed by:
Transport Types
24 Heath Farm Road
Ferndown, Dorset, BH22 8JW
cisgar@btinternet.com

Printed by:
Page Bros Group
Mile Cross Lane
Norwich NR6 6SA

www.pagebros.co.uk

ISBN 978-0-948106-61-3

Tony Young has a lifelong interest in trams which he is fortunate to have been able to follow professionally. After ten years in universities in Leeds, Newcastle upon Tyne, Sheffield and Salford, he joined the fledgling SELNEC PTE in Manchester and developed early plans for light rail in the seventies. He then led the technical team which prepared the plans in the eighties for the Metrolink tram network in Greater Manchester. Then followed twenty years as a consulting engineer advising authorities on light rail proposals in the UK and abroad. He is a Fellow of the Institution of Civil Engineers, a Fellow of the Chartered Institute of Logistics and Transport and a Churchill Fellow.

Front Cover. A 'might have been tram' on a 'might have been tramway'. London County Council tram No. 1 'Bluebird' of 1931 was intended to be the prototype for a new fleet of trams for London. No more were built but Bluebird survives at the National Tramway Museum at Crich, Derbyshire. The Kingsway tram subway might have been extended to other parts of London but remained as the sole example of a tram subway in Britain. It was closed in 1952 but this ramp remains as a listed structure. *Courtesy LCC Tramways Trust, original painting by Richard Berridge*

Contents

Preface

Trams and tramways were a familiar part of urban life for three quarters of a century but then vanished in all cities and towns in Britain, with the notable exception of Blackpool. After a gap of over thirty years they re-emerged in a radically different form in the major conurbations, contributing once again to the social, economic and environmental wellbeing of urban areas.

While large numbers of 'first generation' tramways were built and operated in England, Wales, Scotland and Northern Ireland, there were some that were planned and even obtained parliamentary approval but were not built. Some links between systems that could have created more extensive networks were never built.

Only six street running 'second generation' tramways have been built but many more were planned but not progressed. Even more were aspirations of individuals or authorities which had little chance of being realised. The author was fortunate in being closely involved with the first new tramway, Metrolink in Greater Manchester, seeing it through from the 'back of an envelope' to carrying passengers. Subsequently he contributed to many studies for tramways in towns and cities throughout the country, including extensions to existing systems. Sadly few of these have been built.

In writing this book information has been gathered from many different sources, most published but some unpublished. Photographs and plans have also been collected from a wide variety of sources. Wherever known the sources have been acknowledged but in this day of digital images it is not always possible to determine where things have come from, particularly photographs. Where original costs are quoted, an equivalent current cost is given in italics in brackets.

In July 2017 the Government announced that all diesel and petrol driven vehicles would be prohibited by 2040, subsequently brought forward to 2035. This dramatic decision was an unexpected reaction to the illegal pollution levels applying in London, Leeds and other cities and the obvious need for drastic action. Tramways do not produce any pollutants (at the point of use) and yet there have been few suggestions that modern tramways could be part of the solution. Even worse, while stating that all cars will have to be electric, the government was scrapping rail electrification in the north of England forcing use of diesel trains. The innate British apathy towards electric traction and tramways is alive and well, at least in government circles. And yet where they have been built they are universally popular and well used, taking thousands of car journeys off the roads.

A further irony is that back in the 1930s, the majority of trips in our towns and cities were made on electric vehicles, trams and trolleybuses. But we threw them all away.

Perhaps things are about to change. The rapidly growing realisation that global warming is not only real but potentially devastating to the planet is focusing attention on electric traction. In 2019 the Department for Transport called for evidence to identify opportunities for new light rail and other rapid transit systems in towns and cities in England and Wales. (The DfT does not have any responsibilities in Scotland or Northern Ireland). Could this be the start of the long catch up with France where there are dozens of new tram systems, even in relatively small towns? Or will it just be yet another 'might have been' movement?

Acknowledgements

Most books include acknowledgements to the many people who have assisted the author in any way, providing material, comments and amendments, proof reading or whatever. In this case it is mainly my own research and records which have provided the input to the book. I must retain full responsibility for any inaccuracies or mistakes. Nevertheless sincere thanks are due to the many individuals and authorities who have contributed by pointing me in interesting directions and even employing me to undertake studies of tramways that have become 'might have beens'.

Many of the illustrations have come from various electronic sources where it is frequently difficult or impossible to identify photographer or copyright holder. If anyone recognises anything as theirs which has not been acknowledged please let the author and or publisher know and we will endeavour to correct the matter in any future edition.

Evidence for this book has been gathered over several decades from published reports, publicly available material, the author's own studies and many other sources. It is not a definitive work but rather to paint a broad picture of the state of light rail and tramway projects in Britain, drawing on examples through the ages which all indicate how, with a bit more imagination and funding, we could find it much easier to move about our towns and cities, with rather less environmental damage than we have become used to. There is no shortage of good ideas, technical expertise or enthusiasm in Britain, just an apparent reluctance or inability to find the means to exploit it.

Carl Isgar has provided ongoing advice and assistance in his role as Publications Director for the LRTA. Roger Smith, previously LRTA cartographer, very kindly prepared the maps which help to locate tramway systems and which contribute enormously to the ease of use of the book. Martin Higginson willingly accepted the unenviable job of proofreading the text and made many helpful suggestions. Tim Kendell, LRTA Technical Director, provided information on tram-trains and the proposed tramway in Cardiff. Hugh McAulay unearthed the Glasgow report of 1948 which proved to be years ahead of its time. Many other former colleagues in the tramway and light railway fraternity have, perhaps unwittingly, contributed in different ways to the contents of the book. To all these I offer my sincere thanks.

1. Introduction

Tramways have had a long but intermittent history in Britain. There have been two main eras, the first generation tramways from the 1880s to the 1960s and the second generation from the 1990s to the present day. The modern form of tramway is termed light rail or light rail transit although the terms tram and tramways have enjoyed a renaissance in the current century.

Throughout both eras, while many schemes have been built and carried passengers, there has been an astonishing array of proposals and projects that have not reached fruition. What are they and would our transport systems have been different had they been carried out? Why were they not carried out?

In this book examples are given of many different *'Might have been'* trams and tramways. They range from very minor projects that had no hope of realisation to major metropolitan schemes that were desperately needed and should have been built. Maybe some still will be some day. This is not a comprehensive history, that would require several volumes. Rather it is to give a flavour of what *might have been*, in places ranging from major cities to tiny villages. Extensions to tramways which were built, of which there were many, are not included unless they formed a link to an adjacent tramway, hence potentially creating or expanding a tramway network.

It is now recognised that tramways bring massive social, economic and environmental benefits to the areas they serve. Many towns and cities we know today owe their form and extent to the tram routes that encouraged development beyond the limits of walking or horse drawn carriages. Electric tramways speeded the process to create now familiar extensive conurbations around major cities. But how might things have been even more dramatic if all the unachieved tramways had been built?

This book only considers tramways in the British Isles. There are doubtless many comparable examples around Europe and beyond. There are significant differences; in many European countries the political climate has been more supportive to tramways than in Britain and funding consequently been more generous. In Germany, Switzerland, Belgium and the Netherlands there were not two distinct eras of tramways; development was continuous from the late 19th century to the 21st. France and Spain followed the British trend of scrapping first generation tramways but have since progressed rapidly with second generation systems, quickly overtaking UK developments.

Another key difference is the approach to capital funding. In most European countries there are three levels of government: local, regional and national. The cost of new or extended tramways was often shared between the different levels. If one level didn't come up with enough funds, another level could contribute more. In Britain there has effectively only ever been one level as national government has maintained a stranglehold on investment at local level. However keen a local authority was to build a tramway, if central government said no, it didn't happen. Devolution to the regions may help the situation in Britain but it is painfully slow in emerging.

Before electric tramways there were horse drawn, steam powered and cable hauled tramways in many towns and cities. These are not considered in this book although there were many examples which were planned and not built.

The Economist Intelligence Unit (EIU) publishes an annual measure of liveability in cities, comparing 140 cities throughout the world. The top place has been contested between Melbourne and Vienna for several years and in 2018 Vienna took first place. These two cities have the largest tramway systems in the world; is that pure coincidence? In fact seven of the top ten cities have tramway or light rail systems and the other three have metro systems. The first British city in the list was Manchester at 35th, which happens to have the largest tram system in Britain. The only other British city to feature was London at 48th. This must be strong evidence that tramways contribute to liveable cities.

To document all the tramway schemes that were even thought about would require a second volume of this book. Rather the aim here is to give an outline of the range and types of schemes that were planned to show again what *'might have been'*.

Promoters of tram schemes throughout the 20th century and into the 21st century had to attempt to follow the ever changing rules and policies of the government. Even keeping up with the name of the Ministry of Transport required vigilance. What was the Ministry of Transport until 1970 then became the Department for the Environment for six years before becoming the Department of Transport in 1976. That lasted until 1997 when it became the Department of the Environment, Transport and the Regions. In 2001 another twist saw environment dropped to become Department of Transport, Local Government and the Regions. That only lasted until 2002 when it changed to the Department for Transport which has survived until the present day.

Keeping track of Ministers of Transport was just as challenging. From the time that the first light rail plans were drawn up in Manchester to the day the first tram ran into the city centre there were no fewer than fifteen Ministers or Secretaries of State for Transport with another eight before the turn of the century. They were rarely in post long enough to discover what light rail or tramways were.

The structure of this book is firstly in Chapter 2 to set out some basic principles and features of the tramway scene. In Chapter 3 first generation tramway 'might have beens' are described, that is those from the electric tram era up to 1960. Chapter 4 lists some 'missing links', connections between adjacent tramways, which would have created larger and more extensive networks. Chapter 5 describes various plans to build tunnels for trams, a feature found in many European tramways and in North America. The only example in Britain was the Kingsway subway in London although more were planned in other cities. This Chapter also includes reference to some second generation plans for tram tunnels in Manchester.

By 1960 the only street tramway left was Blackpool, which had been the first back in 1885. This is covered in Chapter 6. Chapter 7 shows that while the last trams had run in British cities, the idea of building modern light rail networks was still alive and well, particularly among members of the LRTL. The first generation networks which could have been developed into modern European style light rail systems, particularly Leeds and Liverpool, are described in Chapter 8. Chapter 9 shows the wide range of new trams which might have been produced for British systems, listing trams for first and second generation networks.

Chapter 10 moves into the second generation street tramways which began with Manchester in 1992. Before then light rail technology was adopted for the Tyne and Wear Metro in 1980 and Docklands Light Railway in 1987 but neither of these had any street tramways. Each of the new systems is described in Chapters 11 to 18, noting routes or plans that did not come to fruition. Some of these may yet be built.

Chapter 19 concentrates on London where there have been many thoughts of new tramways in the past nearly 50 years, many developed by London Transport and subsequently Transport for London, but so far Croydon (now termed London Tramlink) is the only one to be built. Given its undoubted success it is amazing, and very short-sighted, that it has not been copied.

Chapter 20 sets out the tramway projects that should have been built because they were so close to realisation and millions of pounds had already been spent on obtaining Parliamentary powers, detailed designs, planning approvals and even some initial procurements. They are Leeds, Liverpool and South Hampshire, all cancelled by the government.

In Chapter 21 some major cities which have not yet built tramways but which should be strong candidates are outlined. They include greater Bristol, Cardiff and the South Wales Valleys, Cleveland and Glasgow. Of these only Cardiff has firm plans to achieve light rail and contracts are already underway for tram-train operation on some lines and for some street running in the city centre.

The special needs of historic cities are covered in Chapter 22. They include Chester, York, Oxford, Cambridge, Norwich and Bath. While most have had feasibility studies for tramways in the last thirty years, none have current plans although there is an active group in Bath promoting tramways. It is interesting to reflect that many of these cities once had electric trams which even ran through ancient historic gateways.

In the past 25 years several attempts have been made to progress light rail or tramways in Britain by various government related bodies. Although some very good work has been done, sadly none of this has had any positive effects in terms of new tramways. These attempts are outlined in Chapter 23. Chapter 24 lists a number of proposed tramways that will probably never see the light of day.

2. Tramways that might have happened

This Chapter sets the scene, outlining some general principles and the influence that government, both central and local have had on decision making on tramway matters. This applies equally to first and second generation tramways.

Building a new tramway is a complex and demanding task, whether in the late 19th century or the early 21st century. The engineering and operational characteristics must be right for the context but they will be to no avail unless the overall planning, political climate and above all financial support are in place.

A few schemes have fallen by the wayside because the engineering approach was flawed or the planning context was wrong but most failed because the political support was not there and even more the lack of adequate finance. Political support is needed across party lines and at all levels, local, city, regional and national. Public support is also critical, if any proposal attracts strong opposition it is unlikely to succeed. Support must be continuous through the various stages of planning, approvals, funding and construction. Any project that becomes a political football will almost certainly fail.

Early electric tramways in the late 19th or early 20th centuries were often promoted by private companies although most were taken over by local authorities as authorised by the Tramways Act 1870, which allowed acquisition after 21 years. Nowadays tramway schemes nearly always originate at local level, usually promoted by local councils or transport authorities, but they must be approved by national government. Acts of Parliament were required for any tramway or tramway extension until the Transport and Works Act 1992 brought in a supposedly better procedure, but it still needs ultimate approval by the government of the day. Many schemes have fallen at this hurdle, or even later when governments have changed their minds.

As will be revealed, our country is littered with failed tramway schemes, some of which perhaps would not have been greatly missed, but others which would have made a major contribution to the local economy and to the form of our towns and cities. There are no doubt places where traffic congestion and environmental pollution are worse now because a tramway scheme was scrapped, Leeds being the starkest example.

Many first generation electric tramways were converted from horse or steam tramways in the last decades of the 19th century and many more were built new in the first decades of the twentieth century. A rapid expansion of tramways took place between 1900 and 1910, but many proposals did not come to fruition, mainly for lack of capital.

Government influence

One significant influence on later tramway development in Britain was the Royal Commission on Transport Report of 1929 "The Control of Traffic on Roads" (Ref.6). It recommended that *"no additional tramways should be constructed ....and they should gradually disappear and give place to other forms of transport"*. They recognised that trams might have a role in large towns but there were *"many other towns where trams are definitely not necessary...... ..the ultimate abolition of tramways and the substitution of trackless trolleys or omnibuses"*.

The Royal Commission report formed the basis for the Road Traffic Act 1930 which introduced bus service regulation and much more when Herbert Morrison was Minister of Transport. While it did not require the abolition of tramways it was clear that the government did not regard them with any favour. Not surprisingly many tramways in smaller towns disappeared in the nineteen thirties. A significant factor was the need to replace worn out track and vehicles which had been hurriedly built in the tramway euphoria at the turn of the century.

It is not the purpose of this book to describe the reasons for the demise of first generation trams although they did have an impact on *'might have been tramways'*. Right from the start, street tramways were saddled with the cost of providing the roadway between the tracks and for 18ins either side, a substantial cost which effectively meant that in many places the tramway was paying for the cost of the track for its competitors, buses, and all other road traffic. Also the capital cost of tracks was often written off over longer periods than their actual life so funds were not there when needed for renewals (see for example Ref.39).

Many authorities in the early part of the 20th century used profits from the electric tramways to support the rate fund instead of making provision for renewals of life expired assets. Britain has a habit of only looking at initial costs and not whole life costs. This must have been a factor in schemes becoming *'might have beens'*.

Government disapproval of tramways was evident again in the official document on 'Design & Layout of Roads in Built-up Areas', the report of the departmental committee set up by the Minister of War Transport in 1946 (Ref.8). The report commented: *"There can be no doubt that tramcars running on fixed tracks obstruct the free flow of traffic, especially when the tracks are provided with passing loops. In the general interest of the free flow of road traffic, we welcome the tendency to replace tramcars by vehicles of greater flexibility"*.

But it did grudgingly accept that *"tramways may have a proper place in road passenger transport, e.g. on routes serving heavy tidal traffic to or from housing or industrial estates."* They went on: *"We are of the opinion that, taking the long view, there are few towns in which the existence of tramways at surface level should be allowed to determine the future pattern of the road system and the design of its intersections'*.

The report did, perhaps innocently, advocate modern light rail systems when it stated: *"Where tramways are to be retained every opportunity should be taken to locate them within their own fenced reservations which, preferably, should be outside the limits of the highway."* That is what Liverpool had pioneered thirty years earlier and had been followed in Leeds, Birmingham, Glasgow and a few other cities. It also supported tram subways in large cities: *"...there are obvious advantages in making provision for them in subways or tunnels under the carriageway, as was done in Kingsway, London."* Although several cities did have plans for tram subways (See Ch.5), the Kingsway subway remained the only British example.

People may argue that government disapproval of tramways reflected the popular mood of the public. Car ownership was in its infancy in the 1930s but there was already an emerging concern that trams caused congestion and got in the way of cars. A major factor was the common practice of locating double track tramways in the centre of the carriageway. As tram stops were usually on the kerbside, passengers had to walk into the road to board and alight the tram. Cars had to stop and wait until the tram set off again and were not allowed to pass it on the nearside while it was stationary, an essential requirement for safety. This did not of course apply where tramways were segregated in a central reservation or on private right of way, as on most second generation light rail systems.

While it is undoubtedly true that tramways were disliked in many quarters, they were adored in others, especially where they had been modernised with new trams and segregated tracks. This was clearly demonstrated by the crowds that turned out to say farewell to last trams, even in pouring rain as in Glasgow.

Ministry guidance in 1946: "tramways preferably should be outside the limits of the highway." Middleton Woods in Leeds. MoT

The Durham Road extension in Sunderland, opened in 1949 and abandoned in 1954. Sunderland Echo, coloured by Malcolm Fraser

Some larger towns and cities did hang on to their tramways until the late forties or early fifties but in many cases this was merely forced on them by the restrictions of the second world war. In that political climate there was little chance of any *'might have been'* new lines or links being built, although a few did squeeze through the financial limitations, notably the completion of the Middleton-Belle Isle circular route in Leeds and the Durham Road extension in Sunderland in 1949. They had a very short life, classic examples of the British mentality of throwing away sound investments.

Many of the tramways that were built in the first years of the twentieth century constructed extensions to serve new housing areas or industrial estates. Many more extensions were planned but not built, because the funding could not be raised or because of political changes. They are too numerous to list here.

Between the 1950s and the 1980s there were no formal plans for new tramways. Most people assumed that the tramcar had been firmly confined to the museum and would never be seen again. Members of the LRTA, and those who had travelled around European cities, knew better.

The PTEs created in 1969 and 1973 had to submit statutory long term plans and most took the opportunity to consider the potential role of light rail. SELNEC (later Greater Manchester) set the ball rolling with a planned three line LRT network in the early 1970s. Tyneside PTE and London Transport had broken the light rail barrier with their segregated 'light metro' systems in the 1980s and transport planners in most of the PTEs developed plans for street running trams in the 1980s.

The 1990s was the decade when second generation tramway fever was at its greatest. Manchester's Metrolink light rail system had broken the taboo on street running when it burst through the wall at Victoria Station to run along Manchester's city centre streets for the first time in 43 years. Suddenly every town and city wanted one and it was boom time for consulting engineers and economists trying to build a financial case that would satisfy the boffins in Marsham Street in the Department of Transport. They needed a lot of convincing.

In Britain there was an unwritten assumption that tramways could not be justified except in very large cities, at least 500,000 and preferably more. Only Nottingham with a population of 330,000 has so far managed to succeed. In France many of the thirty new tramways are in much smaller cities; Avignon opened its first line in 2019 with a population of less than 100,000. They do not have to contend with the DfT.

The tramway planning boom lasted about fifteen years, until Secretary of State for Transport Alistair Darling started cancelling every scheme on his

Nottingham is the only provincial city in Britain with a population less than 500,000 to achieve a tram network.
Tony Young

desk. When smaller authorities saw that even well planned and justified projects in the conurbations were being thrown out after millions of pounds had been spent on developing schemes and obtaining parliamentary powers, they realised that the chances of smaller and perhaps more marginal projects was virtually nil. Even in London where the need for new investment in tracked transport seemed obvious and had been strongly advocated by Mayor Ken Livingstone, all the schemes under development were unceremoniously thrown out by new Mayor Boris Johnson. It is perhaps not surprising that in the ensuing decade not a single tram scheme has been promoted apart from extensions to existing systems. There are still no new tram schemes planned in the UK.

3. First generation tramway *'might have beens'*

This chapter describes selected examples of 'first generation' tramway *'might have beens'* from the electric tram era up to 1960. They are listed in alphabetical order. The first example is one of the most bizarre, in Canvey Island on the Essex coast.

Canvey Island Tramway

A very unusual, if not unique, transport system was a horse drawn monorail which was built in 1904 from Canvey Ferry to the Winter Gardens and on to Shell Beach on the south side of the island to meet the proposed pier. The brainchild of Estate Agent Frederick Hester, it consisted of a wooden carriage mounted on wheels running on a single rail with the horse held in a wooden frame fixed to the carriage. It was single track with passing places although exactly how that worked isn't clear. The 'Monorail Tramway' was claimed to be the only one-rail tram of its kind in England, a claim probably difficult to disprove.

The unique horse drawn monorail on Canvey Island.
CanveyIsland.Org

Estate Agent Frederick Hester. *Carol Mayers*

This led to the strangest *'Might have been tramway'*, the Canvey Island line between Benfleet Station and Leigh Beck. It is believed to have been promoted by Coastal Developments Limited with a gauge of 3ft.6ins. Single deck trams were delivered but after 200 yards of track had been laid the system was abandoned and the trams returned to the manufacturer.

The electric tramway was intended to replace the horse drawn monorail and a further line was envisaged to cross Hadleigh Marshes to reach Leigh-on-Sea station, (see plan opposite). The engineering challenges of this route would have been enormous. Mr Hester had grand plans to redevelop large parts of Canvey Island and the tramway would have provided much needed accessibility.

The contract was let and by August 1904 4km of sleeper track had been laid. Work was also reported to have started on a depot and generating station at Tewkes Creek. Four 24 seat single deck electric trams were bought and delivered to Canvey in 1904. They were enamelled red with gold lines bearing the livery 'Venice on Sea and Canvey', although at least one was named 'Canvey Island Electric Tramways'. The first were delivered on a trailer hauled by a traction engine but later a horse drawn wagon was used.

Problems arose at the landing stage with the large 30 foot rails and in getting access to land. Planning approvals had been left to the last minute and contractual issues resulted in the contractor removing materials, presumably because he wasn't being paid. In 1905 an auction was held to dispose of some of the sleepers and the rails. The four trams were returned to Brush who had supplied them to the main contractor, and two were then sent to the Llandudno and Colwyn Bay Electric Railway for use as test cars in 1907. They did not enter passenger service and were returned to Brush in Loughborough where the bodies were broken up and the trucks reused.

Who knows how Canvey Island may have developed if the tramway had actually been built and operated. It is doubtful whether it would have survived beyond the thirties in any event as loadings would not have been great. It failed because of over enthusiastic plans and poor project planning. It is amazing that it got as far as it did, but perhaps not surprising that it gained the dubious accolade of England's only tramway that was partly built but then scrapped before a tram ran.

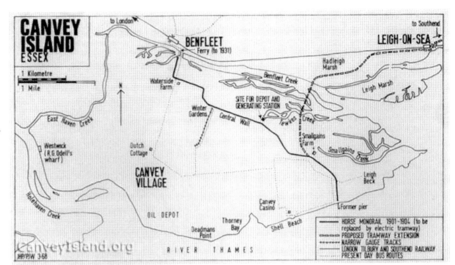

Map showing the planned route for electrification. Canveylsland.Org

Delivery of the new tram cars in 1904 at Benfleet Station.
TMS Photographic Service

Another 1904 picture of one of the electric trams being delivered across Benfleet Creek by cart.
Canveylsland.Org

Cumbrian coast tramways

While Lancashire had the densest network of tramways in the country, the north west of England also had the remotest tramway. The city of Carlisle had a six line tram network serving all the main radial routes into the city from 1900 to 1931. The 3ft.6ins gauge system was nearly 60 miles from the nearest tramway.

A significant *'might have been'* was the West Cumberland Electric Tramways Company's proposed coastal tramway stretching from Cleator Moor south west of Whitehaven through Workington to Maryport, a distance of 17½ miles. An extension northwards to the town of Silloth would have added another 13¾ miles making a total of 31¼ miles, nearly three times the length of the Blackpool coastal tramway.

Powers were granted for the 3ft.6ins gauge line under a Parliamentary Act of 1901 but without the extension to Silloth. Much of the route would have been on roadside reservation or private right of way. It included four depot sites along the line. The one at Silloth would have been 12 miles from the tramway as that section was not approved. It was left in the Act due to an oversight. The powers

were renewed in 1903 and again in 1905. Perhaps not surprisingly the line was not built and the Act was finally revoked in 1923. By then there were bus services along the coast as well as the Cumbrian coast railway which had opened in 1846.

An even more ambitious Lake District tramway project was the Windermere and District Light Railway. Linking Bowness Pier with Windermere railway station and Ambleside it would have been a 3ft 6in gauge boat-tram-train-bus link running mainly on reserved track. Powers were sought in 1900 but local opposition ensured that it did not progress any further and the promoters withdrew their application. It is wholly understandable that hostility to a major engineering project in this highly popular tourist area would force abandonment, but a century later heavy traffic congestion imposes far worse environmental impacts than a tramway would have done.

County Durham

Municipal tramways ran in the towns of South Shields, Sunderland, Darlington, Stockton-on-Tees and West Hartlepool. *'Might have been'* tramways were authorised in Bishop Auckland with a network

Table 3.1.

Tramways authorised and planned but not built in South Lancashire and North East Cheshire.

From	To	Promoter	Route length (miles)	Notes
Blackpool	Garstang	Blackpool & Fylde Light Railway Co.	14.00	
Lytham	Preston	Preston & Lytham Light Railway	12.25	
Southport	Lytham	Southport & Lytham Tramroad Co.	15.38	Including Transporter bridge across Ribble estuary.
Southport	Ormskirk	Ormskirk & Southport Light Railway Co.	6.50	
Preston	Standish & Horwich	Preston, Chorley and Horwich Tramways Co.	23.32	Via Chorley
Preston	Blackburn	Preston & Blackburn Tramways Company	4.57	
Warrington	Northwich	Warrington & Northwich Light Railway Syndicate	19.50	
Whalley	Blackburn, Clayton-le-Moors and Padiham	Blackburn, Accrington, Whalley and Padiham Light Railway Co.	14.25	4ft.0ins gauge.
Bolton	Darwen	Bolton, Turton & Darwen Light Railway	9.17	
Tottington	Turton & Rawtenstall	Turton, Tottington, Ramsbottom & Rawtenstall Light Railway	9.05	Part route later promoted by Ramsbottom UDC
Holcombe Brook	Edenfield	Ramsbottom Urban District Council	5.24	
Newton-in-Makerfield	Warrington, Lowton St Mary's, Haydock & Bamfurlong	South Lancashire Tramways Co.	39.44	Including other links, some built by other tramways.
Todmorden	Summit Littleborough Jumble Hole Clough and Portsmouth	Todmorden Corporation Tramways	9.00	In Yorkshire but would have linked to Lancashire
Gatley	Northenden & Sale	Manchester Southern Tramways Co.	12.75	
Stretford	Urmston & Davyhulme	Manchester Southern Tramways Co.	Included above	
Macclesfield	Hazel Grove, Cheadle and Wilmslow	Macclesfield & District Tramways Co.	11.91	
Lees & Mossley	Saddleworth	Saddleworth & Springhead Tramways Co.	4.06	
Total			210.39	

of 17 miles extending to Shildon, Spennymoor and Croxdale. The Ryhope, Seaham, Murton and South Hetton Light Railway Company obtained powers to build a standard gauge light railway from Ryhope on the Sunderland District Tramway to Seaham Harbour, Dalton-le-Dale and Murton. They had aspirations to continue southwards to South Hetton to join the Sunderland District extension to Easington but neither that nor the Sunderland District extension were authorised.

Lancashire and North East Cheshire

Tramway promoters throughout the country had ideas to extend tramways beyond their current termini or to construct new links between systems. The most extensive network in Britain was in south Lancashire. In the late 1920s it was possible to travel by tram from Liverpool to Rochdale, Oldham or Stalybridge and from Bolton or Bury to Altrincham or Stockport. At its maximum the network was owned by 47 different local authorities and two companies, although this was later reduced to 12 local authorities and three companies. Many smaller authorities leased their lines to larger operators rather than operate them themselves. Nearly all lines were to the standard gauge of 4ft 8½ ins so through running was technically feasible. On at least one occasion a tram did actually travel from Liverpool to Stockport.

Two examples of long-distance journeys by tram to Liverpool were:

1. Bingley to Liverpool in August 1916, 76 miles taking 11 hours, at a total cost of 4s 0d. It did require a 7-mile walk from Hebden Bridge to Summit on the Rochdale system (See Hebden Bridge Chapter 4).
2. Manchester to Liverpool in 1920, 37½ miles taking 4½ hours, at a total cost of 2s 3d and requiring six tram rides.

Many more examples were given by Manchester publisher John Lingard in his booklets "Where to go by tram" in the 1920s. (Ref.5).

If all the lines in Lancashire which were authorised had been built, this network would have been even greater, stretching from Fleetwood to Macclesfield and from Birkenhead and Southport to Colne, Todmorden and Glossop. However, some systems in East Lancashire including Blackburn, Accrington, Burnley and Rawtenstall were built to 4ft.0ins gauge, so through running would have been difficult. The only solutions were dual gauge track, rarely adopted in Britain, or an ingenious engineering solution adopted between Leeds and Bradford, which were different gauges, that allowed the wheels to slide along the axles, with tapered track at the changeover point.

Tramways that were never built, although most did obtain parliamentary authorisation, are listed in Table 3.1 opposite for the South Lancashire and North Cheshire area. They totalled over two hundred miles, more than three times the size of today's Metrolink tram system and would have greatly expanded the catchment areas for employment and wider economic activity. In many cases the railways proved too great a competitor for the slow trams, which rarely exceeded 20 mph on most routes. But as many proposals were semi-rural in nature, this would have created a network similar to the Belgian Vicinal, which served wide parts of the countryside, with direct connections into the major city networks.

Northumberland

To the north of Newcastle upon Tyne the Northumberland Electric Tramway obtained powers in 1902 for a 12½ mile standard gauge network linking Bedlington, Ashington, Morpeth and Newbiggin. However, there would have been a two mile gap in the middle where one section was not approved, which made the network much less useful and no doubt contributed to the whole system being a *'might have been'*.

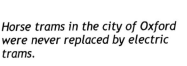
Horse trams in the city of Oxford were never replaced by electric trams.

Most horse tramways were replaced by electric trams, but Oxford and Cambridge never had electric trams. This restored horse tram in the Oxford Bus Museum represents that era. Oxford Bus Museum

Oxford and Cambridge

The renowned ancient university cities of Oxford and Cambridge have much in common. A lesser known fact is that they are both *'might have been'* electric tramway cities. They both had 4 ft gauge horse tramways opened in 1880 (Cambridge) and 1881 (Oxford) with a mixture of single and double deck horse drawn trams. In each case they provided a link between the main railway station and the city centre.

In both cities there were plans to electrify and extend the tramways and convert them to standard gauge, with options considered for overhead wire, stud contact or conduit power supply systems. But both suffered from indecision and lack of agreement between promoters, politicians and shareholders and the deciding factor was competition from bus services which were becoming more reliable. The horse trams soldiered on until 1914 when both cities lost their tramways.

Saddleworth & Springhead Tramways

The already extensive South Lancashire tramway network would have extended even further east if the over-ambitious plans of the Saddleworth and Springhead Tramways Company had come to fruition. The plan overleaf shows the 13 mile

network of lines which were authorised under an Act in 1902 linking into the Oldham tramways at Waterhead and Lees and serving the Pennine townships of Uppermill, Greenfield, Dobcross, Delph and Denshaw. A connection was also planned with the Stalybridge, Hyde, Mossley and Dukinfield tramway at Roaches near Greenfield. The whole network would be single track with passing loops.

Oldham Corporation strongly objected and the line from Waterhead to Denshaw was abandoned, although it was later built under a further Act in 1904. By 1907 little progress was evident and an approach was made to Oldham Corporation to consider operating the authorised tramways. Oldham's General Manager inspected the routes but thought they would not be profitable, a view endorsed by his Tramways Committee. They were no doubt influenced by the difficulties they were having with making a dense urban system pay its way; the sparsely populated Saddleworth area would not produce enough passengers to justify the capital costs.

Southport and Lytham

The tramway towns of Southport and Lytham are only seven miles apart, but by road it is over 30 miles. On a clear day you can see Blackpool Tower from Southport. Winstan Bond describes as the 'maddest tramway never to be built' the plan to bridge the River Ribble estuary with a transporter

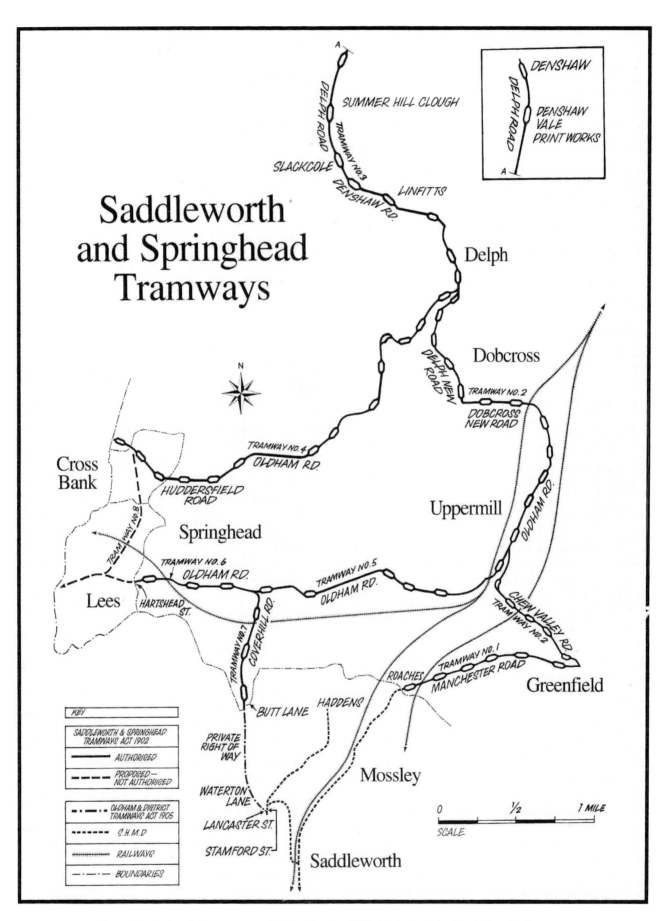

Saddleworth and Springhead Tramways

The Saddleworth and Springhead Tramways authorised by the 1902 Act but not built. Arthur Kirby

bridge for trams. The further inland route would have been 15 miles but still much shorter than the road route via Preston.

The first idea for a bridge link emerged in 1896 for a swing bridge. This was followed by plans for a viaduct with tramway links at each end and a 'Daddy Long Legs' elevated tramway running through the sea, as had been built in Brighton in 1896, which ran until 1901. The Southport and Lytham Tramroad Bill was promoted in Parliament in 1899 but was strongly opposed by Preston Corporation who feared it would badly impact on their plans for Preston Port. The Bill was not successful.

Undeterred the Southport and Lytham Tramroad Company devised an alternative scheme, taking trams from Southport further inland, abandoning the "Daddy Long Legs' device but retaining a transporter bridge. Both routes are shown in the plan below and an artist's impression of the tram transporter. Parliamentary

powers were obtained in 1900 but the ambitious project fell through due to funding problems. The total cost would have been £183,500 (£19.6m) including £53,154 (£5.68m) for the transporter bridge, perhaps on the low side given that the Runcorn-Widnes bridge cost £130,000 (£13.9m) for about the same span only five years later.

A tramway extending from Ormskirk to Fleetwood via Southport, Lytham and Blackpool remained an impossible dream although today it would be a huge tourist attraction as well as relieving congested roads. A further link from the north side of the transporter bridge eastwards to connect with the Preston tramway was not authorised.

Transporter bridges were built in Runcorn (1905), Newport (1906), Middlesbrough (1911) and Warrington (1916) but none of them carried trams although the Warrington transporter did carry rail vehicles until 1940. Runcorn closed in 1961 and was

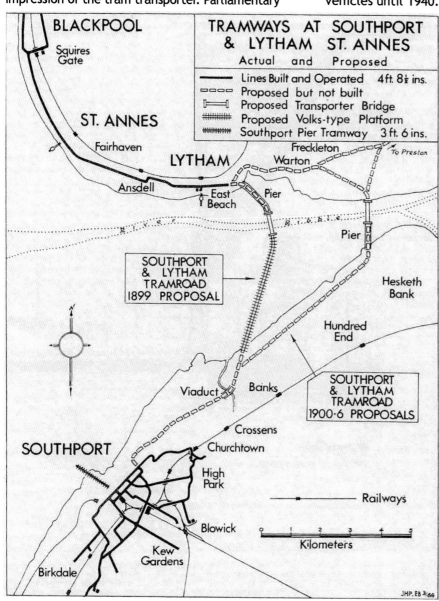

Plans to link Southport and Lytham tramways were described as 'the maddest tramway never to be built'. The 1899 and 1900 options are shown on this plan.
Modern Tramway 379 July 1969

demolished but Newport and Middlesbrough are still in use. The Warrington example is Grade II* listed but is not in good condition. An article giving more detail of this intriguing proposal and including the map reproduced below, was written by Winstan Bond in the July 1969 'Modern Tramway' magazine.

The transporter bridge would have carried trams across the River Ribble enabling them to run from Southport to Lytham and on to Blackpool. Modern Tramway 379 July 1969

First generation tramway "might have beens"

Legend
- operational tramway
- operational tramways with one or more connecting lines
- "*might have been*" tramway, not constructed

Note : 'London' includes the municipal tramways of L.C.C., Barking, Bexley Heath, Croydon, Dartford, East Ham, Erith, Ilford, Leyton, Walthamstow and West Ham, and the company tramways of Gravesend & Northfleet, London United, Metropolitan Electric and South Metropolitan Tramways & Light.

For details of tramways in this area, see separate map.

© R.A Smith & T.Young, October 2020. No. 2438, v1.3.

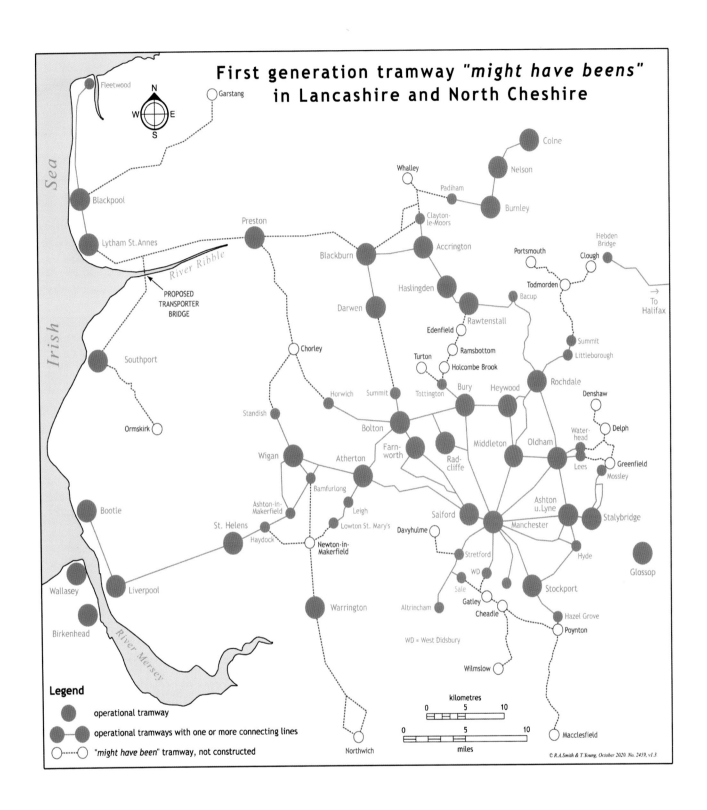

First generation tramway *"might have beens"* in Lancashire and North Cheshire

Irish Sea

Fleetwood

Garstang

Blackpool

Lytham St.Annes

River Ribble

PROPOSED TRANSPORTER BRIDGE

Preston

Southport

Ormskirk

Bootle

Wallasey

Liverpool

Birkenhead

River Mersey

St. Helens

Haydock

Newton-in-Makerfield

Ashton-in-Makerfield

Bamfurlong

Leigh

Lowton St. Mary's

Wigan

Standish

Horwich

Summit

Chorley

Blackburn

Darwen

Haslingden

Accrington

Clayton-le-Moors

Whalley

Padiham

Nelson

Colne

Burnley

Portsmouth

Hebden Bridge

Clough

Todmorden

Bacup

To Halifax

Rawtenstall

Edenfield

Ramsbottom

Holcombe Brook

Turton

Tottington

Bury

Heywood

Summit

Littleborough

Rochdale

Denshaw

Delph

Waterhead

Greenfield

Mossley

Bolton

Farnworth

Radcliffe

Middleton

Oldham

Lees

Atherton

Warrington

Davyhulme

Salford

Ashton u.Lyne

Manchester

Stalybridge

Hyde

Stretford

WD

Glossop

Sale

Gatley

Cheadle

Stockport

Hazel Grove

Poynton

Altrincham

WD = West Didsbury

Wilmslow

Macclesfield

Northwich

Legend

- ● operational tramway
- ●—● operational tramways with one or more connecting lines
- ○---○ *"might have been"* tramway, not constructed

kilometres
0 5 10

miles
0 5 10

© R.A.Smith & T.Young, October 2020. No. 2459, v1.3

4. Missing links

In many parts of the country tramways were developed in adjacent towns and cities which could have been connected with through services, increasing the range of possible destinations for people from both towns. Some examples are described here, set out in alphabetical order.

Birkenhead - Wallasey

On the western banks of the River Mersey opposite Liverpool are two Wirral towns which each had their own municipal tram networks. Both were focused on ferry terminals, Birkenhead on the Woodside Ferry and Wallasey on the Seacombe and New Brighton ferry terminals. They each had about seventy trams.

At their nearest point they were only about a mile apart but there does not appear to have been any enthusiasm to link them together. This would have provided a through route for residents of Birkenhead to visit the sandy beaches and Irish Sea views in New Brighton but the commuter routes to the ferries took much higher priority.

The two tramways closed in the 1930s but jointly operated through bus services were soon established although there was some rivalry between the two towns.

Bolton-Darwen

The largest tram network in Britain, which once stretched from Liverpool to Glossop might have been even larger if a crazy plan by South Lancashire Tramways (SLT) had actually happened. Their straggling network extended from Haydock of racecourse fame in the west, through Leigh to Swinton and Pendlebury in the east and Bolton in the north. Bolton had its own tramway serving all parts of the town and SLT had running rights into Bolton town centre.

To the north of Bolton, across the windswept moors, lies Darwen where a small two route tram system ran into Blackburn. Their most southerly terminus was at Whitehall, about six miles north of Bolton's termini at Dunscar and Tonge Moor. In November 1900 an application was made for a Light Railway Order for a line to link the Darwen and Bolton systems, even though SLT did not run to the north of Bolton and at that point had yet to open its first line. A branch to Belmont was to be on roadside reservation, again across moors with few potential passengers and ending half a mile short

of the village. Another short branch would have served Bromley Cross station, an early example of integration. Most of the line was to be single track with passing places.

Powers for the Bolton, Turton and Darwen Light Railway (BTDLR) were granted but never confirmed and the scheme was quietly forgotten. Not surprising given the difficulties the parent company, South Lancashire Electric Traction and Power Company Limited, was having raising the capital to construct its tram routes through the south Lancashire coalfields, where at least there were plenty of potential passengers. Hardly anybody lived up on the moors and not only that, the route would have long lengths of steep gradients rising to 917 feet.

Even more bizarre was the fact that the Bolton and SLT trams were standard gauge while Darwen and Blackburn were 4ft.0ins gauge, making through running impossible. The section between the Darwen boundary and the terminus of the Darwen tramway was to be mixed gauge, but quite why remains a mystery. It is inconceivable that the new line would terminate at the remote Darwen terminus, or that Darwen would want to extend their line to the borough boundary where nobody lived. There was no mention of a tapered gauge change track as used between Leeds and Bradford.

It was planned to carry freight in addition to passengers to get additional revenue, but the practicalities do not appear to have been thought through. There was no reference to any method of transhipment or of dual gauge vehicles. The Lancashire and Yorkshire Railway, which linked Bolton with Darwen, Blackburn and many parts of south Lancashire, ran only a mile or so to the east and would easily have overcome any attempted competition.

Bristol and Bath

The cities of Bristol and Bath each had sizeable tramway networks serving the built up areas, over 31 miles in Bristol and nearly 15 miles in Bath. Both were standard gauge. Although only twelve miles apart, the two networks were never connected. Bristol trams ran as far as Brislington and were planned to be extended to Keynsham. Bath trams ran to Newton St. Loe and were planned to be extended to Saltford. This would have left a gap of barely two miles between the two systems. Neither extension was built and Bath trams ceased in 1939

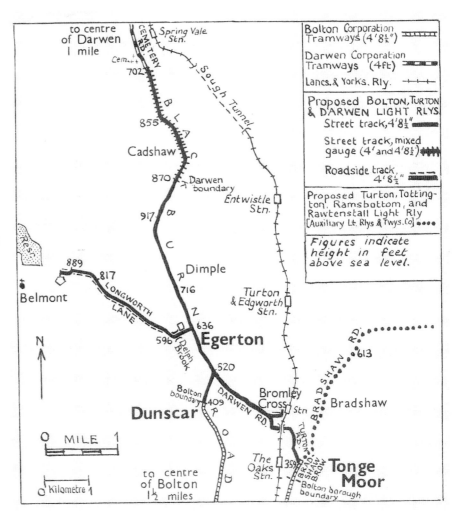

A tramway was proposed across the moors north of Bolton reaching a height of 917ft above sea level. The Bolton, Turton and Darwen Light Railway would have linked the Bolton Corporation Tramway with the Darwen Corporation Tramway, although they were of different gauges.
MTMS

with Bristol following shortly after in 1941. The idea of running trams between Bristol and Bath is still being discussed in Bath.

Burnley Rose Grove – Accrington Cemetery

The vast Lancashire network of tramways encompassed many missing links which could have made it even more extensive although no formal proposal was made. One such was the three-mile gap between the Accrington tramway at Accrington cemetery and the Burnley tramway at Rose Grove. Both were 4ft.0ins gauge so connections would not have presented any problems.

Bury – Rawtenstall

To the south of Rawtenstall the small town of Ramsbottom desperately wanted a tramway to serve its growing development along the River Irwell valley. The Urban District Council obtained tramway powers in 1903 for a six mile route connecting the Bury tramway at Tottington with the Rawtenstall tramway in Rawtenstall town centre via Edenfield.

They could not raise the funds to build it but did construct a tram depot with the title "Ramsbottom Tramways" proudly displayed. The depot was used by trolleybuses but the name was never changed.

Not having succeeded with their tramway scheme the U.D.C. obtained powers in 1912 for a trolleybus route from Holcombe Brook to Edenfield, part of the same route proposed for the tramway. They thus became one of the very first trolleybus operators in Britain, barely a year behind pioneers Leeds and Bradford. The trolleys were not a great success and had all gone by 1931.

Cheltenham and Gloucester

A few miles north of Bristol, the city of Gloucester and the town of Cheltenham each had a small tramway. Both were 3 ft 6 in gauge and both had about ten route miles, Cheltenham with 25 trams and Gloucester with 30 trams. Both had closed by the early 1930s, in common with many small town tramways of that era.

A few miles to the south, the Stroud and District Tramways Company planned a 24 mile 3ft 6in gauge tram network and 15½ miles were authorised to be built in 1903. As well as serving the villages around Stroud, a long route to the north would have connected with Cheltenham's tramway near Leckhampton and it would also have linked into a proposed extension of the Gloucester tramways at Brockworth. It would thus have created a tramway link between Gloucester and Cheltenham, but it was not to be, as the powers were never exercised.

Crossflatts - Keighley (Stockbridge)

On the east side of the Pennine chain, the West Yorkshire conurbation had extensive tramway networks linking all the main towns and cities of Leeds, Bradford, Wakefield, Dewsbury, Halifax and Huddersfield. Through running was more difficult than in Lancashire because of the mix of track gauges, standard in Leeds, Wakefield and Dewsbury, 4 ft 0 ins. in Bradford and Keighley, 3ft.6ins. in Halifax and the strange 4ft.7¾ ins. in Huddersfield. No doubt they all had reasons for their choice but future extension to neighbouring systems was not regarded as important.

One obvious gap was the two miles between the Bradford and Keighley tramways between Crossflatts and Stockbridge. They were the same gauge so it should have been relatively straightforward. The Mid-Yorkshire Tramways Company did obtain powers to construct the link but it was never achieved. Bradford operated trolleybuses to Crossflatts but never extended them to Keighley who also operated trolleybuses, but only until 1932.

East Midlands

Near neighbours Nottingham and Derby each had extensive city tramways, Nottingham being standard gauge while Derby adopted the 4ft.0ins. gauge. A 14 mile light railway from Derby to Ashbourne was authorised in 1901 and even reported as being under construction but it was never built. As it was proposed to be a standard gauge line, working over the city tracks would not have been feasible anyway. Various plans to link Derby and Nottingham tramways, either east west via Long Eaton or to the north via Belper and Ripley, were not authorised. A link may yet be built, more than a century later, as the planned station on HS2 at Toton is very close to the Nottingham Express Transit tram terminus at Chilwell. There are already plans to extend the tram line to Derby city centre.

The Nottingham tramway served a range of suburban destinations but was also connected to the Nottinghamshire and Derbyshire Tramways line (the Notts and Derby) extending 14 miles north-westwards to Heanor and Ripley. Powers were obtained for another 27 miles taking trams to Belper, Alfreton and to link into the Mansfield and District tramway at Sutton-in-Ashfield. Thoughts for yet a further 40 miles of tramway were withdrawn from the planning process. None of these ambitious ideas bore fruit.

Roughly midway between Derby and Nottingham is the small town of Ilkeston, which achieved a small 3ft.6ins gauge tramway from Cotmanhay in the north to Hallam Fields in the south, a distance of less than four miles, with a short spur to Ilkeston Junction railway station. Its operation was taken over by the Notts and Derby company which sought powers in 1922 to construct a link between the two tramways, only 2½ miles apart, and to convert the whole Ilkeston line to standard gauge. This could have been a step towards creating a network of tramways in the East Midlands but before anything could be done, modern progress in the thirties introduced the trolleybus as a more efficient mode. The Ilkeston route was also converted to trolleybus but this was relatively short lived as in 1953 all the Notts and Derby trolleybus routes were converted to motor buses. Trolleybuses continued to serve the cities of Nottingham and Derby until 1966 and 1967 respectively.

Fareham and Portsmouth

Three tramways served the naval port and busy city of Portsmouth and its neighbouring towns of Fareham, Gosport, Cosham and Horndean. All were built to the unusual gauge of 4ft.7¾ins, chosen to allow railway freight wagons and locomotives to run in the streets, as also in Glasgow and Huddersfield. The Portsmouth and Horndean Light Railway ran as a rural tramway with sleeper track on roadside reservation for much of its route, including the steep climb over Portsdown Hill to Horndean. Extensions to Petersfield and Hambleton were not authorised.

Powers were obtained by the Portsmouth and Horndean Light Railway and the Gosport and Fareham Tramways for a line linking these two systems between Fareham and Cosham. It would have completed a circular route from Gosport Ferry via Fareham, Cosham and Portsmouth to the floating bridge in Portsmouth. It was not built and all the trams on all three systems had gone by the late thirties.

Another route which was authorised but not built would have taken trams onto Hayling Island, to the east of Portsmouth on a four mile line connected to the Portsmouth city network. It included a suspension bridge to cross the Langstone Channel to connect the two islands, but the high cost of such a structure no doubt resulted in the tramway remaining a *'might have been'*.

To the west on the other side of Portsmouth Harbour ran the Gosport and Fareham Tramway linking those two towns along the A32 main road to a gauge of 4ft.7¾ ins. Like the Portsmouth and Horndean light railway it was mainly single track with passing places on roadside reservation but with street running through the town centres. Authorisation was obtained in 1903 for a link between Fareham and Cosham which would have produced a continuous line from the Gosport ferry terminal via Fareham, Cosham and Portsmouth city centre to the ferry terminal on the Portsmouth side of the harbour, a distance of some fifteen miles. The powers were not exercised and the opportunity to create a tramway around the harbour was lost.

A century later, Hampshire County Council obtained powers to construct a light rapid transit line, a modern tramway, from Fareham to Gosport and thence through a tunnel under Portsmouth Harbour, continuing on street to Portsmouth city centre. Once again progress was thwarted and the scheme was cancelled by the government in 2004. This is described further in Chapter 20.

Glossop - Hyde/Stalybridge

To the east of the Manchester conurbation was the jointly run Stalybridge, Hyde, Mossley and Dukinfield Tramways and Electricity Board with a small network serving these industrial towns. Stalybridge was in Cheshire and further east in Derbyshire was the small Glossop tramway. The three mile gap between them was never filled so the eastern extremity of the South Lancashire network remained with S.H.M.D.

Great Yarmouth and Lowestoft

The remote towns of Great Yarmouth and Lowestoft on the east Norfolk coast each had a small 3ft.6ins gauge tramway owned by their respective corporations, with terminals only about seven miles apart. The Drake and Gorham Electric Power and Traction Company, known as the East Anglian Light Railway Company, sought powers in 1900 to build a light railway between the two towns from Gorleston to Lowestoft and an extension to the south of the Lowestoft tramway to Kessingland. This would have created a 22 mile coastal tramway to rival the Blackpool and Fleetwood coastal tramway and given a massive boost to Great Yarmouth as a seaside resort. The southwards extension powers were authorised although the line was never built, but the vital link between Great Yarmouth and Lowestoft was not authorised.

Halesowen Tramways

An extensive 3ft 6in gauge tramway network served Birmingham and surrounding areas. Adjacent towns West Bromwich, Wolverhampton, Walsall, Dudley and Stourbridge were all linked by trams, forming a Black Country network. This might have been even greater if powers obtained by Halesowen Rural District Council in 1902 had come to fruition. These powers, which passed to the Halesowen Lighting and Traction Company Limited, authorised the construction and operation of an 11 mile network of tramways between Stourbridge and Birmingham with links northwards to the Dudley tramways at Cradley Heath and Blackheath.

Despite several attempts over the next few years, and the purchase of the company by the mammoth British Electric Traction Company (BET), the finance was not forthcoming, so it never progressed beyond the drawing board. The opportunity to create a narrow gauge network to rival industrial conurbation tramways in other parts of Britain and in Europe was lost. Halesowen was one of at least five tramways owned by BET that were never built including Durham, Gower Peninsular, Wellingborough and Worthing.

Nearly a century later, Cradley Heath is the home of the Parry Peoplemover, a lightweight tram system that has finally found a role as the shuttle service between Stourbridge and Stourbridge junction. If you wait long enough some sort of tram might eventually arrive.

Hebden Bridge - Summit

Rochdale tramways reached the Pennine town of Littleborough and continued up the hill to Summit on the road to Todmorden. At the western end of

A view reminiscent of Blackpool's promenade but on the opposite coastline. Trams once ran along the sea front in Great Yarmouth and could have been linked to the Lowestoft tramway and beyond.

the Calder Valley the Halifax trams reached Hebden Bridge. The seven mile gap between these termini would have been almost filled by the Todmorden Corporation Tramway proposed in 1902. Todmorden's proposed route to Portsmouth would have been only four miles from the Burnley terminus at Townley. However the three potential links with adjacent tramways were all different gauges, Burnley on 4ft.0ins, Rochdale on 4ft.8½ ins and Halifax on 3ft.6ins. That would have been a difficult decision for them, only one through connection could have been made. The tramway was never built and Todmorden became one of the first municipalities in the country to run buses.

Huddersfield - Dewsbury

Huddersfield had become the first municipal tramway operator in Britain in 1883 and developed a 39 mile network of electric tramways serving all parts of this hilly town. The longest route stretched way up into the Pennines at Marsden, only about seven miles from Oldham's Waterhead terminus and even closer to the proposed Saddleworth terminus. In 1912 Parliamentary powers were sought for a number of extensions including one from Bradley to Mirfield, close to the Ravensthorpe terminus of the Yorkshire Woollen District tramway from Dewsbury. Through running would not have been feasible due to the gauge problem although in this case the difference was only ¾ in.

Powers were granted but the link was never built and the chance for a tramway linking Huddersfield with the towns of Dewsbury, Batley and Birstall, albeit with a change of tram, was lost.

London

Over 300 miles of electric tramways were operated in the London area with nearly 3,000 tramcars and a further 50 miles were authorised but not built. There were many extensions planned, some running well into adjacent counties and into rural or semi-rural locations. Most never reached approval stage and probably would not have survived long if they had.

The story of tramways in London, including the 'might have been' lines, would need a book of its own. Many books have been written on tramways in various parts of London including the major operators Metropolitan Electric Tramways, London United Tramways and London County Council Tramways as well as many local authority operations. All were subsumed in the London Passenger Transport Board in 1933.

In his book on London's trams, James Joyce (Ref.33) describes London's tramways as they might have been. Ambitious plans would have taken trams well out into the surrounding counties in Surrey, Berkshire and Middlesex and further into the heart of the city. London trams reaching Watford, Staines, Slough, Leatherhead, Epsom and Maidenhead must have been firmly in the realm of fantasy. High costs and public opposition in leafy suburbs would have ensured that they remained 'might have beens'.

Slightly more realistic were the tram subway plans from Victoria to Marble Arch and the four miles from Knightsbridge to Aldgate, described in a later chapter. The latter would have served a similar function to Crossrail, finally built over a century later, illustrating the far sightedness of some early tram planners. The Royal Commission on London Traffic in 1905 (Ref.3) considered far reaching plans for tramway development. Most spectacular would have been entirely new 140ft. wide avenues incorporating four track tramways east-west from Bayswater Road to Whitechapel and north-south from Holloway to Elephant and Castle.

An ongoing problem with tramways in central London was a result of the refusal to allow trams to cross the city (apart from the Kingsway subway) or to serve the West End. A ring of nine inner city terminals from Paddington to Aldgate were dead ends, causing operational difficulties and traffic congestion. Suggestions to link these terminals with a connecting tramway could have greatly eased the situation but it was never approved. In 1914 a proposal to link no fewer than 22 tram terminals in the central area was overtaken by the First World War and when it was reconsidered in 1919 enthusiasm for tramways was beginning to wane.

Some plans to operate express trams for commuters in the 1920s were not pursued because of the lack of overtaking tracks. Instead interest turned to segregation of tracks from road traffic, surprisingly absent on any scale in London. A delegation to Birmingham and Liverpool inspected their newly constructed sleeper tracks in the median strips of dual carriageways and were greatly impressed. Negotiations began to construct similar tracks along Uxbridge Road where there was plenty of carriageway width to accommodate reservations. Some of the potential tramway reservations can still be seen between Southall and Hillingdon but they never had trams, surely one of the saddest 'might have beens' in London, a great lost opportunity. They were nearly used for trams decades later by West London Tram but that is also a 'might have been', see Ch.19.

Maidstone & Chatham

In north Kent, an electric tramway linked Chatham with Rochester, Gillingham and Rainham with a branch to Chatham Dockyard, familiar to generations of sailors. A few miles to the south was the small tramway of Maidstone Corporation Tramways. An ambitious plan was launched in 1903 to link the two systems with a 3ft.6ins overhead electric tramway, this being the gauge of the existing tramways in the area. The Rochester, Chatham, Gravesend, and Maidstone Tramways Company envisaged a roadside tramway along the main road between Maidstone and Chatham. Objections from the companies resulted in parts of the route being withdrawn and although some powers were authorised, none was built.

Perhaps they were very far sighted because nearly a century later, Kent County Council proposed a light rail line linking Chatham and Maidstone, which is described in Chapter 21.

Margate and Dover

The Isle of Thanet Tramways ran from Margate through Broadstairs to Ramsgate, partly along the seafront using the popular 3ft.6ins gauge. Dover had a small municipal tramway serving this important seaport. It was one of the first electric tramways in the south of England, both routes opening in 1897.

Probably the most ambitious tramway plan in Britain was launched in 1899 by the Cinque Ports Light Railway for a 3ft.6ins gauge line from Ramsgate Harbour through Sandwich, Deal, Dover, Folkestone, Hythe, Dymchurch, Romney, Lydd and

Rye to Hastings, a total distance of nearly 68 miles. Through running could have extended from Margate to Bexhill but Dover Corporation blocked the way and the scheme was dropped in in 1900. East Kent buses replaced Dover trams in 1936 and Isle of Thanet trams in 1937.

Rawtenstall-Burnley

Back in the East Lancashire network, another potential link was the two mile gap between the Rawtenstall tramway at Dunnockshaw and Burnley tracks at Burnley Summit. This was another windswept Pennine moorland route with few potential passengers, only sheep. The line would have been single track with passing places but connected to Burnley's double track. It reached a height of 984 ft and some gradients were as steep as 10.5%. Powers were granted under the Rawtenstall Corporation Act 1907 to construct the line to Burnley Summit, the terminus of the Burnley Corporation tram route but they were never exercised.

South Coast

The largest town along the South Coast was the town of Brighton which had a small 3ft.6ins gauge tramway network. It continued profitably until closure in 1939. A string of coastal towns could have been served by a Blackpool style tramway but a plethora of various proposals all came to nothing, due in large part to negative attitudes of local councils opposing schemes in their area. A few sections were authorised but not built and then in 1903 BET (British Electric Traction Ltd) proposed a 22 mile tramway from Littlehampton to Brighton via Worthing, Shoreham and Hove. Most of it was

An extract from the Parliamentary plans for the Rawtenstall extension to Burnley.
Richard Hargreaves

authorised but none built, due again to council opposition and the powers lapsed in 1910. Plans to take the tramway even further east through Rottingdean to Newhaven were not authorised.

South Shields - Sunderland

The town of South Shields on the south bank of the River Tyne estuary was a busy and compact industrial, commercial and leisure centre, popular with visitors from nearby Newcastle upon Tyne and the County Durham hinterland. It was served by a 7½ mile tramway network with one modern reserved track route towards Cleadon. Adjacent tramways were in Jarrow to the west and Sunderland to the south. There was through running to Jarrow which itself was only a short distance from the Gateshead system, but that connection was never made.

The Cleadon terminus of the South Shields sleeper track route (actually at The Ridgeway, Cleadon Park, about a mile from Cleadon village) was less than three miles from the Fulwell terminus of the Sunderland tramway. As early as 1903 there was talk of linking the two systems and in 1913 three route options were discussed between the two councils. They could never agree on which option to progress and despite ongoing talks over several years, nothing was achieved.

South Shields tram No.7 must have had a lucky number because it led the procession when the system opened and then survived to become the only remaining example of the original trams, but sadly its luck ran out before tram preservation became popular. It was not preserved. In the view below at The Ridgeway, the last street of the council estate, the track it is standing on was meant to carry on into Cleadon Village and then on

South Shields open top four wheel tram No.7 at The Ridgeway, within sight of Sunderland. Dr Hugh Nicol, Monday 16th July 1934; colour by Malcolm Fraser

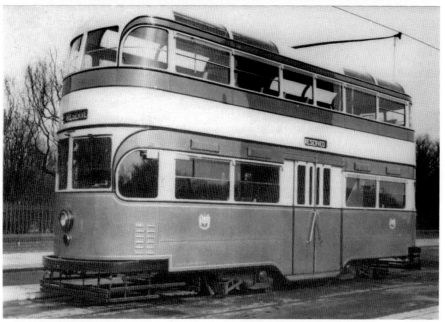

South Shields No. 52 built by Brush in 1936 was the newest tram in the South Shields fleet and copied Sunderland's penchant for streamlined centre entrance cars.

When South Shields closed in 1946 No. 52 found a new life as Sunderland No.48 thus being the only tram that ran in both towns even though the link between them was never built. If the link between the two systems had been built, Sunderland 48 could have been on its way to its former home in South Shields instead of terminating at Roker and Seaburn.

South Shields' attractive blue livery has been recreated in this colourised depot view of No. 52. *Malcolm Fraser*

A side view and interior views of South Shield No. 52. *R. Brook*

Sunderland tram No.87 is on its way from Fulwell to Seaburn, about to turn right from Dene Lane into Dykelands Road. The trees on the horizon are close to Cleadon and the terminus of the South Shields Ridgeway tram route. Malcolm Fraser

to Sunderland, but it never happened. The only bit of Cleadon in sight is the water tower on the hill, Cleadon Chimney.

South Shields trams finished in 1946 and tram No. 52, the only modern car in the fleet, was sold to Sunderland. It was repainted from South Shields blue and cream into Sunderland's red and cream as their No.48 and fitted in well with their fleet of modern centre entrance streamlined trams. It wasn't only a tram that went to Sunderland; some of the rails from the Ridgeway central reservation were sold to Sunderland for use on the Durham Road extensions. No. 48 ran until 1954 when the Sunderland system closed, despite a new extension along Durham Road being only five years old. So while the two systems were never connected, one tram did run on both tramways!

Trams may yet run from South Shields to Sunderland. At a meeting in March 2014, the Leader of South Tyneside Council, Councillor Iain Malcolm, described his vision for a tramway from South Shields to Cleadon and Sunderland, which was under discussion with Nexus, the Tyne and Wear transport authority.

Wakefield - Normanton

Another less obvious missing link was between the Wakefield tramway and Castleford. A tramway was

built by United Kingdom Tramways from Normanton through Castleford to Pontefract. UK Tramways obtained powers to extend it from Normanton into Wakefield, linking with the West Riding trams, but it was never built; neither were proposed extensions to Featherstone and Knottingley. UK Tramways was short-lived and the Castleford tramways were abandoned in 1925.

South Wales

Although several towns and cities in south Wales had tramways, there were never any plans to link any of them together. The Oystermouth tramway between Swansea and Mumbles was the oldest passenger railway system in the world, having begun operation with horse traction in 1807. It later had the largest double deck trams ever operated on a British electric tramway but sadly closed in 1960. It was not even connected to the Swansea town tramway although they were very close at the town end of the line.

Cardiff, Swansea, Llanelly, Neath, Pontypridd, Aberdare, Merthyr Tydfil and Newport all had their own tramways and some extensions were authorised but none that would have linked networks. This was at least in part due to the topography of the valleys which constrained route opportunities.

Missing Links

Legend
- ○ operational tramway
- ○ proposed tramway, not built
- ○—○ operational tramways with one or more connecting lines
- ○—○ "*might have been*" missing link, not built

Scotland

Perth
Dundee Broughty Ferry
Wemyss
Dunfirmline Kikrcaldy
Falkirk Leith
Dumbarton
Greenock Edinburgh Musselburgh
Glasgow Airdrie
Paisley Motherwell
Rothesay
Ardrossan
Kilmarnock
Ayr

Irish Sea

Sea (Wales)

North Sea

Carlisle

Tyneside
Newcastle Tynemouth
Gateshead South Shields
Jarrow
Sunderland
Sunderland District

Stockton West Hartlepool
Darlington Middlesbrough

Scarborough

Barrow in Furness Lancaster
Morecambe

Keighley York
Blackpool Bradford
Preston Burnley Dewsbury
Lytham St.Annes Leeds
Southport Halifax Castleford
Wakefield
Barnsley Dearne District
Huddersfield Doncaster
Sheffield Mexborough
Rotherham
Chesterfield Lincoln

Hull
Immingham Grimsby
Cleethorpes

For details of tramways in this area, see separate map.

Llandudno & Colwyn Bay
Chester
Wrexham
Pwllheli

Matlock Mansfield
Ripley (Notts & Derbys)
Ilkeston
Stoke on Trent Derby Nottingham

Burton upon Trent Burton & Ashby

Wales

Leicester Peterborough
Norwich Great Yarmouth
Wolverhampton Walsall Lowestoft
Dudley
Halesowen Birmingham
Kidderminster & Stourport Coventry
Warwick & Leamington
Worcester Northampton Cambridge

Ipswich
England Colchester

Gloucester Cheltenham
Oxford Luton
Swindon London
Swansea Merthyr Tydfil
Llanelli Aberdare Newport Reading
Neath Bristol Southend-on Sea
Rhondda Bath Sheerness
Mumbles Pontypridd Cardiff Rochester Margate
Weston-Super-Mare Chatham
Maidstone
Dover
Taunton

Fareham Horndean Littlehampton Hastings
Southampton Cosham Brighton
Poole Bournemouth Portsmouth Worthing
Gosport
Exeter

Torquay

Devonport Plymouth
Camborne & Redruth

English Channel

N
W E
S

0   50   100
kilometres

0   50   100
miles

Note : 'London' includes the municipal tramways of L.C.C., Barking, Bexley Heath, Croydon, Dartford, East Ham, Erith, Ilford, Leyton, Walthamstow and West Ham, and the company tramways of Gravesend & Northfleet, London United, Metropolitan Electric and South Metropolitan Tramways & Light.

© R.A.Smith & T.Young, October 2020. No. 2462, v1.2.

Scotland

In Scotland the cities of Edinburgh and Glasgow each had large tramway networks which extended well into adjacent towns. Aberdeen and Dundee each had their city tram systems but were not close enough to be linked to any other tramway. There were no 'missing links' as such although there were some authorised extensions which were not built.

Dunfermline and Kirkaldy.

Two towns on the north bank of the Firth of Forth, Dunfermline and Kirkaldy, each had small tram systems serving their respective local areas and extending into the rural hinterland and to Rosyth Dockyard. Dunfermline and District Tramways progressively expanded north eastwards to the communities of Lochgelly, Kelty and Lochore by

1910. The gauge was 3ft.6 ins. and service was provided by 45 4-wheel double deck cars on the 18½ mile network.

A few miles further up the Firth of Forth coastline the municipality of Kirkaldy had a six mile 3ft.6ins. gauge system running from Linktown in the south to Leven in the northeast. A Bill was promoted to join the two systems with a line from Lochgelly to Kirkaldy and Dunfermline did obtain powers for an extension from Lochgelly to Kinglassie, about half way to Kirkaldy. The opportunity to create a 30 mile line from Rosyth to Leven was lost for ever. While it was mainly rural at that time, much development has taken place over the past century and improved forms of public transport were considered in a study of options for Cardenden in 2008. The existing bus services follow a similar route to the 'might have been' tramway and there are good local rail services.

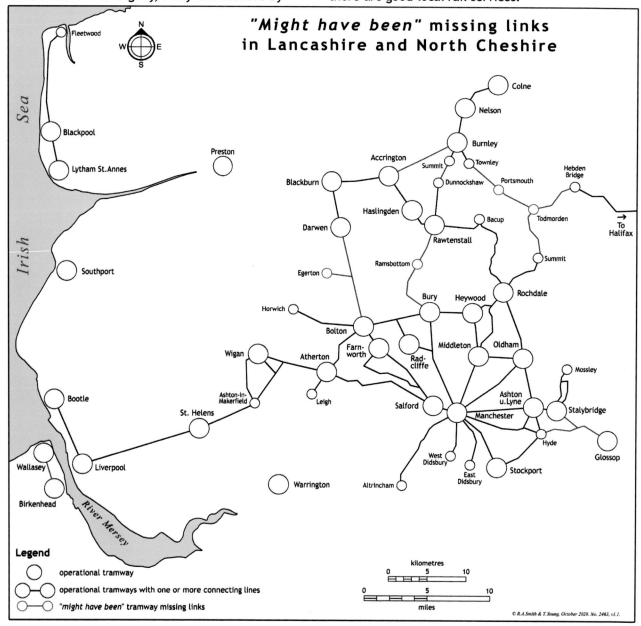

5. Tram Tunnels - only one made it

While underground railways have become commonplace in large cities and conurbations since the early examples in the nineteenth century, tunnels for tramways have been much less common. A few examples can be found in European cities and Boston, Philadelphia and San Francisco have had tram tunnels for a century or more. In Britain the only example was a relatively short tunnel in London but it might have been much longer.

Some modern light rail systems have tunnels including Croydon Tramlink and Manchester Metrolink but they are former railway tunnels and do not include any stations.

The Kingsway Tram Subway

London's only tram subway, and the only one in Britain to this day, was authorised by a London County Council Act in 1902. The concept was modelled on similar projects in New York and Boston following visits by LCC officers. Its construction was integrated with the reconstruction of Kingsway and Aldwych, an early example of integrated transport and land use.

Before the Kingsway subway was approved, a more ambitious plan was proposed in 1901 running from an underground loop under Parliament Square, under Whitehall and then under Strand, Fleet Street, St Paul's Churchyard and Cheapside to Moorgate Street. The total cost for the 5 mile (8 km) tunnel would have

been £1.75m *(£1.73bn)*. The cut and cover double track tramway for single deck trams was flanked on each side by pipe subways for services, an advanced concept that has still not been adopted for modern tramways. Although this route was not built, the design concept was used for the Kingsway subway.

Services began in 1906 with single deck cars, it being assumed that double deckers would not be feasible and that single deck trams coupled together could handle the projected demand. There were two underground tram stations at Holborn and Aldwych. These had island platforms, with passengers boarding and alighting through the offside front doors.

The tunnel enabled tram services in the north to be linked with tram services in the south so direct journeys could be made from Highgate, Hackney and Leyton to Tooting, West Norwood, Camberwell and Catford. However to achieve this network with adequate capacity it was necessary to enlarge the tunnel to allow double deck operation and this was completed in 1931. Trailer operation with single deckers was technically satisfactory but was vehemently opposed by the Metropolitan police. This set Britain against common practice in the rest of Europe for nearly a century.

Trams displaying the sign 'Via Kingsway Subway' became a familiar sight across wide parts of London but, after only 21 years of full use, the last tram

A tram station in the Kingsway tram subway in London, closed in 1952.

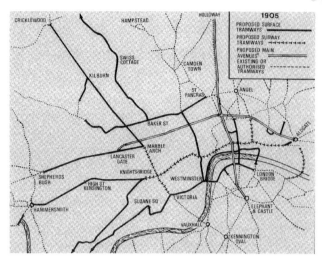

Proposed tram subways in London in 1905.

ran through the subway on 5th April 1952, prior to London's last tram on 5th July 1952, another example of Britain's unfortunate habit of throwing away infrastructure assets long before they were life expired.

Even before trams started operating through the Kingsway subway, the Royal Commission on London Traffic recommended in 1905 that shallow tram subways should be built running north-south and east-west under central London to link the existing tramways which did not penetrate the city centre. One would run from Victoria to Marble Arch under Grosvenor Place and Park Lane and another from Aldgate under Cheapside, Ludgate Hill, Strand and Piccadilly to Knightsbridge. The latter was similar to the 1901 plan and was eight times the length of the Kingsway subway then under construction. A north-south tunnel would run under the Thames from Leman Street near Aldgate East to Tower Bridge Road on the south side.

Yet another scheme would have linked Southwark and Aldersgate but the route passed close to St Paul's Cathedral so it was quickly dropped. Other routes were considered too expensive or not really needed, only the Victoria – Marble Arch tunnel was favoured. The Commission said it was highly desirable and would not be too expensive as it would run under Hyde Park and avoid the carriageway in Park Lane. The LCC considered this plan again in 1918-19 but decided to develop a surface tramway through the Park instead. That was also rejected.

The Kingsway tram subway ran from Southampton Row to Victoria Embankment underneath Kingsway, Aldwych and Lancaster Place. Plans for further tram subways in London were never realised.

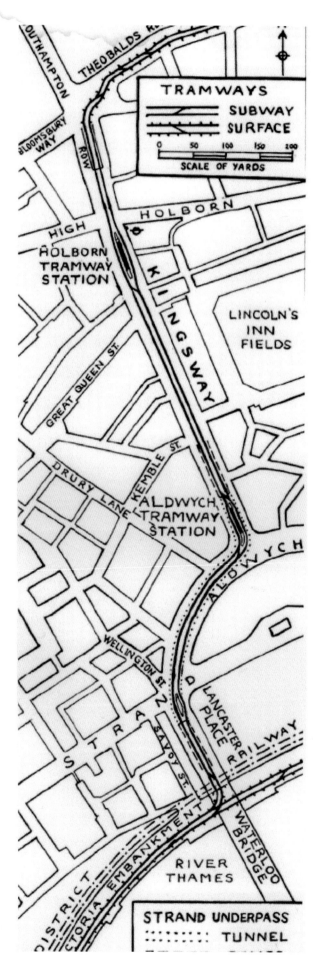

Manchester Tram Subways

While tram subways were seen as a solution to London's congested streets, very similar ideas were being proposed to relieve congestion in central Manchester. The Manchester Courier for 5th May 1903 showed a plan for underground tramways linking Piccadilly (then London Road), Victoria, Exchange, Central and Oxford Road stations (figure below). An interchange station between the three tunnels would be located on the Royal Infirmary Hospital site in Piccadilly, later known as Piccadilly Gardens. The outer ends of each tunnel line would have been at surface level to minimise costs. The route into London Road station was remarkably similar to the present Metrolink route from Aytoun Street to London Road, although Aytoun Street had not then been completed.

An Act of Parliament was to be sought for powers to construct tramways or light railways partly underground and partly on the surface. Some tunnel sections would be in bored tunnel and only single deck cars would be operated. Total cost, excluding trams, was estimated at £750,000 (£484m). Like so many schemes this one was never progressed.

With the Kingsway subway already in operation, Manchester considered another tram subway plan in 1914. Manchester City Tramways Manager J.M.McElroy undertook an extensive study tour of tramways in major European cities and some in the USA including New York and Boston. On his return he prepared a report for the Tramways Committee which set out a range of options for coping with the growth in tramway traffic. As well as various rapid transit lines another option was shallow tram subways.

A contemporary plan published in the Manchester Guardian on 14th March 1914 (figure overleaf) shows an east-west tram subway running under London Road, Piccadilly and Market Street with a tunnel ramp in London Road south of Fairfield Street and a ramp in Victoria Bridge Street between Deansgate and Chapel Street. The length was 1¼ miles (2 km) and there would have been two or three subway tram stops with staircase access from street level.

Subways would be preferable to deep level tubes as they were more easily accessible to passengers. However McElroy did not favour the idea of tram subways in the city centre as they would be high cost and low capacity and cause severe disruption

The 1903 Tram Tunnel proposal was termed a railway on the plan but the key refers to 'Underground Tramway' and 'Overground Tramway'.
Manchester Courier May, 1903

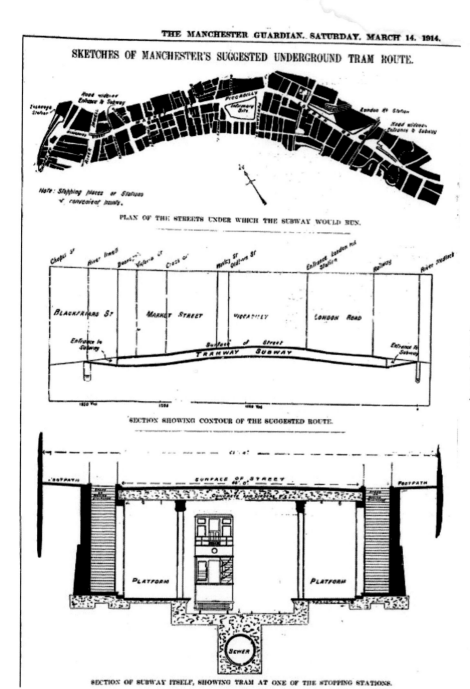

SKETCHES OF MANCHESTER'S SUGGESTED UNDERGROUND TRAM ROUTE.

PLAN OF THE STREETS UNDER WHICH THE SUBWAY WOULD RUN.

SECTION SHOWING CONTOUR OF THE SUGGESTED ROUTE.

SECTION OF SUBWAY ITSELF, SHOWING TRAM AT ONE OF THE STOPPING STATIONS.

A report in the Manchester Guardian for 14 March 1914 showed the proposed route and cross sections for a Market Street tram subway, quite different from the 1903 plan.

during construction. They would probably be limited to single deck cars with much less capacity than the standard double deck trams although the cross section of a tram 'stopping station' shows a double deck tram with side platforms. At that time the London subway only had single deck trams with island platforms so Manchester's design was more advanced. But he did envisage the need to plan for major integrated transport systems. The 1914-18 war no doubt put paid to any investment at least in the short term and tram subways slipped off the agenda for the next seventy years.

There were several attempts at developing an underground railway for Manchester from the turn of the 20th century. A well planned scheme was

proposed in 1928 by Henry Mattinson, General Manager of Manchester City Tramways, to link the suburban railways. A north-east to south-west tunnel and a north-west to south-east tunnel would have intersected at an interchange station at Albert Square and would have linked all the mainline railway stations.

Mattinson explained that these tunnels would accommodate nine suburban railway routes with 27 services carrying 200,000 passengers a day, nearly ten times today's crowded trains. It was a remarkably far sighted plan and would doubtless have given Manchester the foundations of an integrated public transport network for the next century. It pre-dated the Picc-Vic tunnel project

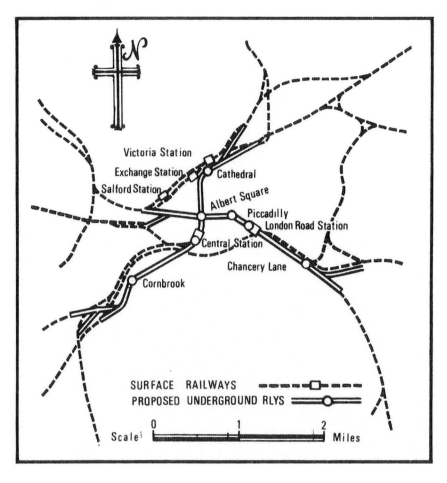

Manchester Tramway Manager Henry Mattinson's plan for underground railways in Manchester in 1928, an excellent plan that was shelved like the rest.

by 45 years, but it is to Manchester's discredit that neither of these schemes were built.

Seventy years after the 1914 tram tunnel proposal, yet another project for tram tunnels was mooted. As part of the Rail Strategy Study which led to the selection of the Metrolink system, options for light rail tunnels were included to link Piccadilly, Victoria and Deansgate stations (figures below). A sub-surface option would have followed the present Metrolink route fairly closely with underground tram stops at Piccadilly Gardens, High Street and St Peter's Square. A bored tunnel option would follow a different route with underground stations at Piccadilly Gardens, Royal Exchange and Albert Square. The resulting light rail network would have closely resembled the Tyne & Wear Metro with its tunnels under Newcastle and Gateshead. Manchester City Council favoured an underground option as they were concerned about the practicability of street running light rail but the street running option was selected and nobody would now suggest going back to tram tunnels.

Manchester is still the largest conurbation in Europe with no rail tunnels of any description, tram, light rail, metro, underground or 'S'Bahn' (suburban rail). This may yet change as the latest strategy document 'Greater Manchester Transport Strategy 2040 launched in 2016 includes the possibility of rail tunnels which could be for Metrolink or heavy rail. However it is only a long term option.

Researchers at Manchester University have added some of the various cross city tram and underground options from the twentieth century onto one plan to show the range. The red line, Metrolink tramway, is the only one to have been built (see page 39).

LRT Tunnel Alignments

(A) Mosley St. alignment

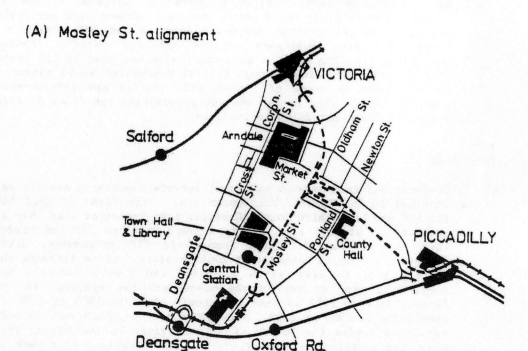

(B) Cross St./Corporation St. alignment

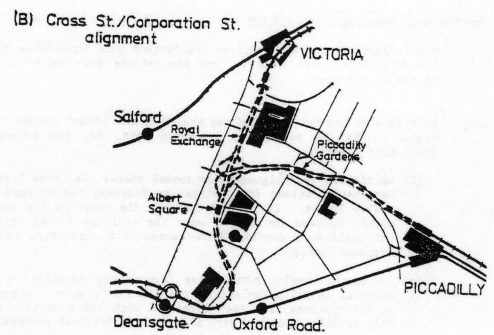

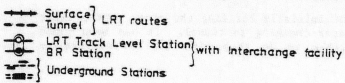

Surface ⎱ LRT routes
Tunnel ⎰

LRT Track Level Station ⎱ with interchange facility
BR Station ⎰

Underground Stations

Light rail tunnel alignment options for Manchester in January 1984. GMC/GMPTE

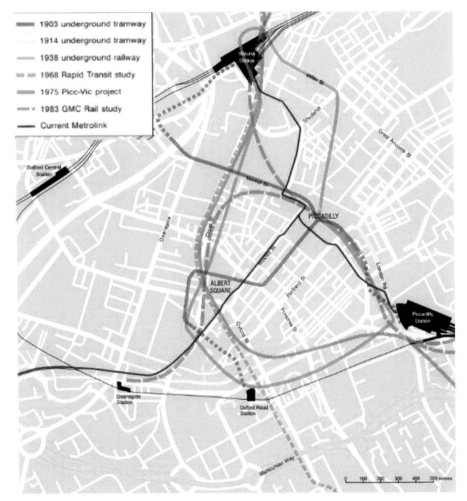

Tunnels planned under Manchester from 1903 to 1983 and the Metrolink route.
Martin Dodge, Manchester University

Legend:
- 1903 underground tramway
- 1914 underground tramway
- 1938 underground railway
- 1968 Rapid Transit study
- 1975 Picc-Vic project
- 1983 GMC Rail study
- Current Metrolink

Liverpool Mersey Tunnel

A rail tunnel under the River Mersey opened in 1886 but by the nineteen twenties pressure was growing for a road tunnel. Construction started in 1925 to a design by civil engineer Sir Basil Mott in association with John Brodie, renowned City Engineer of Liverpool. Mott, Hay and Anderson were the consulting engineers who went on to become one of the leading light rail and tramway engineers in Britain, (now Mott MacDonald), designing Manchester's Phase 1 Metrolink amongst others.

John Brodie was famous for designing the standard dual carriageway with tramway reservation in the centre and footways on each side (see chapter 8) and was credited with being one of the first to propose electric trams for Liverpool. He became City Engineer in 1898 and was the first local authority engineer to be made President of the prestigious Institution of Civil Engineers for 1920/21. He died in 1934.

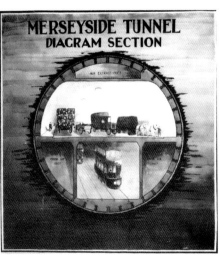

Cross sections for trams in the Mersey Tunnel.

Liverpool tram 757 was the Priestley Subway car of 1929.
Alan Robson

Liverpool 757 bore a close resemblance to Blackpool tram 167 built in 1928. *Alan Robson*

No doubt through John Brodie's influence, the Queensway Mersey Tunnel was designed for road traffic **and** trams. Road vehicles would use the upper deck while trams would have their exclusive tracks on the lower deck (figure page 39). This would have connected the vast Liverpool network with the smaller Birkenhead system and potentially the Wallasey tramway.

The cross section sketches produced at the time showed double deck trams (figure page 39) although it was probable that only single deck cars would have been used, as in the original Kingsway subway in London. Liverpool Corporation even built a prototype single deck tram intended as the forerunner of a fleet to operate the tunnel routes. Number 757, known as the 'Priestly Subway Car'

after the General Manager Percy Priestly, was built in 1929 by English Electric in Preston (figure above). Its design was similar to Blackpool's long single decker 'Pantograph' cars (figure above) but with various technical improvements for high speed running and multiple unit operation. It was probably the closest that any British operator came to adopting the European standard of single deck multiple unit operation which could have transformed the economics of UK tramways.

Some rather optimistic costings were produced and disagreements between the authorities on each side of the Mersey resulted in the tramway being removed from the plans and when the Mersey Tunnel opened in 1934 it was for road vehicles only. Car No. 757 was withdrawn in 1935.

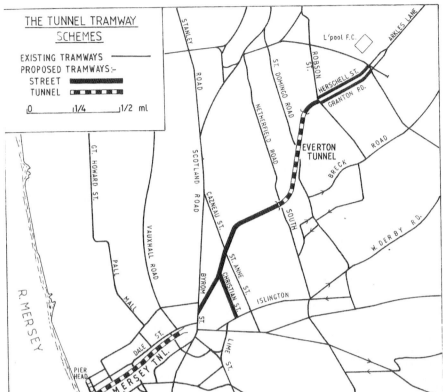

Tram tunnel schemes for Liverpool in 1927.

Liverpool might have had two tram tunnels. While trams under the Mersey were being debated, plans for a tram tunnel under Everton (figure above) were progressing. Parliamentary powers were granted in 1927 to construct the tunnel including a double track tramway and connecting tracks to the adjacent tram routes. It would have connected to the Mersey tram tunnel on street tracks and could have formed the nucleus of a rapid transit network for the city. Prevailing economic considerations once more stopped a visionary project. Priestley's untimely death in 1933 may have left the tunnels with fewer supporters.

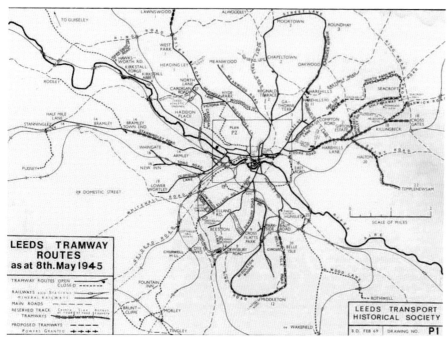

Leeds tramways in 1945 included many miles of reserved tracks. LTHS

Leeds

The City of Leeds had one of the largest tram networks in Britain which could have been developed into a European style light rail system. Over 70 miles of routes included many miles of reserved track tramways on central reservations in dual carriageways, side reservations or private right of way. Routes to Lawnswood, Roundhay Park, Cross Gates, Halton and Temple Newsam, Belle Isle, Middleton and Bramley had significant lengths of segregated tracks. More were planned and three separate routes to the massive housing area at Seacroft were authorised, but not built.

In 1945 an imaginative plan was developed by Leeds City Engineer, Colonel W.S.Cameron, working closely with Tramways Manager William Vane Morland, for tram subways in the city centre which would have replaced most of the street running routes (figure opposite).

A northwest to west tunnel would have linked Woodhouse Lane to Wellington Street with underground stations at Woodhouse Lane, Briggate and City Square, for interchange with rail services. A northeast to east tunnel would link North Street to York Street with underground stations at North Street, Briggate (interchange with western tram tunnel), Corn Exchange and Leeds Bus Station. A third single track loop tunnel would link lines from the south with underground stations at City Square, Briggate and Corn Exchange, each giving interchange with the west and east tunnel routes. Tunnel ramps would be located in the streets, about half a mile from the city centre.

Leeds City Tramways even ordered three prototype single deck trams for possible use in the tunnels (see Ch 9). However financial constraints and political changes combined to ensure that the far sighted subway proposals were lost. Instead a progression of tramway cutbacks ensued, although in 1948 a new section of route was opened linking the Middleton and Belle Isle services, both of which would have fed into the tunnel system.

Following the retirement of Vane Morland, Alexander Findlay was appointed General Manager of Leeds City Tramways in December 1949. He had been Chief Engineer of the Glasgow Tramways and was closely involved in the planned tram subways in that city, a concept very similar to that for Leeds. The subway plans were briefly reconsidered but there was not sufficient political or financial support to see them through.

Vane Morland died in 1962 aged 78. 'Modern Tramway' commented: "if his ideas had been followed through to the end, Leeds would have been one of the best equipped cities in the world then and now. It would have been the envy of Britain's cities and the undisputed leader in transport planning. Vane Morland stood out as perhaps the most far-sighted manager of a large city transport system that Britain has ever known".

Leeds is the ultimate *'might have been'* tramway in Britain. Ironically after another 65 years Leeds still does not have any form of light rail or tramway, probably the largest city in Europe which is dependent on buses for its urban public transport.

Proposed tram subways in Leeds city centre in 1945.

City Square in Leeds would have had a multilevel underground tram station if the City Engineer's plans had been built. Leeds City Engineer

The prototype subway trams were eventually delivered in 1953 but by then not only had the tunnel plans been scrapped but a decision taken to scrap the whole tram network, a staggering waste of infrastructure investment. Leeds last tram ran in November 1959.

Glasgow

Scotland's largest first generation tram network, Glasgow, is also home to the smallest underground railway in Britain. It is commonly called the Glasgow Subway (or the 'clockwork orange'!) and runs in a circle for six and a half miles of 4ft.0ins gauge double track, entirely underground. It might have been accompanied by tram subways with interchanges at key locations.

In 1943 during the second world war, a new dynamic general manager was appointed to Glasgow Corporation Transport Department, one E.R.L.Fitzpayne. His father had been general manager of Edinburgh Corporation Tramways, so trams ran in the blood. He made the jump from one of the smallest tramways in the country at South Shields to assistant manager at the largest, quickly becoming General Manager.

Fitzpayne's vision was based on the upgrading of the tram network with reserved track routes in the suburbs feeding into tram subways through the central area. Underground tram stations would be integrated with underground railway stations where appropriate. Reserved tracks already existed on some outer suburban routes. Models illustrating the concept were exhibited at the Kelvingrove Art Galleries in August 1944. Trams would continue to provide the primary public transport network, integrated with bus services and the underground. An American PCC car was shown as a possible type of rolling stock.

His plan was even more ambitious than the Leeds subways the following year. It would have given Glasgow a magnificent public transport network to rival the best of European city systems.

Another attempt to introduce modern trams to Glasgow was made in 1948 when a report by Eric Fitzpayne on the future development of passenger transport in Glasgow (Ref.10) was presented to the Glasgow Transport Committee. It made scant mention of the massive tram network although it did accept that Glasgow's trams were regarded with pride by its citizens and had efficiently and cheaply met the problem of mass transportation. The report commented 'it cannot be lightly thrown aside unless there is something better to take its place'. He proposed a 'new electric vehicle' which is described in Chapter 9 but is clearly a modern light rail vehicle. Among the routes was the reserved track tramway to Anniesland and tunnels through the city centre. When nothing came of this plan, Fitzpayne appears to have given up hope of modern trams as ten years later he agreed to scrap the whole Glasgow tram network.

Glasgow was the last city tram system in Britain but like the rest it was confined to history and the last trams ran in 1962, some long before they were life expired. Miles of relatively new reserved track and post war trams with plenty of years left were all consigned to the scrapyard, a huge *'might have been'*.

A Glasgow Coronation tram on sleeper track on Mossbank Boulevard, abandoned in 1960.
Dr Neil Clifton

6. Blackpool, sole survivor

The seaside town of Blackpool is renowned as having the very first electric street tramway in Britain in 1885 and the last first generation tramway in the sixties. As tram routes closed in other cities up and down the country, so too tram routes closed in Blackpool until the last complete street tram route in the UK, to Marton, finally succumbed to buses in October 1962. The street section along Dickson Road to Blackpool North Station followed in October 1963. This left just the long seafront route from Starr Gate to Fleetwood, incorporating most of the original Blackpool and Fleetwood Tramroad.

The system could have been extended in 1941 when wartime pressures nearly resulted in a tramway extension along Squires Gate Lane from Lytham Road to the Vickers Armstrong factory at Common Edge Lane. Now the site of a large trading estate, then it produced much needed Wellington bombers. But it was a mile from the nearest tram stop and fuel shortages ruled out feeder bus services. A reserved track tramway, partly single track and partly double track in a central reservation, would have been a valuable addition to the system, and would still be very valuable today to serve the retail park and Blackpool airport.

Blackpool manager Walter Luff was enthusiastic and even had enough tram rail in stock. Blackpool Council were less keen and insisted that it should only be temporary and that Vickers should pay the whole cost. Like so many good ideas it never came to fruition.

The history of the decline of the British street tramway was researched by the late Richard Buckley for his PhD thesis (Ref. 32). He showed why Blackpool became the last surviving tramway in Britain, identifying the reasons for the gradual demise of all other tramways, the smaller ones before the second world war and even the larger city systems in the post war period. By 1961 only Blackpool was left. Its extensive reserved tracks and modernised fleet of trams had combined to give the tramway an advantage over buses that ensured its survival, features that could have saved tramways in at least a few other towns and cities.

The remaining historic trams in Blackpool were dispersed to various museums including several in the USA and some even carried passengers again on city streetcar systems, notably along Market Street in San Francisco. A substantial number were retained in Blackpool to operate vintage tours along the promenade.

The sixties were not a good time for Blackpool's trams, being the last remaining British system was not easy. On more than one occasion there were serious fears that even Blackpool would close completely and leave Britain completely tramless apart from museums. The fact that the last remaining route was mainly on reserved track, apart from the section through Fleetwood town centre, and trams were the only way of handling the heavy loadings during the Blackpool Illuminations, saved the system. It would not have been achieved

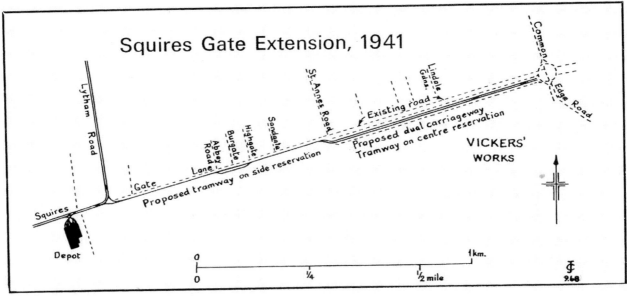

A tramway extension along Squires Gate Lane to the Vickers Armstrong factory would be valuable today to serve the retail park and airport.

without the enormous skill and dedication of their tramway engineers who managed to keep an aging fleet serviceable. Ironically the streamlined trams built in the 1930s outlived the post-war trams built in the fifties and even those built in the eighties.

The sixties saw the introduction of motor and trailer combinations using rebuilt pre-war railcoaches as towing cars with new build trailers from Metro Cammell-Weymann. The attempt to emulate continental practice was not entirely successful and they only operated in summer periods and had a relatively short working life. The

1970s saw a major programme of rebuilding pre-war trams to create one man operated trams and modernised double deckers, keeping the system going through hard times.

By the mid-1980s the future of the tramway was more secure and new trams were ordered from East Lancashire Coachbuilders of Blackburn, more familiar as bus builders. These Centenary cars were designed for one man operation with a front entrance and centre exit and intended to replace the converted OMO cars. Only eight cars were built before the 1986 Transport Act resulted in Blackpool

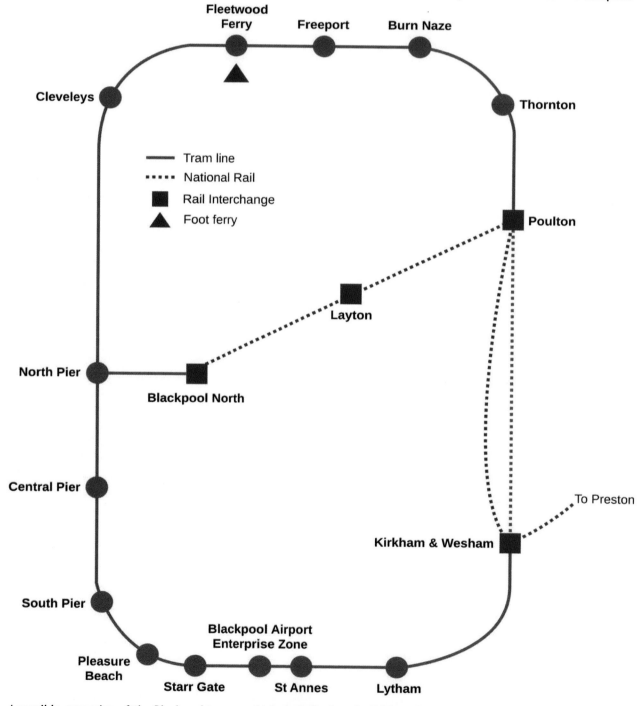

A possible expansion of the Blackpool tramway to include Poulton-le-Fylde and Lytham St Annes.

Transport being separated from Blackpool Council and no more Centenaries were ordered. They were not the most successful of trams so perhaps it was a sensible decision but another *'might have been'* situation if a larger fleet had been obtained.

In the 1990s various plans to extend the Blackpool Tramway began to be considered. A favourite was to build a link to Pleasure Beach Station and take over the heavy rail line to Lytham St Anne's. Other thoughts have been to take trams to Poulton-le-Fylde or the Poulton to Fleetwood branch line. None of these ideas were progressed but a major upgrade on the Starr Gate to Fleetwood route was approved by the government in 2009 and completed in 2012 with a new fleet of articulated low floor trams.

The most obvious extension was to link North Pier and the promenade tramway with Blackpool North station, the main inter-city terminal for the town. Blackpool North lost its tram service when the Dickson Road route closed in 1963. Provision was made in the upgrade for the junction at Talbot Square although it remained unused for over five years. After some false starts work finally began in 2017 and should have been completed in 2019 but will not open fully until 2022 because of delays to the programme. At least one *'might have been'* has become a *'will be'*.

A major EU project termed 'Sintropher' between 2007 and 2014 examined a range of extension options using various forms of tram-train running on the tramway and extending onto heavy rail tracks. All the existing Fylde rail routes from Blackpool North and Blackpool South were considered together with disused or unused alignments up to Fleetwood. No firm proposals have emerged.

Discussions have taken place at the Blackpool, Fylde and Wyre Economic Prosperity Board to support the three local councils to fund a feasibility study into creating a light rail loop embracing the existing coastal tramway, the former railway from Fleetwood to Poulton-le-Fylde, the existing railway to Kirkham and Wesham and the South Blackpool line. This would revolutionise public transport on the Fylde peninsular but will it remain a *'might have been'?*

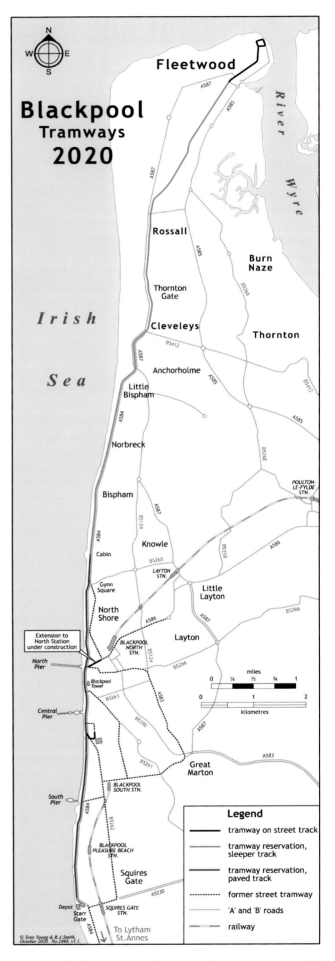

7. Gone but not forgotten - light rail plans not dead yet

The demise of once extensive tram networks in London, Liverpool, Leeds and Glasgow left most to conclude that the tram in Britain was dead, never to rise again. Transport and land use studies became the way forward in all the major conurbations. They evaluated every possible mode option but stubbornly refused to acknowledge the existence of light rail or tramways. Heavy rail or metro solutions were advanced for some major cities or improved bus systems. Light rail was eventually selected for Tyneside in the early seventies but as a segregated light metro, not with any street running.

There was a commonly held view amongst tramway advocates, still persisting into the 21st century, that officialdom in government and many local authorities deliberately denied mention of trams, often substituting 'public transport' for the word 'tram', or even just 'buses'. Major conurbations like Leeds and Bristol have stubbornly held onto bus based networks when trams could have offered a so much more attractive solution.

It was left to enthusiasts in the Light Railway Transport League (LRTL, changed to LRTA in 1979) to keep the concept of street running tramways alive during the sixties and seventies. Nobody dared to mention the word 'tram' as it would instantly brand the promoter as a backward looking crackpot totally out of touch with reality. Instead the term 'light rail' was used or in the case of Manchester 'duorail' to combat the short lived enthusiasm for monorails.

An excellent report was published by the LRTL in 1969 (Ref.18), just before the creation of the first Passenger Transport Executives. Entitled 'The New Tramway' it described many of the new light rail developments in Europe and beyond to show what was being achieved abroad. There was little technical literature in the UK and this document was intended as a general introduction. Although planners and engineers were beginning to recognise that new public transport systems were needed, many had little knowledge of light rail. Modern trams, traction forms, track, stations and forms of segregation were described with examples and operating capacities, speeds and frequencies and fares. Outline capital and operating costs were set out with an indication of profitability.

LRTL Members had tried hard in all the major tramway cities including London, Liverpool, Leeds, Sheffield and Glasgow to persuade councillors to retain and modernise their tramways, but without success. After they had all gone, light rail plans were suggested by LRTL members for Manchester, Norwich and Cleveland and no doubt other cities. Some examples are described here.

Manchester MARTIC

A monorail was proposed by Taylor Woodrow in 1965 (Ref.15) to link Wythenshawe and Langley through the city centre of Manchester. While it was not received with great enthusiasm (elevated structures through Manchester's historic centre would not have enhanced the cityscape) it did spur the authorities on to commission a major study of public transport options. The Manchester Rapid Transit Study report appeared two years later in 1967 (Ref.16). It recommended a conventional underground line, based on the technology of lines in Toronto. While it was a very good study it studiously ignored the one option that could have offered the most cost effective solution, namely light rail.

A small group of LRTL members in Manchester set up the Manchester Area Rapid Transit Investigation Committee (MARTIC) in 1964 to investigate the main public transport arteries in Greater Manchester. They coined the term 'duorail' to distinguish their proposal from the monorail, and to avoid the despised word 'tram'.

For an amateur group with no representation from 'officialdom' their short report was amazingly farsighted and proposed many features which are now an accepted part of the Metrolink tram system. They included the Bury electric railway line, links through the city centre, and a line to Wythenshawe and Ringway Airport, via Princess Parkway rather than the circuitous route via Sale Moor followed by Metrolink.

The MARTIC vehicle was an articulated double ended light rail vehicle capable of street running, powered through overhead wires and with a passenger capacity of 200, anticipating the Metrolink tram of nearly thirty years later.

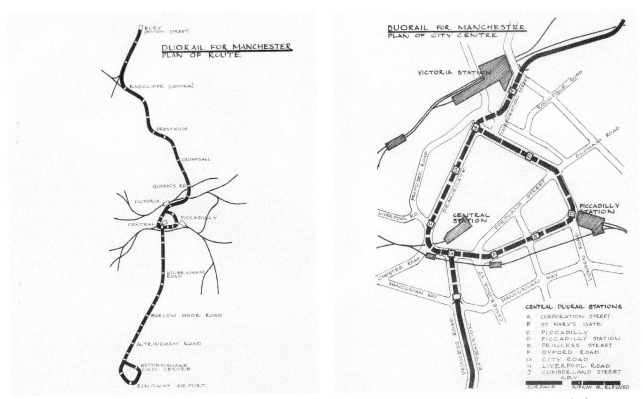

MARTIC's 'Duorail' route from Bury to Wythenshawe and Ringway Airport bears a close resemblance to today's Metrolink lines. In the city centre it would have followed a two way circular route linking the then three main railway stations. MARTIC

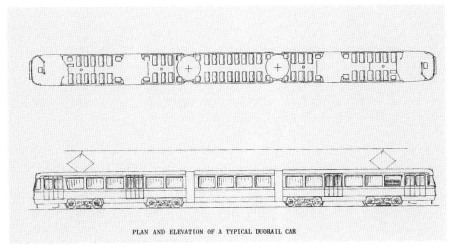

The type of vehicle envisaged by MARTIC was in effect an articulated tramcar similar to today's Metrolink trams. Metrolink trams have reached the Airport but via a circuitous route. MARTIC Brian Yates

Might Have Been Trams and Tramways 49

Transit for Norwich

A report published in 1970 by the LRTL (Ref.20) described a feasibility study for a modern tram system for the city of Norwich. A well-attended exhibition was held in Norwich Central Library and the plans were reported on radio, television and in the local press with some enthusiasm. They even coined the name 'Supertram', nearly 25 years before it became common language in Sheffield.

Three cross city routes were proposed (Fig.1 opposite) linking through the city centre (Fig.2 below) and each serving two outer termini, giving twelve destinations. Alignments were selected to support the linear patterns of development then being advanced, with a high level of segregation from road traffic.

The 46km network would have included 5km of tram only streets and a substantial amount of single track to ease creation of reserved track and minimise costs. The total cost was put at over £9m, about £300m at current prices, assuming 5 minute services in peak times and 10 minute off-peak.

Thirty three years later a study was carried out for Norfolk County Council which proposed a cross city light rail line (see Ch. 22). None of the schemes for Norwich have materialised.

A feasibility study
Editor: Peter J. Walker

Transit for Cleveland

In the early 1970s as work was beginning on Britain's first new generation light rail system, the Tyneside Metro, another report from the LRTL proposed a transit system for Cleveland (Ref.22). The emerging County of Cleveland resulted from the 1972 Local Government Act, which created the new non-metropolitan county comprising Stockton-on-Tees, Middlesbrough and Hartlepool. This was short lived as in 1996 another reorganisation created four separate unitary authorities, although the name Cleveland was retained for some functions including Police and Fire Service. To add further confusion the name 'Teesside' is used for some things such as the University.

The Teesside Structure Plan admitted that the transport system was inadequate and proposed express buses to improve public transport, the local rail system offering little benefit. The LRTL proposal was for a light rail network of routes linking all parts

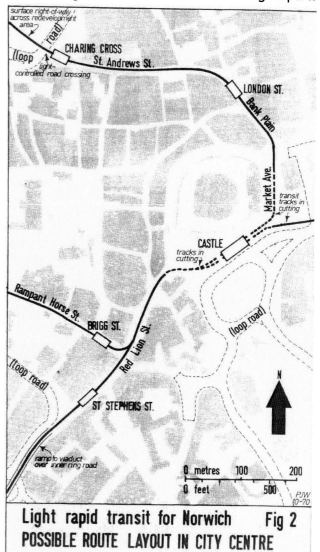

Transit for Norwich LRT Proposal Fig 2

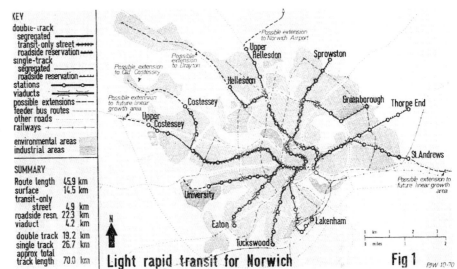

of the county and extending to Yarm, Guisborough, Redcar and Saltburn.

A 27 mile network would be operated with double articulated light rail vehicles with 94 seats and 160 standing. Estimated total cost was £9.7m, (£250m at current prices). The idea was not progressed, but seeds were sown as Cleveland later commissioned their own studies for light rail, but no proposals were taken any further.

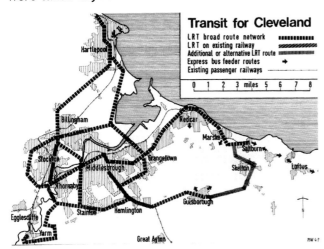

The Transit for Cleveland Report and the proposed network serving Middlesbrough, Redcar and Hartlepool. LRTL

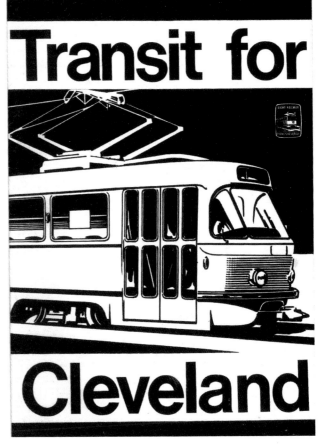

Light rapid transit vehicle for Cleveland

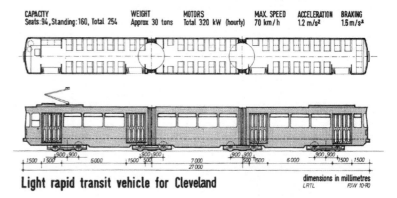

Light rapid transit vehicle for Cleveland

The type of vehicle envisaged for Cleveland. LRTL

A tramway for Sheffield

Sheffield's last tram ran in October 1960, the last city tramway in England. While they had lost favour with the city authorities they were still held in great affection by the travelling public. In 1965 Prime Minister Harold Wilson appointed Barbara Castle MP to be Minister of Transport. She had radical plans for urban public transport and to help formulate her ideas, she commissioned some transport studies, one of which was the 'Passenger Transport Integration Pilot Study, Sheffield Area'.

A Steering Committee of senior representatives from the Ministry, Yorkshire and Humberside Economic Planning Council, British Rail and others included Mr Chaceley Humpidge, General Manager of Sheffield City Transport. He was a lifelong supporter of tramways and trolleybuses having moved from Bradford where he had been responsible for extending the trolleybus network to be the largest outside London. It had often been rumoured that if he had taken over at Sheffield a bit earlier, the trams might have survived.

The Study was led by Dr Tom Constantine in the Civil Engineering Department of Sheffield University, later to become Professor and Pro Vice Chancellor of Salford University. It concluded that there was a case for a detailed engineering and economic study of a tramway, particularly to serve the new

town development at Mosborough. Mr Humpidge was known to favour a tramway to Mosborough and had sketched out his own plans. Dr Constantine had visited Frankfurt in Germany and had been impressed by the efficiency of their extensive tram system.

The local press latched on to the study conclusions, even making it their front page news in the Star, not noted for its pro-tram stance. It may have sowed some seeds, but Sheffield had to wait another 28 years before trams returned to its streets and reached Mosborough. Sadly Reverend Chaceley Humpidge (he was ordained in the Church of England after retiring) died in 1972 so did not see his dream realised. He had served as the first President of the Tramway Museum Society from 1958.

The Sheffield Study had a longer term influence, which eventually led to new tramways in Manchester, Sheffield and Birmingham. Barbara Castle used the results to inform a Transport White Paper 'Public Transport and Traffic' (Ref.17) which led to the 1968 Transport Act that set up Passenger Transport Executives in the major conurbations. Each of the new PTEs drew up plans for investment in new public transport systems, starting with the Tyneside Metro in 1980. It is likely that without the PTEs, none of the tramways which are now so familiar would have been carrying passengers.

The Sheffield Star banner headline on 5th May 1967 announcing the return of trams to Sheffield, only six and a half years after the last one had been sent to the scrapyard. The Sheffield Morning Telegraph repeated the story in November.

A narrow gauge 'might have been'

A rather different kind of 'might have been' had its origins in a factory in Barnet in North London. While full sized tramways were fast disappearing across Britain, a miniature tram was being built by tram visionary Claude Lane. His trams had run at various

fetes and in St Leonards near Hastings and Rhyl in North Wales, but a permanent home was found in Eastbourne on the south coast.

Eastbourne was the first municipality in the country to operate its own buses but never had trams, until in 1954 Modern Electric Tramways opened their 2ft.0ins gauge route from Royal Parade at Princes Park Gates to Crumbles. The mile long route linked car parks with the Golf House, Sailing Club and depot with a separate headquarters building and workshops.

Plans to extend the tramway in both directions were never realised and relations with Eastbourne Corporation were difficult. Although the tramway was popular with tourists the Corporation was worried about competition with its own buses. After a series of annual lease renewals and failure to obtain a seven year lease, the tramway finally closed in September 1969.

While Eastbourne trams proved to be another 'might have been', the tramway lived on to become an enormous success. An alternative location for the tramway was found along a disused railway in the picturesque River Axe valley for three miles between Seaton and Colyton in south Devon. The entire tramway including trams, track, overhead line and poles and depot was moved from Eastbourne to Seaton and the track re-gauged to 2ft.9ins.

Trams began carrying passengers again in May 1970, only eight months after the last tram had run in

Eastbourne. The line was extended in stages to reach the final terminus at Colyton in 1980. The fleet of twelve trams operate from March to October and December with 2 or 3 trams per hour serving the villages of Colyford and Colyton with exquisite views of the riverside, much appreciated by ornithologists.

The Seaton Tramway continues to expand its successful operations and a new £2 million tram terminal has been built to handle the increasing numbers of passengers, supported by Heritage Lottery funding.

While the Seaton tramway is clearly a tourist attraction, it does provide a valuable public transport link to the villages it serves. Its classic tramway technology is low cost, reliable and easy to install, operate and maintain. The concept could easily be applied to many other locations in rural or urban areas, particularly where there is an abandoned railway or tramway alignment. Some of the 'might have been' tramways described in this book could have adopted the Seaton approach which was pioneered nearly three quarters of a century ago by the far sighted Claude Lane.

Modern Electric Tramways Car No.6 at Princes Park between Crumbles and Royal Parade in Eastbourne in 1961. Tony Young

The former tram terminus in Seaton, Devon, opened in 1995. It has now been replaced by a more futuristic building. Tony Young

8. Potential Light Rail Networks

While our European neighbours were busily modernising and upgrading their tramway systems in the post war period, Britain was intent on getting rid of its trams. The death knell was sounded way back in 1930 with the Royal Commission, which encouraged all but the largest systems to replace trams with buses, or perhaps trolleybuses. Not all continental countries kept their trams. France and Spain followed the British trend except for a very small number of cities which retained a line or two, but they both reversed their policies in the eighties and nineties and now have new and expanding tram systems in many cities.

A key feature of new and upgraded European tramways is reserved track, segregated from the effects of traffic congestion. As cities have expanded and road networks extended, separate tracks have been included in the highway and traffic layouts for trams so that in many places they have a protected alignment over most of their networks. In Britain buses were not given this advantage so that now they are severely affected by congestion and buses are slow, unreliable and expensive to operate. For the majority of public transport users, the bus is the only option. No wonder that people take to their cars at the earliest opportunity, making the problem even worse for the poor bus passenger. But things could have been very different.

The greatest *'might have beens'* are the light rail networks which could so easily have been built in the largest British cities, notably Leeds and Liverpool but also Birmingham and Glasgow. All these northern industrial cities had miles of segregated alignments, particularly Liverpool's extensive central reservations in dual carriageways and similar routes in Leeds which also had private right of way routes. Liverpool, Leeds and Glasgow also had plans for central area subways which, together with their reserved tracks, would have taken them three quarters of the way towards creating light rail systems akin to those of Cologne, Zürich, Brussels or Gothenburg.

Liverpool

Liverpool's far-sighted City Engineer, John Brodie, designed a 120ft wide dual carriageway arterial road with a central tramway reservation on grassed tracks protected by continuous hedges (figure overleaf). A total of 25.5 miles, (40.8 km) were built in Liverpool over the thirty years from 1914 (Bowring Park) to 1944 (Kirkby) including Utting Avenue, Townsend Lane, Muirhead Avenue, East Prescot Road, Bowring Park Road, Menlove Avenue, Mather Avenue and The East Lancashire Road. Most still exist, sadly without the trams. They have been nibbled away at junctions to give yet more space for cars to get in the way of buses.

New trams were being built in Liverpool throughout the 1930s although the long association with eight wheel bogie cars was broken with a move to four wheelers. The body styling was similarly modern in appearance, 'Streamliners' and 'Baby Grands'. One hundred Baby Grands were built between 1937 and 1942. But while Leeds and Glasgow continued building new trams after the war, Liverpool carried on with its pre-war fleets.

In 1948, only six years after their newest tram had entered service, a decision was taken to scrap the entire tram network, on the

JOHN A. BRODIE, M. ENG. (L'POOL), WH. SC.,
PAST PRESIDENT INST. C.E., M. I. MECH. E.,
PRESIDENT OF THE LIVERPOOL ENGINEERING SOCIETY.

John Alexander Brodie, 1858-1934.

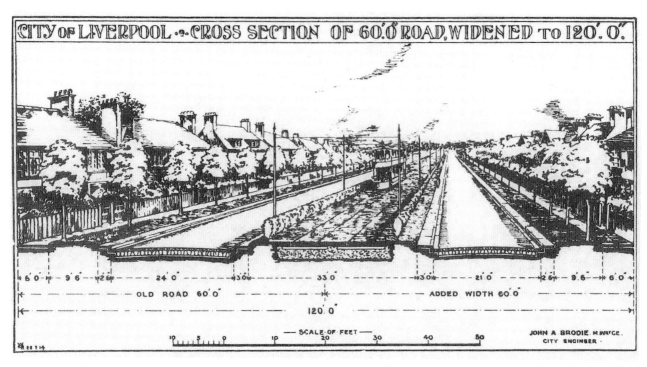

Reserved tracks in Liverpool designed by John Brodie, City Engineer.

Liverpool tram 869 built in 1936 ran in the city until 1954 along John Brodie's reservations. It is now in the National Tramway Museum at Crich in Derbyshire. Tony Young

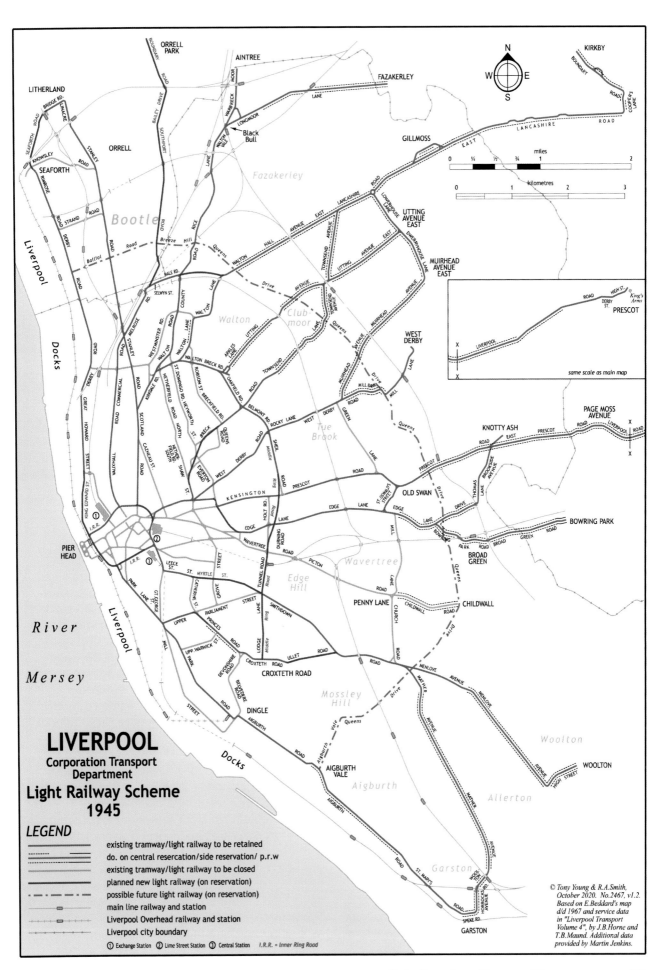

LIVERPOOL
Corporation Transport Department
Light Railway Scheme
1945

LEGEND

existing tramway/light railway to be retained
do. on central resercation/side reservation/ p.r.w
existing tramway/light railway to be closed
planned new light railway (on reservation)
possible future light railway (on reservation)
main line railway and station
Liverpool Overhead railway and station
Liverpool city boundary

① Exchange Station ② Lime Street Station ③ Central Station   I.R.R. = Inner Ring Road

© Tony Young & R.A.Smith,
October 2020. No.2467, v1.2.
Based on E.Beddard's map
d/d 1967 and service data
in "Liverpool Transport
Volume 4", by J.B.Horne and
T.B.Maund. Additional data
provided by Martin Jenkins.

Leeds had many miles of reserved tramways and could have had a modern light rail system. Dr. M.Harrison

Mayor's casting vote. A petition from 250,000 Liverpudlians to keep the trams had no effect. Liverpool's last tram ran in 1957 and John Brodie's magnificent contribution to the city was unceremoniously thrown away.

If the tunnels described in Chapter 5 had been built and if some of the traffic free streets later created had been made tram and pedestrian streets, like many around Europe, then Liverpool would have been well on the way to a segregated light rail network. The gaps in between could easily have been gradually filled in as inner city regeneration progressed. Instead the city, like so many others in the UK, is left with a polluting mass of congestion where buses cannot offer any attractive solution.

Similar designs of reserved track tramways could be seen on Princess Parkway and Kingsway in Manchester, Bristol Road and Tyburn Road in Birmingham, York Road, Selby Road and Belle Isle Road in Leeds, Durham Road in Sunderland and Great Western Road in Glasgow. By the end of the fifties they had all been consigned to the scrapyard, their invaluable contribution to urban infrastructure simply not understood. At today's prices they would be worth billions of pounds.

Leeds

Over the first half century of Leeds trams, an impressive stock of tramway infrastructure had been amassed with a substantial proportion of the network on some form of segregated track totalling 11.5 miles (18.4 km). There were the Liverpool style dual carriageways to Crossgates, Halton, Gipton, Lawnswood, Stanningley, and Belle Isle and the unique off highway route through Middleton Woods to the Middleton housing estate. Various forms of side reservation supported the routes to Roundhay Park, Temple Newsam and West Park.

Leeds were even building new tram routes until 1949 when the Middleton to Belle Isle link was completed, thus creating a circular route. The City Engineer's plans for tram subways under the city centre, as described in Chapter 5, were still fresh and it looked as though the future of trams in Leeds was assured. There were plans for new single deck trams to run in the subways and three were actually being built. These are described in Chapter 9.

As in other northern industrial cities, the inner suburbs including rows of back to back terraces

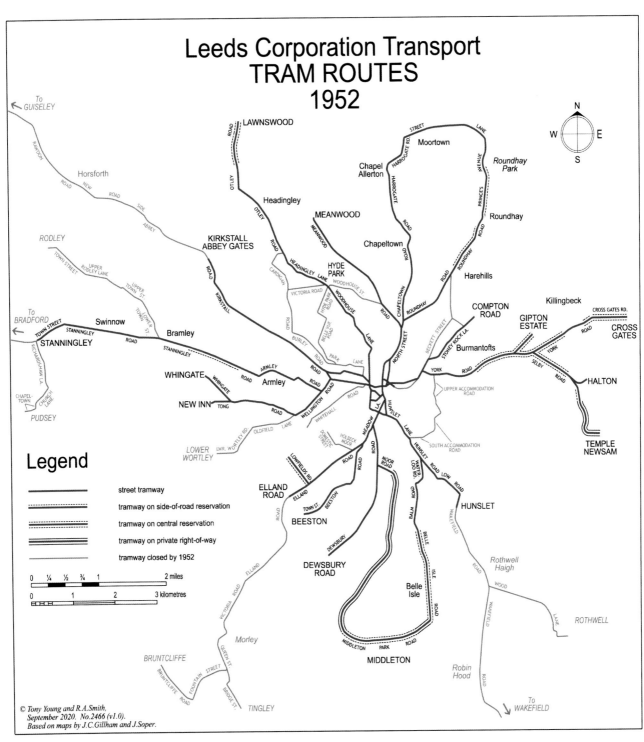

Leeds Corporation Transport
TRAM ROUTES
1952

Legend

————————	street tramway
- - - - - - - -	tramway on side-of-road reservation
══════════	tramway on central reservation
═══════════	tramway on private right-of-way
————————	tramway closed by 1952

0 ¼ ½ ¾ 1   2 miles
0   1   2   3 kilometres

© Tony Young and R.A.Smith,
September 2020. No.2466 (v1.0).
Based on maps by J.C.Gillham and J.Soper.

were systematically demolished and replaced with modern dwellings, often high rise. Massive new estates were constructed on the outskirts of the city, notably in Middleton and Seacroft. While two tram routes did reach Middleton and Belle Isle, plans for three routes to Seacroft, via Compton Road, Gipton Road and York Road, were never realised. Parliamentary powers were granted for some sections but by 1947 any thoughts of tramways to Seacroft had evaporated, even though the new subway trams were on order. Trams had once again become a political football only on opposite sides

of the political spectrum to Liverpool, conservative pro-tram and Labour anti-tram.

If like Liverpool existing reserved tracks in the suburbs had been joined to new tunnels in the city centre, linked by new tracks through regenerated inner suburbs, Leeds could also have been the proud owner of a light rail system on a par with the best in western Europe. But this is Britain!

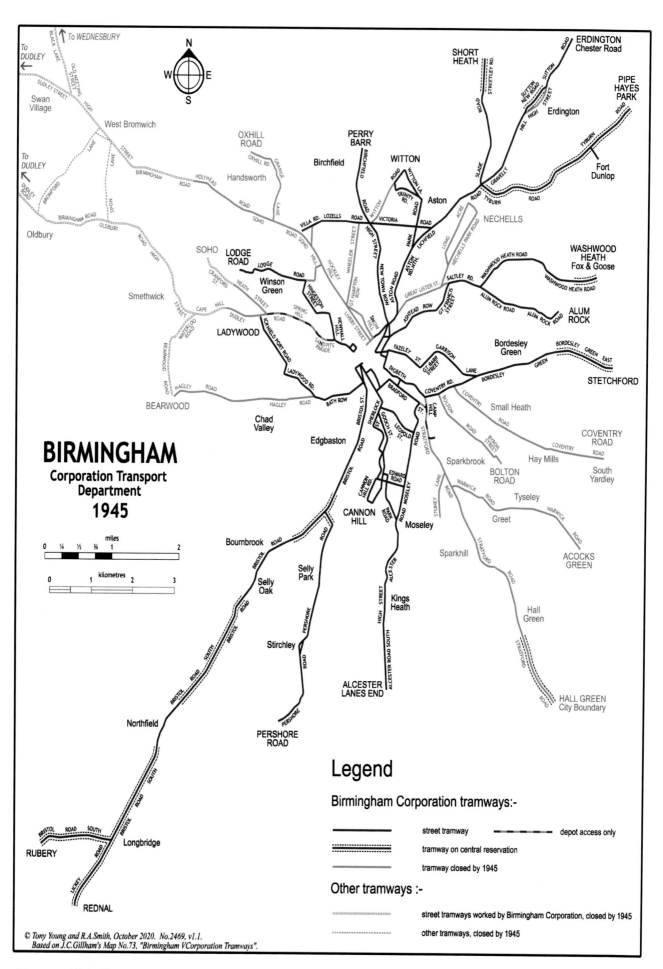

BIRMINGHAM
Corporation Transport
Department
1945

Legend

Birmingham Corporation tramways:-

street tramway

depot access only

tramway on central reservation

tramway closed by 1945

Other tramways :-

street tramways worked by Birmingham Corporation, closed by 1945

other tramways, closed by 1945

© Tony Young and R.A.Smith, October 2020. No.2469, v1.1.
Based on J.C.Gillham's Map No.73, "Birmingham VCorporation Tramways".

A central tramway reservation in a dual carriageway, Bristol Road in Birmingham. MoT

Birmingham

While not quite on the scale of Liverpool or Leeds, Birmingham did have extensive tramway reservations on dual carriageways, notably along Bristol Road from Selly Oak to Rednal and Rubery in the south west. Other sections could be seen on Tyburn Road and Streetly Road in the north west, Bordesley Green to Stechford, and Stratford Road to Hall Green in the south, giving a total of 11.4 miles (18.3 km). The narrow gauge of 3ft.6ins, the largest network in Britain, made the large double deck bogie cars look a little unstable. Unlike Liverpool or Leeds, Birmingham did not obtain any modern trams, their newest dating from 1930.

With major redevelopment taking place in the inner suburbs, the opportunity could have been taken to extend the tramway reservations to create a segregated light rail network, but that would have been years before its time and the last tram ran in 1953. Another example of abandoning miles of valuable reservation worth millions at current prices.

Sixty years later Birmingham does have trams running on street again but they are unlikely to ever run down Bristol Road. It does not feature in current West Midlands Metro expansion plans.

Other British cities

In other major cities in Britain, some tramways managed to survive the war but in many cases they were in a terrible state, desperately in need of renewed track and rolling stock. Faced with economic stringency the only way open to operators, who were all municipally owned (outside London),

was to buy buses which were much cheaper to purchase and in many cases also cheaper to operate. That was the British way of doing things; in Germany, Netherlands, Belgium, Sweden, Switzerland and many Eastern European countries, trams were not only replaced by new ones but networks expanded into the suburbs. The common use of long articulated trams, or trams with two or three trailers, gave them a greater capacity and hence cheaper operating costs than double decker buses.

The greater resources of London Transport were not used to upgrade its tramways, as they might have been, because the decision to get rid of them had already been taken. Londoners loved their trams but London motorists didn't, neither did their transport managers. The British disease of anti-tram-itis was alive and well. The last one ran in 1952.

9. Rolling stock

The Presidents Conference Committee car (PCC)

There has never been a shortage of British engineering expertise and imagination in producing new concepts or designs for tramcars. But putting them into practice, and even better into series production has too often proven difficult or impossible, usually for financial or political reasons, or both. Meanwhile our continental friends have continually developed trams from the earliest electric four wheelers to multi-section articulated cars and reaped the benefits.

Before the demise of the last British first generation tramways, some operators were eyeing the developments in the USA with the ubiquitous PCC car (Presidents Conference Committee). Designed in the nineteen thirties by operators, for operators, some five thousand were built for North American cities and thousands more in western and eastern European cities in the post war period when the designs were licensed to European

manufacturers. Although a pre-war design, the PCC could outperform any British tram and was more comfortable and smoother to ride. They could outshine any other design on technical, ergonomic and economic performance. No wonder it was so popular, on both sides of the Atlantic.

Large numbers of PCCs could be seen in Brussels, The Hague, Antwerp and Barcelona and in Moscow, Warsaw, Prague, Kiev, Dresden, Leipzig and many other Eastern European cities. But attempts to bring one to Britain were never successful even though Liverpool, Leeds and Glasgow had all shown interest. In 1945 when the Leeds and Liverpool light railway plans were being developed, English Electric produced a drawing of a British PCC car hoping to attract orders to establish the design in the UK. It was double ended, unlike most American examples, because few tram routes in Britain had turning circles at terminals and was shorter and narrower than the standard American model.

If English Electric's plans had come to fruition and a PCC car had been produced for the British market,

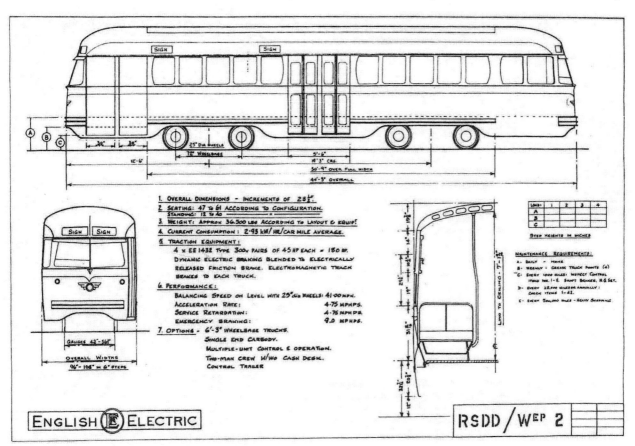

In 1945 English Electric produced a plan for a British double ended PCC tram. None were ever built. English Electric

Madrid tram 1051 is a PCC tram built in 1952 by Fiat, seen in 1966 at Cuatro Caminos. *Tony Young*

A PCC type tram still operating in Prague in 2014, a 'might have been' in Britain. *Tony Young*

it would probably have revolutionised the remaining city tram systems, particularly Liverpool, Leeds and Glasgow. In North America conventional tramways (streetcars) had been in rapid decline, as in Britain, but the PCC car provided the revolution needed to revitalise big city networks and prolong their useful life. No double deck PCCs were ever built although Glasgow Corporation came close (see later in Ch 9).In some cities, Boston, Philadelphia, Pittsburgh, Cleveland, San Francisco and Toronto, the PCC saved the trams long enough to bridge the gap into the second generation and they all now have modern light rail systems. Their modern LRVs retain some features of PCCs but have half a century of improvements. Imagine what Liverpool, Leeds and Glasgow would look like now if that had happened in Britain. Sadly that's another *'might have been'*.

The London Felthams

The year before LCC No.1 (see below) entered service, a fleet of 100 Feltham trams was launched, 46 for the London United Tramways (LUT) and 54 for Metropolitan Electric Tramways (MET). They were the result of several years' research and development and three prototypes and were the finest tramcars then built in Britain. They were produced by the Union Construction Company's Feltham works and were soon known as 'Felthams'.

They were the longest trams in London at 40ft.6ins (12.3m) and seated 64 passengers, 22 downstairs and 42 upstairs with up to 20 standing giving a maximum capacity of 84. At least another 100 Felthams would have been built and even Walthamstow Corporation might have bought some, but the setting up of London Transport in 1933 ensured that the production lines

The only remaining London Feltham tramcar, MET 355, is in the London Transport Museum in Acton. Tony Young

One of the prototype Felthams, MET 331, the one with centre entrance doors, is preserved at the Tramway Museum at Crich. Tony Young

were closed. By far the most comfortable and efficient public transport vehicle in London was denied to Londoners by short sighted bureaucrats. Most of the Felthams lasted until London trams closed in 1952, when many found further service in Leeds until that system closed in 1959. One prototype, MET 331, the only centre entrance version, was sold to Sunderland in 1936 becoming their 100 and is now at Crich.

London County Council No. 1 'Bluebird'

Just before the London Passenger Transport Board (LPTB or the familiar 'London Transport') was created in 1933, London County Council Tramways developed a new design of double deck bogie tram using the latest technology. It had a flat floor in the lower deck, air operated brakes and doors and upholstered seats on both decks. Seating totalled 66, 28 downstairs and 38 upstairs, at least ten more than a typical bus of its day. Numbered 1 in the LCC fleet, it entered passenger service in 1932 and ran through the Kingsway Subway on routes 31, 33 and 35 linking, Hackney, Manor House and Highgate in the north with Wandsworth, West Norwood and Forest Hill in the south.

No.1 was intended to be the forerunner of a large fleet of trams to replace vehicles that were reaching the end of their useful lives, some over 30 years old. It could also have strengthened the fleet to operate through newly planned subways. Painted in a striking streamlined livery of blue and white, it was quickly nicknamed 'Bluebird' and became very popular with passengers and drivers although some drivers were a little frightened by its turn of speed and unfamiliar brakes. It reverted to London red in 1938.

A 'might have been tram' on a 'might have been tramway'. London County Council tram No.1 'Bluebird' was intended to be the first of a new fleet while the Kingsway tram subway could have been the first of a number of subways in London. Courtesy LCC Tramways Trust, original painting by Richard Berridge

London Transport tram No.1 at Archway on a special tour in 1949. It remained the only one ever built. *David Bradley*

London Transport No.1 is being restored at the National Tramway Museum in Derbyshire and is expected to return to passenger service in 2021. *Tony Young*

It ran in London until 1939 but only ran on special journeys after the war until it was sold to Leeds City Transport in 1951. No more were ever built and No.1 remained a tantalising example of what *'might have been'* in the capital city. It ran in Leeds until 1957 and was then acquired for preservation. It now resides at the Tramway Museum at Crich in Derbyshire and is undergoing a major overhaul before once more carrying passengers, resplendent in its original blue colours.

The Glasgow new electric vehicle

Long before the term 'light rail vehicle' had become accepted, what was probably the first example of a light rail vehicle in Britain was proposed by Eric Fitzpayne, General Manager of Glasgow Corporation Transport in his far sighted report in May 1948. (Ref.10). His drawing is shown opposite.

Although termed a 'single deck two coach unit', it is clearly equivalent to an articulated light rail vehicle or modern tram. It was probably not politically acceptable to use the word 'tram'. The two coaches would be permanently coupled

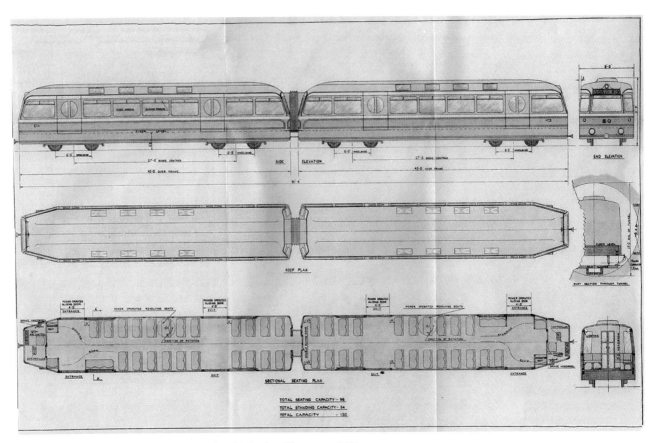

Eric Fitzpayne's drawing of a light rail vehicle for Glasgow. GCT

with a cab at each end. It would be 91ft 4ins (27.8m) long and 9ft 0ins (2.74m) wide with seats for 96 passengers and total capacity of 130. Maximum speed would be 42.5 mph (68 km/hr) and power supply would be overhead at 600 V dc (the same as the existing trams). A novel feature was power operated revolving seats which would automatically reverse at the terminus so that all passengers would always face forwards.

Not only was nothing more heard of this plan for Glasgow, but when the LRTL proposed articulated trams ten years later the Transport Committee seemed to have forgotten that their own manager had proposed a modern electric vehicle.

Glasgow 1005

In 1947 Glasgow Corporation Tramways built an experimental tram to test various novel features. It was the only single ended double decker in Glasgow and the only double deck car in Britain to be fitted with VAMBAC (Variable Automatic Multinotch Braking And Control) control. The only other VAMBAC cars were in Blackpool and the solitary Leeds rail coach 602. It was the nearest thing to a double deck PCC car and the Maley and Taunton bogies had similarities to PCC bogies. Some commented that 1005 was the finest double deck tram ever built.

Its two doors were both on the nearside, initially with front entrance and rear exit, intended to demonstrate the potential of passenger flow. As all other trams in Glasgow had rear doors for boarding and alighting, passengers could not get used to this innovation and it was reversed to allow boarding from the rear and alighting at the front. The VAMBAC control was unreliable and was replaced with conventional control equipment in 1950 and in 1956 it was converted to double ended so that it could be used on any route and not just circular routes, or routes with turning circles or wyes. It continued in service until 1962 when the system closed. One bogie was preserved as an exhibit in the Transport Museum.

This tram probably never had a chance of being the forerunner of a new generation of Glasgow trams, it had too many unproven and unsatisfactory features. The LRTL tried to persuade Glasgow Corporation to consider modern articulated trams in their paper on The Future of Glasgow's Tramways' in 1958, showing contemporary examples from Cologne, Stuttgart, Rotterdam, Amsterdam, Dusseldorf, Vienna and Rome, all of which had introduced articulated trams in the fifties (Ref. 11). It fell on deaf ears because Glasgow's General Manager Eric Fitzpayne had already decided in 1957 to abandon the whole system. The Transport Committee agreed the plan in 1958.

The experimental single ended tram 1005 for Glasgow in 1947, the nearest thing to a double deck PCC car. GCT

The LRTL was way ahead of its time, it took another thirty five years before articulated trams were acceptable in Britain, and fifty five years before they would be accepted in Scotland. Sadly for Glasgow that was in Edinburgh, trams have yet to reappear in Glasgow. Tram 1005, or articulated trams, were *'might have beens'*.

Leeds railcars

The imaginative but ambitious plans for tram subways in Leeds spawned a revolutionary (for Britain) type of tramcar to run in them. The brainchild of Leeds' farsighted General Manager William Vane Morland, it was to be a 'British PCC car' following the design of the most successful streetcar (American for 'street tram') in the USA and Canada. He had visited North America in 1936 and was convinced that the combination of PCC cars and central area tunnels, as in Boston and Philadelphia, would be the right solution to the transport problems of Leeds.

Developing a new tram during the war years would have been a daunting task, so a single deck tram was purchased from Sunderland Corporation. Although built in 1931 it had not seen much use in Sunderland and had been in store for several years before moving to Leeds in 1944. Sunderland 85 eventually became Leeds 600 after an extensive and protracted rebuild in Leeds' workshops, although it carried the fleet number 288 until 1950. The end entrances were replaced by central entrances, the end profiles changed to tapered profile and new seating installed and new bogies.

It was finally completed in 1954, when it carried its first passengers, but only three years later was taken out of service and stored until the system closed in 1959. Tram 600 was acquired for preservation, given its historic significance as the forerunner of a potential fleet of British subway trams. Now owned by the Tramway Museum Society it is currently in their store at Clay Cross in Derbyshire awaiting restoration.

While 600 was a heavily rebuilt tram, Nos. 601 and 602 were brand new trams, built by Charles Roe at Crossgates in Leeds, famous for their bus and trolleybus bodies. They followed the precedent set by 600 in being double ended central entrance bogie single deckers but in all other respects were entirely different. They were the only trams ever built by Charles Roe.

Both trams seated 34 with 36 standing, the total of 70 being higher than contemporary double deck buses but very low compared to modern articulated trams. But they could have been coupled in two or three car trains which buses cannot be. Nor could buses operate through tunnels.

The two single deckers, 601 and 602, were painted in a special purple livery for the Coronation of Her Majesty Queen Elizabeth II in 1953. They entered passenger service on 1st June 1953, just in time for Coronation day on 2nd. No 601 had relatively conventional electrical and mechanical equipment and performed reliably for its short life. On the other hand 602 was considered to be the most advanced tram of its time in the world

Leeds tram 602, the prototype for the light rail system that was never built. Tony Young

and required a lot of attention, perhaps it was too sophisticated. All three single deckers were withdrawn in 1957 after very short working lives, their original purpose having gone. Nos 600 and 602 have been preserved but 601 was sadly vandalised beyond repair in Leeds and eventually scrapped.

In hindsight it would have been much easier, and perhaps more game changing for Britain, if Vane Morland had brought an American PCC car home with him instead of just bringing the drawings. Car 602 was intended to be a prototype British PCC car but it couldn't match the pedigree of the American version, it did not have the weight of the Presidents Conference Committee behind it. Belgium and Holland built PCC cars under licence and they lasted for decades. Britain could have done the same.

Blackpool

As the only first generation tramway to survive continuously into the second generation, the optimum type of rolling stock has been a recurring issue over the decades. A drawing of a modern tram as envisaged by the LRTL (Light Railway Transport League) in 1947 to encourage the remaining British systems to update their fleets clearly owes much to the popular Blackpool 'Balloon' trams of the thirties, some of which are still operational well into the twenty first century. While this design never left the drawing board, another double deck concept was prepared nearly sixty years later.

When the upgrade to a modern light rail line became a realistic possibility, a range of options was considered, including a modern version of the renowned and popular 1930s 'balloon' double

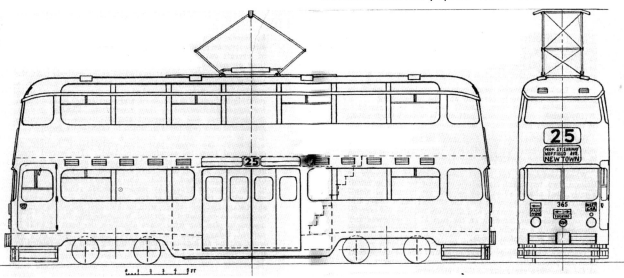

A modern double decker for British tram systems. LRTL 1947

Drawn: Matthew. J.A. Morton 2005

A modern double deck 'Balloon' type tram for Blackpool. *East Lancashire Coachbuilders*

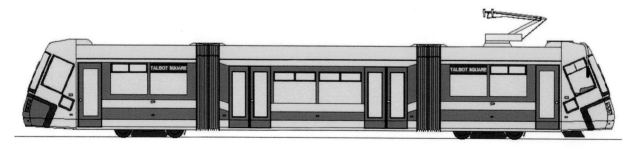

Škoda 14T-3 articulated tram for Blackpool. *Škoda Transportation s.r.o.*

A single deck tram for Blackpool based on the Leyland National bus body. *Garry Luck*

Škoda type 10T tram for Blackpool.
Škoda Transportation s.r.o.

decker. East Lancashire Coachbuilders produced a design for a double ended bogie car in 2005. While this came to nothing it did perhaps encourage the retention of a few 'Balloon' cars to supplement the fleet of new articulated trams.

Following the successful application of bus body parts to create the hated 'Pacer' trains, it was not surprising that the possibility of a Leyland National tram was proposed. What it might have looked like is well illustrated in Garry Luck's 'photograph'. A later proposal for a tram based on the Leyland Lynx bus for Manchester also never left the drawing board.

At that time one possible new tram design for Blackpool was the Škoda 10T, as supplied in various forms to new street running tramways in the USA. Škoda also proposed their 14T design with more modern styling, although arguably not as attractive. In the event, the contract was awarded to Bombardier with their Flexity 2 model and the Škodas remained *'might have beens'*.

Manchester Light Rail Vehicles

After the failed attempts at creating a modern tram in London and Leeds, trams faded into oblivion for the next thirty years. The last city trams were erased from the streets of Leeds, Sheffield and Glasgow leaving only Blackpool to soldier on as an assumed anachronism. Britain had fallen out of love with the tram, largely because they got in the way of the new god, the motor car. The tram was seen as contributing to congestion.

Cars increased in such volumes that they created congestion themselves, eventually resulting in a dramatic policy reversal and the rehabilitation of the tram. Manchester led this revolution although Newcastle and London pioneered the introduction of light rail technology with the Tyneside Metro and the Docklands Light Railway (DLR). But they did not venture onto city streets, the major breakthrough that was left to Manchester to achieve.

GMPTE planners and GMC officers together with senior council members visited many light rail systems around Europe and North America to gain an understanding of the rolling stock options available, their characteristics and operational performance. British Rail Engineering (BREL) engineers recognised the potential market for light rail in the UK and were keen to assist the PTE's investigations. In February 1985 they prepared a comparison of eleven light rail vehicles then in production from seven manufacturers in six countries. Two were 15m bogie cars, the rest single articulated cars ranging between 21m length and 30m. Interestingly all were high floor cars as at that time there were no low floor light rail vehicles available, although the first prototype low floor street trams had been delivered to Geneva in 1984. The question is often asked, why didn't Manchester buy low floor trams? The answer is simple, there weren't any! A couple of years later and Manchester Metrolink might have looked very different.

The first light rail vehicle to run in Manchester was in fact a DLR vehicle, fitted temporarily with a pantograph and driving controls to operate on a demonstration line for three weeks at Debdale Park, Gorton. It ran in Manchester in March 1987 before it ran in London. Although it ran in the DLR blue and red and white livery, GEC who provided the vehicle produced a 'fictitious' photograph of the car, No.11, in GMPTE livery to illustrate what a light rail vehicle would look like in Manchester's orange, brown and white colours.

When Manchester's trams did eventually arrive, not only did they not look anything like a DLR car (which could not run on street), they were not in orange livery, the enforced privatisation of the operation bringing a totally new livery.

The Manchester demonstration, termed 'Project Light Rail', was the brainchild of a group of companies who could see the potential of light rail. One was British Rail Engineering Limited (BREL) who researched vehicle specifications and produced a model of a LRV which they could build under license based on the successful German Stadtbahn 'B' vehicle. It had been intended to bring a prototype Santa Clara, California, LRV manufactured in Canada by UTDC (later Bombardier) to demonstrate light rail technology in Manchester. The production was running late and it would not have been ready for the programmed demonstration in March 1987 so the DLR LRV was brought to Manchester instead.

When bids were invited for Metrolink Phase 1, BREL were included in one of the private sector consortia and proposed a design based on Stadtbahn 'B'. Although it would have been by far the best vehicle for Manchester, the Design, Build, Operate, Maintain (DBOM) form of contract which was imposed by the government meant that the best package was awarded and that included the Firema T68 which was similar in specification but inferior in quality. While all the T68s were withdrawn long before their design life of 30 years, Stadtbahn 'B' cars in Germany were still running after more than 40years in service.

Another unsuccessful design was produced by Hawker Siddeley, more attractive than the chosen T68. Leyland Motors had also produced outline designs based on the Leyland Lynx single deck bus but they did not bid for the contract.

Ironically, the effective successor design to the Stadtbahn 'B' which entered service with Cologne Transport in Germany (KVB) in 2002, the Bombardier K5000, was selected for the fleet replacement for Metrolink in 2009. So twenty years later, with greater freedom on purchasing policy, Greater Manchester got what it wanted in the first place. The Manchester version is the M5000 and by 2017 there were 120 in service. They quickly proved more reliable than the vehicles they replaced. In 2020 another 27 were on order for delivery by 2021.

A failed experiment that should never have happened was the purchase of two surplus San Francisco Municipal Railway Boeing LRVs in 2002 to provide much needed additional capacity on the Phase 1 Metrolink system. Only No.1326

DLR Car No.11, which ran in Manchester in 1987 before it ran in London, was never painted in Manchester's orange livery. Tony Young/GEC

The BREL design for Manchester based on the Düwag Stadtbahn 'B' LRV. BREL

BREL's bid design for Metrolink. BREL

The Hawker Siddeley LRV design for Manchester. Hawker Siddeley

A Light Rail Vehicle for Manchester based on the 1986 Leyland Lynx single deck bus design. Leyland Motors

A tram design that was built, the Bombardier M5000, but in a livery that was never used. Bombardier Transportation

Muni 1326 at the Queens Road Depot of Manchester Metrolink in 2002. Tony Young

arrived in Manchester and a test run to Eccles soon demonstrated that it was not suitable. It was too wide for a British tramway and the end doors were on the tapers making direct boarding from a straight platform impossible. Furthermore everybody in the light rail industry knew that these were some of the worst LRVs ever produced with a very poor reliability record. The second vehicle Muni No.1226 was sent to Derby for tests but both were eventually scrapped without carrying a passenger.

South Yorkshire Supertram

While Greater Manchester was speeding ahead with its Metrolink high floor system, South Yorkshire was following not far behind with the first UK low floor tram system. The steep hills of the city required a capability to climb 10% gradients which meant only designs with all axles motored could be considered. A contemporary artist's impression shows a three section articulated layout with two double doors in the low floor sections, allowing full size motor bogies to be located under the central high floor section. This is the design that was adopted for the production of Supertram fleet.

The only potential British manufacturer of light rail vehicles in the mid 1980s was British Rail Engineering Ltd at their Derby works. They were keen to get into the new light rail market and produced plans for a high floor vehicle for Manchester and a low floor articulated car for Sheffield. The model below indicates the type of vehicle they proposed.

In the event the contract for Sheffield's trams went to long established German tram builder Düwag.

Artist's impression of the three-section articulated car.

 A BREL design for a partial low floor tram for Sheffield. BREL

A British PCC, again?

A standard British tram was never achieved for first generation tramways but several attempts were made to develop a standard British light rail vehicle specification in the 1980s. Forty years after English Electric's plans, a 'British PCC car' still seemed an exciting prospect. In 1991 the PTEG Light Rail Group, the Railway Industries Association (RIA) and the Institution of Mechanical Engineers undertook a survey of light rail promoters with a view to developing a standard light rail vehicle template.

Some debate over terminology, template, specification or standard, did not affect the aim which was to simplify system design, increase competitiveness of light rail as a public transport option, simplify sharing of assets and the creation of a second hand market for light rail vehicles. The template would have specified a six axle articulated double ended vehicle capable of street running and multiple unit operation. It would include overall dimensions, performance, alignment characteristics, low floor and power supply. Whether a standard or a specification it would have become a RIA standard including access arrangements, ride quality, crash worthiness, controls and instrumentation and environmental issues.

It is not difficult to see why agreement was not reached. Each system being developed had its own particular characteristics and to require all promoters to adopt the same features would impose some that were not needed on their system. For example Manchester Metrolink was the only system with multiple unit operation and is still the only one twenty five years later. It is perhaps instructive to note that attempts to produce a national standard in other countries, notably France, also failed as technology advanced too quickly. The PCC remains still the only example of a standard tramcar specification. Despite many good intentions the concept came to nothing. Worse still, the first seven UK light rail systems each produced their own specification and all were different and incompatible.

Parry Peoplemover

Some might dispute the inclusion of a 'peoplemover' in a book on tramways, but it is in effect a form of tram. A lightweight low speed peoplemover was developed by Parry People Movers Ltd at Cradley Heath in the West Midlands in the early nineteen nineties. Small tram-like vehicles are powered by a flywheel using battery, electric pickup or internal combustion power in various combinations. A prototype was demonstrated in

Birmingham in 1993 and then in many towns around Britain using simple temporary track. No overhead power supply is needed.

Intended as a low cost system for smaller towns or as a feeder or car park link in larger cities, the system failed to find any commercial application until it was finally selected to operate the Stourbridge to Stourbridge Junction rail line for London Midland in the West Midlands.

The type PPM60 is class 139 for Network Rail purposes and uses a flywheel powered by a small LPG engine. Seated capacity is 20 to 25 with a further 30 to 35 standing in the 9m long high floor vehicle. Regular public service began in June 2009 with a fleet of two units for the short ¾ mile branch line. Maximum speed is 20 mph with 6 trains per hour all day on a journey of three minutes. Reliability has proved to be very high with substantial reductions in operating and maintenance costs and emissions.

Despite its apparent success, the Stourbridge service remains the only commercial application of this tramway technology. This is not for the lack of trying as the following lists demonstrate. A prototype vehicle has been demonstrated at a number of these locations, mostly for a short period. The longest demonstration was for thirty months over about a mile on the Bristol Harbour Railway using a PPM35 vehicle. There are no plans for further demonstrations.

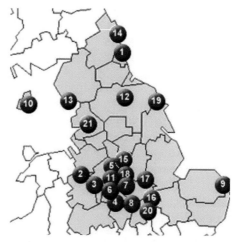

Locations in Northern England and the Midlands where PPM systems have been proposed. Parry Peoplemovers Ltd
1. Newcastle (ref. *Local Transport Today, 23rd March 2006*)
2. Oswestry (*proposal submitted by Pre Metro Operations Ltd to Shropshire County Council, March 2006*)
3. Bewdley (*demonstrated, 2002*)
4. Stourbridge (*experimental operation 2005-06, full service to commence 2008*)

An early Parry Peoplemover flywheel driven minitram demonstrated in Birmingham in November 1993. Tony Young

A Parry Peoplemover was operated on the Bristol Harbour Railway for 30 months in 1997-98. Tony Young

Older enthusiasts remember with great affection the Llandudno and Colwyn Bay tramway. A 'might have been' re-incarnation was planned for Llandudno using Parry minitrams but did not progress beyond the model stage. Tony Young

5. Amerton
6. Dudley (ref. Express & Star, 13th September 2002)
7. Quorn (demonstrated, 2003)
8. Coventry
9. Great Yarmouth (ref. Eastern Daily Press, 22nd April 2004)
10. Isle of Man
11. Wolverhampton Airport (ref. Stourbridge News, 20th May 2004)
12. Bedale (demonstration on Wensleydale Railway, 2005)
13. Dalton-in-Furness (ref. North-West Evening Mail, 18th July 2005)
14. Alnwick (ref. The Journal, 24th March 2006)
15. Wirksworth (ref. Heritage Railway, September 2001)
16. Corby (ref. Lightweight Suburban Railways, JPM Parry & Associates Ltd, January 2006)
17. Loughborough University (ref. Loughborough Echo, 3rd December 2004)
18. Brownhills (ref. Express & Star, 26th March 2005)
19. Scarborough (ref. Tramways & Urban Transit, November 1999)
20. Northampton (ref. Northampton Chronicle & Echo, 19th May 2006)
21. Preston (ref. Lancashire Evening Post, 22nd August 2008)

11. Gloucester (ref. Tramways & Urban Transit, March 2005)
12. Brighton (demonstrated, 1994)
13. Bournemouth & Boscombe (ref. Daily Echo, 4th February 2006)
14. Banbury (ref. Banbury Guardian, 24th October 2002)
15. Cheltenham (ref. Gloucestershire Echo, 29th November 2003)
16. Bourne End - High Wycombe (ref. Bucks Free Press, 27th April 2007)
17. Bordon-Bentley (ref. Bordon Post, 15th August 2007)
18. Folkestone Harbour (ref.www. theremembranceline.co.uk)
19. Ludgershall-Andover (ref. RAIL, 24th February 2010)

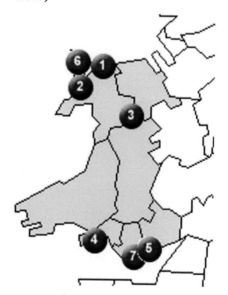

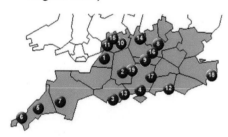

Locations in Southern England where PPM systems have been proposed. Parry Peoplemovers Ltd
1. Bristol (passenger operation on harbourside railway, 1998-2000)
2. Stonehenge
3. Weymouth (trial operation on harbour tramway, 1997)
4. Hythe (study by Atkins for Hampshire County Council, 2004)
5. Bodmin (ref. Lightweight Suburban Railways, JPM Parry & Associates Ltd, January 2006)
6. St Ives (ref. The West Briton, 11th March 2004)
7. Tavistock
8. Dunstable
9. Wallingford (ref. Lightweight Suburban Railways, JPM Parry & Associates Ltd, January 2006)
10. Winchcombe (ref. Lightweight Suburban Railways, JPM Parry & Associates Ltd, January 2006)

Locations in Wales where PPM transport systems have been proposed. Parry Peoplemovers Ltd
1. Llandudno (ref. Daily Post, 10th February 2000)
2. Welsh Highland Railway (demonstrated, 1999)
3. Welshpool Llanfair (demonstrated, 1995-96)
4. Swansea (demonstrated, 1994)
5. Cardiff Bay (ref. Local Transport Today, 23rd March 2006)
6. Llangefni (ref. Lightweight Suburban Railways, JPM Parry & Associates Ltd, January 2006)
7. Barry Island (ref. Modern Railways, August 2007)

West Midlands 'Tracline 65' guided busway, operating 1984 to 1987.
Tony Young

Germany, fitted with a temporary pantograph and driven manually, before it ran in London.

A survey for the House of Commons Transport Committee in 1990 listed 38 towns and cities with studies of light rail or segregated transit of some form. A summary is shown in Table 10.1 (overleaf).

Twenty five years later, only six of these thirty eight towns and cities had tram systems (shown yellow) and a further three had guided busways (shown blue). The remaining thirty still had no segregated public transport system.

Streetly Road, Birmingham was a reserved track tramway until 1953.

DLR No. 11 ran in DLR livery in Manchester before it ran in London. Tony Young

Table 10.1. Potential tram schemes identified in a survey for the House of Commons Transport Committee, 1990. (yellow – tram schemes built; blue – busway built.)

System	Promoter	Status	System	Promoter	Status
Aberdeen	Grampian RC	None	Leicester	Leicestershire CC	Study
Bedford	North Bedfordshire District Council	Study	Luton	Luton & District Transport	Study
Belfast	NIR & NI DoE	Studies	Maidstone	Kent CC	Study
Bristol	ATA & Avon CC	Bill in Parliament	Manchester	GMPTE	Under construction
Cambridge	Cambridge CC & City Council	Study	Middlesbrough	Cleveland CC & Teesside DC	Parliamentary Bill preparation
Cardiff	South Glam CC & Cardiff Bay DC	Study	Milton Keynes	Milton Keynes DC	Study
Chatham	Kent CC	Study	Norwich	Norfolk CC	Study
Chelmsford	Chelmsford Borough Council	Study	Nottingham	Nottingham CC, Nottingham City C Nott Dev Enterprise	Parliamentary Bill preparation
Chester	Cheshire CC & Chester City Council	Study	Plymouth	Private sector	Study
Coventry	Coventry CC West Midlands PTE	Preparing Bill	Portsmouth	South Hants Metro & Hants CC	Bill in Parliament
Croydon	LT & LB Croydon	Study	Preston	Private sector	None
Edinburgh	Lothian RC	Study	Reading	Berkshire CC	Study
Exeter	Private sector	Study	Sheffield	South Yorkshire PTE	Bill in Parliament
Gateshead	Gateshead MBC & local businesses	Study	Southend	Essex CC	Study
Glasgow	Strathclyde PTE	Study	Stoke	Stoke City Council, Staffs CC	Study
Gloucester	Gloucester CC	Study	Swindon	Wiltshire CC	Study
Hull	Humberside CC & Hull City C	Study	Watford	BR & LUL	Finance awaited
Kingston	LT & LB Kingston	Study	West Midlands	West Midlands PTE	Powers obtained, Bills in Parliament
Leeds	WYPTE, Leeds City C	Study	Wimbledon	LB Merton	Study

A plan prepared by the TAS Partnership in 2002 (page 86) showed 45 places where some form of rapid transit was under consideration, including the seven schemes then in operation. Two were the segregated light rail lines in Tyne and Wear and London Docklands which do not have street running and one was the long established original Blackpool tramway which had not then been upgraded. That left 38 schemes which were 'might have beens', only two of which, Nottingham and Edinburgh, have since been built.

Ten years after the 1990 survey, the Department for the Environment, Transport and the Regions

(DETR) published its Ten Year Plan, 'Transport 2010' (Ref.48), brainchild of John Prescott who by then had been appointed Deputy Prime Minister. It envisaged up to 25 new rapid transit lines in major cities and conurbations to more than double light rail use. They included new lines or extensions in Manchester, London (DLR), Newcastle and Nottingham. Also in the list were new systems in Leeds, West Midlands, Bristol/South Gloucestershire and Portsmouth and South Hampshire. All the extensions were built (although Alistair Darling tried to cancel some) but none of the new systems except the West Midlands which had already opened

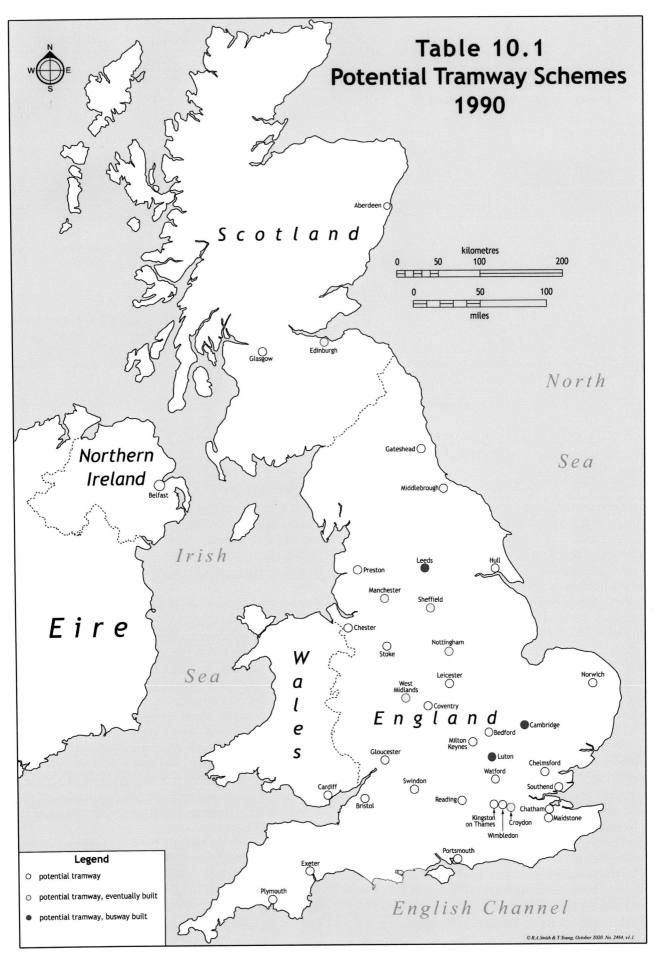

Table 10.1
Potential Tramway Schemes
1990

Legend

○ potential tramway

◐ potential tramway, eventually built

● potential tramway, busway built

© R.A.Smith & T.Young, October 2020. No. 2464, v1.1.

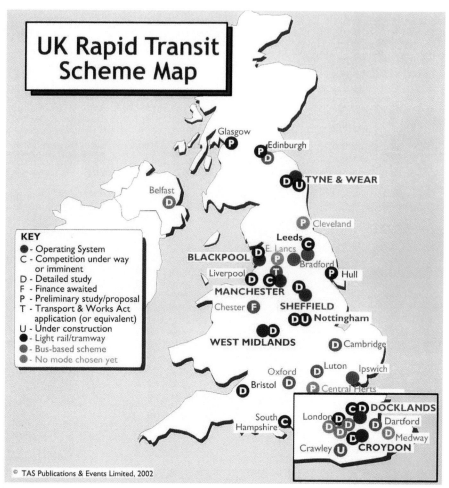

UK Rapid Transit Scheme Map

KEY
- ● - Operating System
- C - Competition under way or imminent
- D - Detailed study
- F - Finance awaited
- P - Preliminary study/proposal
- T - Transport & Works Act application (or equivalent)
- U - Under construction
- ● - Light rail/tramway
- ● - Bus-based scheme
- ● - No mode chosen yet

Glasgow, Edinburgh, TYNE & WEAR, Belfast, Cleveland, Leeds, E. Lancs, BLACKPOOL, Bradford, Liverpool, Hull, MANCHESTER, Chester, SHEFFIELD, Nottingham, WEST MIDLANDS, Cambridge, Oxford, Luton, Ipswich, Bristol, Central Herts, South Hampshire, London, DOCKLANDS, Dartford, Medway, Crawley, CROYDON

© TAS Publications & Events Limited, 2002

Potential light rail schemes in UK in 2002. TAS Partnership

in 1999. Leeds, Bristol and South Hampshire still do not have any kind of rapid transit system.

Although Labour retained control until 2010 by when the Transport 2010 Plan was supposed to be implemented, it was effectively abandoned long before then. Alistair Darling, the Labour Secretary of State for Transport, cancelled major tram schemes in Leeds, Liverpool and South Hampshire in 2004 and tried to cancel all the extensions in Greater Manchester. Politicians, the media and supporters in Manchester mounted a massive campaign to get Darling to change his mind and they won. All their planned extensions are now built but Liverpool, Leeds and South Hampshire still have no trams. Millions was spent on Parliamentary plans and advanced works, with government approval, only to be thrown on the scrap heap. Merseyside even bought the tram rails which languished on a quayside for years afterwards and very nearly signed the order for the trams. Liverpool and Leeds were not 'might have beens', they were 'should have beens.

The reason given by Alistair Darling for pulling the rug from the three light rail schemes was the old chestnut of cost increases. There is no doubt that project costs do increase with time but a comparison of light rail and highway scheme cost

increases in the same period Table 10.2 (opposite) shows that light rail increases were fairly modest and highway cost increases in most cases were far worse. And yet all these tram schemes were cancelled but none of the highway schemes.

Another cost comparison is between different tram schemes. In Table 10.3 (overleaf) the costs per km for contemporary tram projects show that the three cancelled projects were of a similar order of costs to the Manchester Metrolink extension costs. But they were barely half the costs of the Edinburgh tram scheme which was built. The only conclusion that can be drawn is that the Secretary of State for Transport was biased against tram schemes. Ironically Alistair Darling was an Edinburgh MP where the most expensive tram project *was* built, admittedly against considerable opposition, but it is now judged a great success and local residents and businesses want it extending. An extension is now under construction.

Yet another list of potential tram systems was presented at the All Party Parliamentary Light Rail Group (APPLRG) in November 2007, see Table 10.4 (overleaf). Proposals in 65 towns and cities were reported of which 14 had tram schemes of some kind, three had their tram plans cancelled by Alistair Darling, four had busway schemes and the remaining

While Liverpool and Leeds accepted the Government refusal, Manchester fought back and won. Oldham and Rochdale Councils hung huge banners on their respective town halls. Tony Young

Table 10.2. Cost increases for light rail and highway schemes.

Light rail scheme cost increases		
System	2004 Cost*	Increase
South Hampshire	£214m	26%
Leeds	£500m	41%
Liverpool	£314m	38%

* public sector cost

Highway scheme cost increases March 2007 – March 2008		
Project	2008 Cost	Increase
A21 Kippings Cross – Lamberhurst	£103m	158%
Handcross Warninglid widening	£69m	72%
A21 Tonbridge-Pembury	£112m	75%
M25 J16-J23 widening	£697m	41%
A5-M1 Dunstable Northern By-pass	£124m	156%
M1 J10-J13 widening	£601m	57%
M40 J15 Longbridge roundabout	£71m	25%
A14 Ellington-Fen Ditton	£944m	93%
M25 J27-J30	£583m	45%

44 still had nothing. The list included Birkenhead which only has a heritage tramway and Luton which has since achieved a busway project.

These lists demonstrate that the potential for tramways, or at least something significantly better than buses, is considered by local authorities or other local interests to be needed, usually to combat traffic congestion, reduce environmental impacts and support the local economy. Most will remain as *'might have beens'* for the foreseeable future.

Table 10.3. Comparative costs of light rail projects per km, 2004.

Light rail project	Cost per km	Decision
South Hampshire	£15.0m/km	Cancelled
Leeds	£17.8m/km	Cancelled
Liverpool	£16.5m/km	Cancelled
Metrolink extensions	£18.1m/km	Built
Edinburgh	£32.9m/km	Built

Table 10.4. Potential light rail schemes identified in All Party Parliamentary Light Rail Group presentation, 12 November 2007.

Key: Green – tram/light rail scheme implemented.
       Blue – busway scheme implemented.
       Red – tram scheme cancelled by Alastair Darling.
       Black – no scheme implemented (in 2007, Luton implemented 2013).

Scope for new public transport systems		
Aberdeen	Docklands	Milton Keynes
Barking	Doncaster	Newcastle upon Tyne
Bedford	Dundee	Norwich
Belfast	East Lancashire	Nottingham
Birkenhead	Edinburgh	Oxford
Birmingham	Exeter	Plymouth
Blackpool	Gateshead	Portsmouth
Bournemouth	Glasgow	Preston
Bradford	Gloucester	Reading
Brighton	Guildford	Runcorn
Bristol	Kettering	Sheffield
Cambridge	Kingston upon Hull	Southampton
Cardiff	Kingston upon Thames	Southend
Chatham	Lancaster	Stoke on Trent
Chelmsford	Leeds	Sunderland
Chester	Leicester	Swansea
Cleveland	Liverpool	Swindon
Corby	London	Walsall
Coventry	Luton	Watford
Crawley	Maidstone	West Midlands
Croydon	Manchester	Wimbledon
Dartford	Middlesbrough	

While the 1990s and the first decade of the 21st century saw large numbers of possible tram schemes put forward by local authorities, most have now given up any hope of achieving schemes. Alistair Darling's refusal to allow well thought out projects for Leeds, Liverpool and South Hampshire to proceed cast a deep shadow over any future attempts by other authorities. These large authorities were able to support the very high project costs but then lost millions of wasted investment due to a reversal of government policy. This has discouraged most authorities from even thinking about trams.

The light rail schemes that were constructed in the 1980s and beyond in the major conurbations have all been successful in attracting passengers from cars and contributing to the local economies of their regions. But the potential was considerably greater as the next chapters will indicate.

A separate chapter is included for each of the new generation light rail projects.

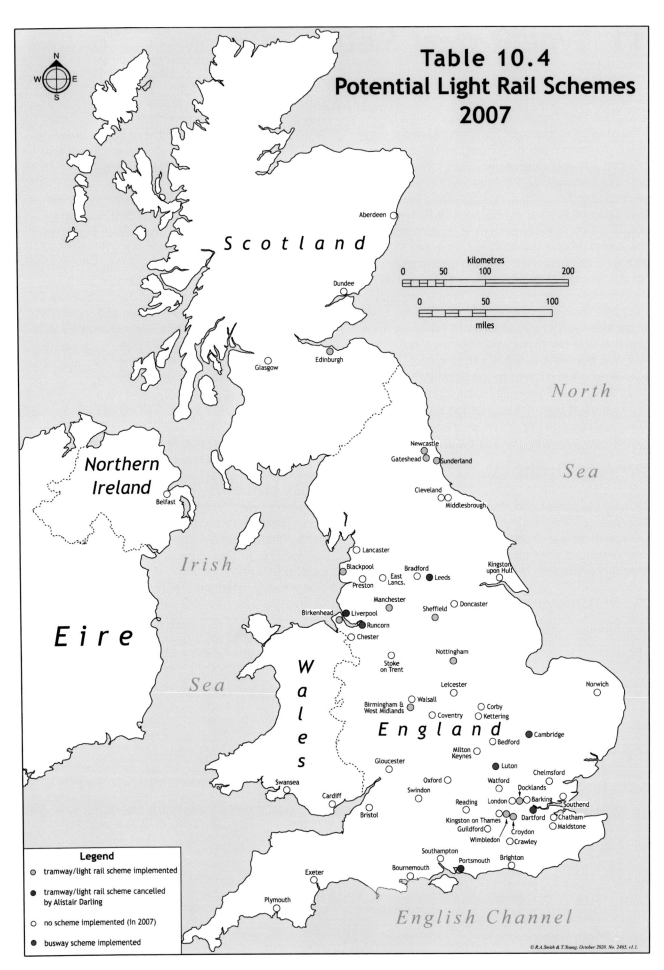

Table 10.4
Potential Light Rail Schemes
2007

kilometres

0   50   100   200

0   50   100

miles

Scotland

Aberdeen

Dundee

Edinburgh

Glasgow

North

Sea

Northern
Ireland

Belfast

Irish

Newcastle

Gateshead   Sunderland

Cleveland

Middlesbrough

Eire

Sea

Lancaster

Blackpool   Bradford

Preston   East   Leeds
          Lancs.

Birkenhead   Liverpool   Manchester   Sheffield   Doncaster

          Runcorn

          Chester

Wales

Stoke
on Trent

Nottingham

Kingston
upon Hull

Norwich

Leicester

Birmingham &   Walsall
West Midlands

Coventry   Corby
           Kettering

England

Cambridge

Bedford

Milton
Keynes

Gloucester

Luton

Chelmsford

Swansea

Cardiff

Bristol

Oxford

Swindon

Reading

Watford

London   Docklands

          Barking

Kingston on Thames
Guildford

Wimbledon

Dartford

Croydon

Crawley

Southend

Chatham

Maidstone

Southampton

Bournemouth

Exeter

Portsmouth   Brighton

Plymouth

English Channel

Legend

○ tramway/light rail scheme implemented

● tramway/light rail scheme cancelled
  by Alistair Darling

○ no scheme implemented (in 2007)

● busway scheme implemented

© R.A.Smith & T.Young, October 2020, No. 2465, v1.1.

11. Tyne & Wear Metro

Tyneside Metro was the first system in the UK to adopt light rail technology and was the first to be promoted by a Passenger Transport Executive using the provisions of the 1968 Transport Act. It was also the first and only example of a fully integrated public transport network as the Metro and bus services worked together with integrated fares. That feature was destroyed by bus deregulation in 1986 and the Metro lost some thirty percent of its patronage. The integration of transport and land use, the only true example in Britain, was also destroyed with the abolition of the Metropolitan County Council in 1986.

Tyne and Wear Metro, as it became following local government reorganisation in 1974, is a fully segregated urban railway with no street running and does not therefore count as a tram system. However the vehicles were based on the German Düwag Stadtbahn 'B' LRV which is capable of street running, but that ability was not included in the Tyneside specification. Also the system operates at 1500 V dc rather than the usual 750 V dc for street running.

Project Orpheus

In the early part of the 21st century, Tyne & Wear PTE initiated Project Orpheus to reinvigorate the Metro system and develop an enhanced bus network. Also envisaged were extensions to the Metro using tramway technology, as shown in the diagram below.

The existing Metro is shown in yellow and green and possible tramway extensions in blue. They include a long overdue extension to the west to Denton, a line to the MetroCentre (which currently

is not on the Metro and not in the centre), a link between Gateshead and South Hylton via Washington, also long overdue, a route to Ryhope via Doxford Park, a line to Killingworth and two additional lines to Newcastle Airport.

This plan would have given Tyne & Wear a light rail network on a par with some of the best in Europe. In 2005 it was estimated that the project would cost £500m spread over twenty years, quite modest for a major rail project and petty cash compared to the sums being spent in London and the Southeast, but it soon emerged that by British provincial standards it was far too ambitious. The need to maintain and upgrade the existing Metro would take all likely resources for the foreseeable future and Project Orpheus was quietly dropped. The new trains to be supplied by Stadler up to 2024 will not be capable of street running.

Other studies in Tyne and Wear

Some other studies have been undertaken of possible light rail routes, for example the Coalfields Link Study carried out for South Tyneside District Council with Nexus in 2002. Preliminary alignments were suggested from South Shields to West Boldon with a view to extending southwards to the Doxford International development in Sunderland. At least part of the route could have been tramway.

The primary objective was to link Metro and bus services in South Shields with socially deprived communities and employment opportunities. Important traffic objectives were Shields ferry terminal, South Tyneside District Hospital,

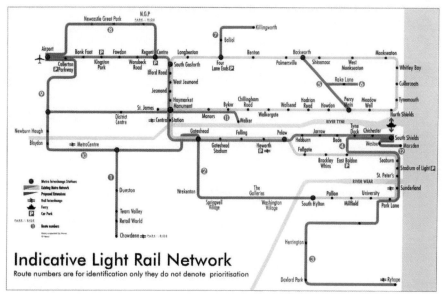

Possible tramway extensions to the Tyne & Wear Metro in Project Orpheus. Tyne & Wear PTE

Urgently needed replacement Metro trains for Tyne and Wear Metro will not be capable of street running. NEXUS

South Tyneside College, Boldon Colliery Asda development, the Nissan car plant and a park and ride site on the A19 trunk route.

Another proposal was studied for South East Northumberland using former rail alignments to Blyth and Ashington and these are still being pursued by Northumberland County Council and Nexus but are unlikely to feature any form of tramway.

The North East Combined Authority and Nexus (Tyne & Wear PTE) have produced a 'Metro and Local Rail Strategy' which describes the works planned to upgrade the existing Metro. It includes possible extensions to cover some of the Project Orpheus routes and some additional lines, but most using the existing fully segregated Metro type operation. No provision is being made for any street running and it will remain a high floor metro. Consideration will be given to dual voltage rolling stock but this would be 1500 V dc/25 kV ac to allow the Sunderland line to be electrified at the

Network Rail standard voltage. This would make any tramway extensions even more unlikely. The imaginative Project Orpheus Metro extensions on tramway will remain '*might have beens*'.

Tyne & Wear Metro could be extended on several fronts but none will involve street running tramways. Tyne & Wear PTE

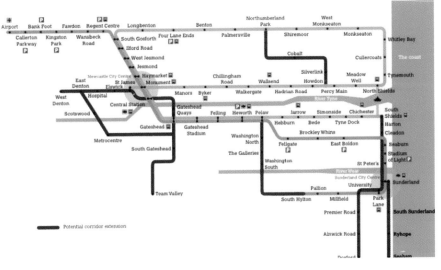

12. Docklands Light Railway

Several light rail concepts were considered by London Transport during the 1980s. The first to be approved was the now well-known Docklands Light Railway (DLR) in the east end serving the once derelict docklands area. It was an essential ingredient to the economic regeneration of this once thriving port.

The DLR was originally conceived as a conventional light rail system with overhead power supply and some street running sections. The northern terminus of the initial three line system was going to be Mile End Underground station on the Central and District lines with street running along Burdett Road or possibly part of Mile End Road. Some route options within the Isle of Dogs could have included short sections of street running. These plans were dropped when it was realised that operating on street on these busy roads would not have been practicable. The concept of modern street running which is now well established in Manchester, Sheffield and Nottingham was a bit before its time in London. The rail centre of Stratford was chosen instead as the northern terminus of the DLR, which offered interchange with British Rail services as well as the Underground.

As plans progressed for the DLR, objections to the overhead wires on the high level elevated viaducts across the docks emerged and the power supply was changed to third rail. Then the radical step of driverless operation under computer control was taken. These changes ruled out any thoughts of street running for all time. But elsewhere in Greater London, the idea of on street operation was very much alive and London Transport had not given up on re-introducing trams to London.

Possible extensions to the DLR would all be on fully segregated railway, no street running. DLR

13. Greater Manchester Metrolink

1970s light rail plans

The Transport Act 1968 created the first Passenger Transport Executives and their Passenger Transport Authorities in 1969. The PTE covering the Manchester area was named SELNEC, South East Lancashire North East Cheshire, and took over all the municipal bus operations on 1st November 1969.

Each PTE had a statutory duty to prepare a Long Term Plan setting out investment in all forms of public transport for the future. SELNEC's plan, 'Lifeline 2000', set out the major rail investment planned, with the Picc-Vic tunnel as its centre piece. In addition to electrification of most of the suburban rail lines, a new network of light

rail lines was proposed to serve corridors which had no rail lines.

The University line would connect the Universities of Manchester and Salford along the Wilmslow Road corridor through St Peter's Square and extend to Eccles and Walkden and Withington and Didsbury. The North-East line would serve Broughton and Droylsden while the Wythenshawe line would run along the Princess Parkway corridor to Wythenshawe town centre.

When the Picc-Vic network was finally abandoned due to costs (although the similar costing Tyneside Metro was given the go ahead) the light rail network was quietly forgotten and no further

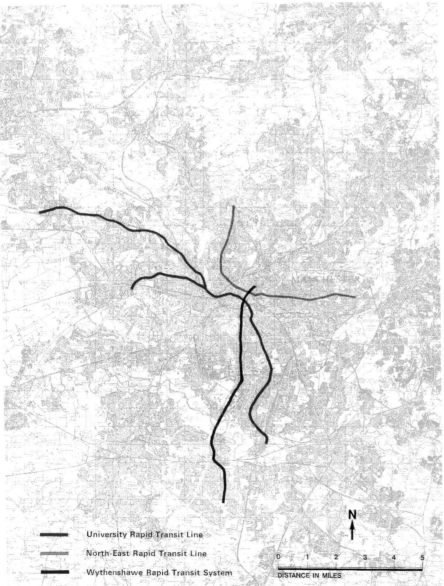

The three line rapid transit network proposed for Manchester to supplement the heavy rail network.

University Rapid Transit Line

North-East Rapid Transit Line

Wythenshawe Rapid Transit System

N

0   1   2   3   4   5
DISTANCE IN MILES

The rolling stock envisaged was a standard German tram design.

work undertaken, until the light rail concept was resurrected ten years later. Droylsden, Eccles and Wythenshawe do now have tram lines but the classic Wilmslow Road and Princess Parkway corridors are still the preserve of slow and unreliable bus services. They both had first generation tram services and plans to extend the tram lines from Southern Cemetery towards Wythenshawe were approved in the 1920s. Sadly the then General Manager Henry Mattinson died suddenly in 1928 and his ambitious plans for Liverpool style central reservation tramways never materialised, except Princess Road and Kingsway. Some roads in Manchester were constructed with central reservations but the trams were never installed. One of these, Mauldeth Road West, now does have trams in the central reservation for a short distance on the Airport Metrolink line. The rest of Mattinson's plans remain *'might have beens'*.

Metrolink success brings light rail to Greater Manchester

Abandonment of Picc-Vic left Manchester with its still unsolved problem of lack of central area rail accessibility and absence of north-south rail links. Yet another Study was set up jointly between GMC, GMPTE, and British Rail termed 'a Rail Strategy for Greater Manchester, The Options', under the direction of Councillor Andrew Fender, then chairman of the GMC Transportation Strategy Committee.

The first report in April 1983 was followed by further reports in January and November 1984 and such was the speed of progress that the first Parliamentary Bill seeking powers to construct and operate trams in central Manchester was deposited in November

Greater Manchester's Railways in the year 2000

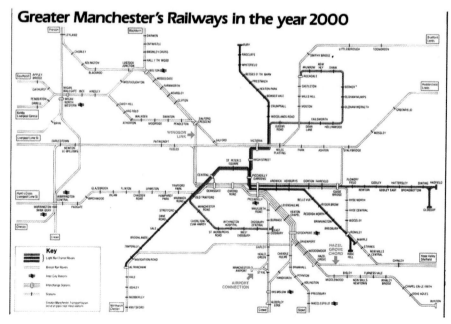

Greater Manchester's rail strategy for light rail lines and heavy rail links in 1984. Four of the six lines were built but Glossop and Marple are 'might have beens'.

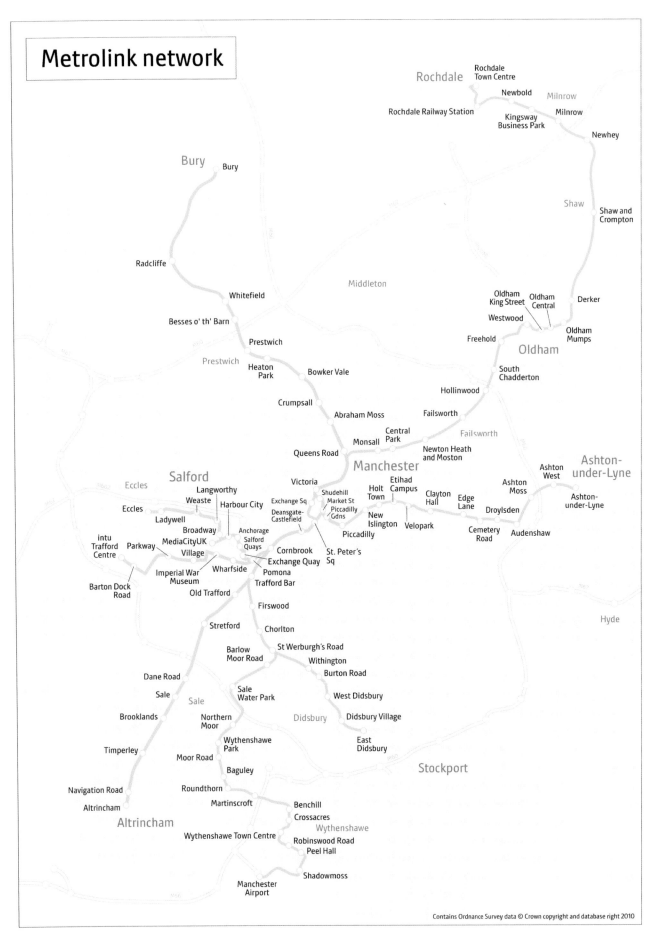

Metrolink network

Rochdale
Rochdale Town Centre
Newbold
Rochdale Railway Station
Kingsway Business Park
Milnrow
Milnrow
Newhey
Shaw
Shaw and Crompton

Bury
Bury

Radcliffe

Middleton

Whitefield

Oldham King Street
Oldham Central
Derker
Westwood
Besses o' th' Barn
Oldham Mumps

Prestwich
Prestwich
Heaton Park
Bowker Vale
Freehold
Oldham

South Chadderton

Crumpsall
Hollinwood

Abraham Moss
Failsworth

Central Park
Failsworth

Monsall
Newton Heath and Moston

Queens Road

Eccles
Salford
Manchester
Ashton West
Ashton-under-Lyne

Langworthy
Victoria
Etihad Campus
Ashton Moss

Weaste
Shudehill
Holt Town
Clayton Hall
Edge Lane
Ashton-under-Lyne

Eccles
Harbour City
Exchange Sq
Market St
Piccadilly Gdns
Droylsden

Ladywell
Deansgate-Castlefield
New Islington
Velopark

Broadway
Anchorage
Piccadilly
Cemetery Road
Audenshaw

intu Trafford Centre
Parkway
MediaCityUK
Salford Quays

Village
Cornbrook
St. Peter's Sq

Imperial War Museum
Wharfside
Exchange Quay
Pomona

Barton Dock Road
Old Trafford
Trafford Bar

Firswood

Stretford
Chorlton
Hyde

Barlow Moor Road
St Werburgh's Road
Withington

Dane Road
Burton Road

Sale
Sale
Sale Water Park
West Didsbury

Brooklands
Northern Moor
Didsbury
Didsbury Village

Timperley
Wythenshawe Park
East Didsbury

Moor Road
Stockport

Baguley

Navigation Road
Roundthorn

Altrincham
Martinscroft
Benchill

Altrincham
Crossacres
Wythenshawe

Wythenshawe Town Centre
Robinswood Road
Peel Hall

Shadowmoss

Manchester Airport

Contains Ordnance Survey data © Crown copyright and database right 2010

The Metrolink network as it has developed in the 21st century.

1984. This heralded the return of street running trams to British cities although it took another eight years before the first ones ran in 1992.

The light rail network comprised six radial routes: Bury, Rochdale, Glossop/Hadfield, Marple/Rose Hill, Altrincham and East Didsbury, all except the last being existing operational railways. The rail strategy also included heavy rail links: the Windsor Link in Salford, the Hazel Grove Chord in Stockport and the Airport Rail Link from the Styal line.

All these schemes have since been built and operated except the Glossop/Hadfield and Marple/Rose Hill lines which remain as 'might have beens'. The Marple line may yet be converted for tram-train operation but Glossop/Hadfield will probably continue as a conventional suburban railway. It has in effect been replaced in the light rail network by the street running Ashton tram route which serves East Manchester and Droylsden more directly than the existing rail route.

While two of the originally proposed light rail lines are still 'might have beens', the Metrolink network has been a huge success and contributed enormously to the economy of the region. Three new lines were added to the network, Salford Quays/Eccles, Ashton-under-Lyne and Manchester Airport and a short branch to Media City. One further route opened in 2020 through Trafford Park to the Trafford Centre. In the city centre an additional cross city route has been built linking Victoria Station with St Peter's Square via Exchange Square and Cross Street.

The 1984 strategic plan only proposed conversion of existing railway lines to light rail and the only section of street running was through the city centre. Once the concept of street running was demonstrated to be acceptable it could be applied on other routes. The success of Market Street with trams was quickly recognised as a cost effective and environmentally positive way of giving good access to a thriving shopping centre, so much so that the buses were soon removed to create a tram and pedestrian precinct.

The Oldham Rochdale route was expanded to divert the tramway through the town centre in Oldham and extend it down Drake Street into the town centre

A replica Manchester standard bogie tramcar No. 1007 (Manchester's last tram) stands at the terminus at St Peter's Square, alongside Metrolink tram 1006. Nothing remains of this scene except the Town Hall extension as the Metrolink stop has been moved northwards and expanded to a four platform layout and all the T68 class trams have been withdrawn.

The tram route linking MOSI with the city centre would have run up Liverpool Road and across Deansgate.

of Rochdale. The new routes to Ashton and Eccles include significant street running sections which would not have been considered acceptable only a decade or more earlier.

Metrolink is now the largest tram system in Britain with 120 trams operating over nearly 100 km of route serving seven of the ten districts of Greater Manchester with 99 tram stops. Future plans may well include tram trains running on other existing suburban rail lines and perhaps even tram tunnels under the city centre. Manchester is the largest city in Europe with no rail tunnels of any description. All this is a far cry from the *'might have been'* light rail plans of the early seventies.

A Manchester tram re-incarnated?

When Manchester's last first generation tramcar ran its final journey in 1949, nobody thought to retain an example for history. The tramway preservation movement was in its infancy and the significance of the Manchester standard bogie car in the city's development was not appreciated. Several hundred of these impressive trams were built at Hyde Road works in the 1920s and 1930s, many a Mancunian will have travelled to school or work on them, but suddenly they were all gone.

First generation trams from other major cities, London, Leeds, Liverpool and Glasgow, have been preserved and many are in running order. But although Manchester had one of the largest tram systems in Britain with nearly 1,000 trams, the only one to be fully restored is the non-typical single

decker 765. None of the familiar double deck bogie cars which were built by the Corporation Tramways Department and served the city faithfully for decades escaped the breakers yard.

In 2008 Steve Davies was appointed as Director of the Manchester Museum of Science and Industry (MOSI). His main interest was railways but he saw an opportunity to recreate a little bit of Manchester tramway with a replica standard double deck tram. It would run on a line from the Museum, past the main entrance, up Liverpool Road to cross Deansgate and continue to terminate in St Peter's Square, alongside the Metrolink stop (before it was moved in 2016). The replica tram could have been built with assistance from members of the Manchester Transport Museum Society who are experienced in restoring old trams and operating them, including the vintage Manchester single decker, at the tramway museum in Heaton Park.

While perhaps impossibly ambitious, it would have given the city centre an unrivalled tourist attraction as well as bringing to life an important element in its history. All that remains are some enticing photomontages of what might have been. Steve left MOSI in 2010 and nothing more was heard of his exciting plans. At least Manchester does have a thriving tramway museum in Heaton Park, uniquely incorporating a section of original first generation tramway. Many North American cities have reintroduced trams to city streets, perhaps Steve's far sighted dream will be realised someday. Until then it remains as a *'might have been'*.

14. South Yorkshire Supertram

The second new generation tram system was South Yorkshire Supertram in Sheffield which opened in 1994. The three line network linked Middlewood, Malin Bridge and Hillsborough in the north west, Halfway in Mosbrough in the south east and Meadowhall Shopping Centre in the north east with the city centre. It was the first UK system to use low floor trams with low platforms in the street, a pattern followed by all subsequent tram systems.

Extensions were planned to Sheffield University, the Hospitals and Ranmoor in the west, Dore in the south west, Rotherham and Parkgate in the north, and Hellaby in the north east. A more detailed study was undertaken in 2000 of route options to serve Sheffield's Royal Hallamshire Hospital. A short double track spur along Glossop Road could terminate in the Hospital grounds. Alternatively a single track loop would run via Hounsfield Road, Western Bank, Whitham Road, Newbould Lane and Glossop Road. The first option gave a positive rate of return but it was not progressed.

After years of further studies and debate, the Parkgate route was finally selected as the tram-train trial route and began operation in 2018. If demonstrated to be successful, the tram-train concept could be extended to other existing rail routes. Meanwhile the other three extensions remain as 'might have beens'.

Early extension plans would have served the major hospitals and Stannington.

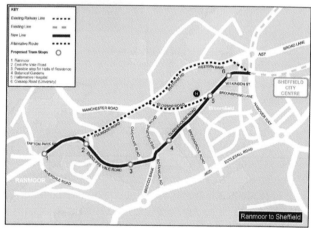

The most recent Ranmoor extension plan serving the university and hospitals.

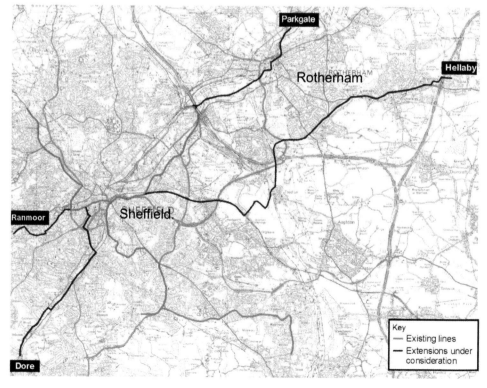

Extensions under consideration to South Yorkshire Supertam in Sheffield in 2001.

15. West Midlands Metro (formerly Midland Metro

Birmingham once had an extensive tram network with 3ft 6ins gauge trams along most of the main radial roads with links to Dudley, West Bromwich, Walsall and Wolverhampton. Long lengths of reserved tracks along Bristol Road and Tyburn Road with shorter lengths through Erdington and Hall Green could have formed the basis for a modern light rail system. But the last trams ran in 1953, another example of millions of pounds worth of infrastructure being abandoned.

The case for rapid transit in the West Midlands was set out in a report 'Rapid Transit for the West Midlands' in June 1984. The first light rail plans were launched in 1985 with a starter 10 km line from Fiveways through the city centre to Castle Bromwich. The section from Fiveways to Aston University would have been in tunnel, a distance of 3 km. Stations would have served the Science Park and University at Gosta Green, New Street, Paradise Circus, the proposed Convention Centre (opened in 1991) and Five Ways. Extensions eastwards would serve Castle Vale and Chelmsley Wood and westwards towards Harborne and Hagley Road. A Parliamentary Bill would be deposited in November 1985.

A network of priority routes would take trams to West Bromwich, Sutton Coldfield and Chelmsley Wood with further extensions to Wolverhampton, Dudley, Stourbridge, Walsall, Halesowen, Bartley Green, Bristol Road to Rubery, Warstock, Shirley and Solihull. The light rail network would complement the heavy rail suburban network, much of which was either already electrified or planned to be electrified.

This plan would have given the West Midlands an excellent tram system but was far too ambitious.

Midland Metro was re-launched in September 1987 with a Bill deposited in Parliament in November 1988 for a route from Birmingham Snow Hill to Wolverhampton. Most of the route is on former railway which closed in 1972 with a short section of street running along Bilston Road into Wolverhampton.

A 20 year strategy produced in 1992 included for the first time the city of Coventry, often left out of West Midlands proposals. Three routes were identified but only as 'corridors to be investigated'. Similar status was given to a number of other corridors in Birmingham and the routes for Line 2 to Birmingham Airport and Line 3 to Walsall and Dudley were shown. Twenty five years later these routes are still 'might have beens'.

A revised plan for extensions was published in 2002 showing a short extension in the city centre from Snow Hill to New Street and a line from Wednesbury to Dudley and Brierley Hill, again following the route of a former railway. Other extensions bore some similarities to the 1985 plan serving Walsall and Wednesfield, Great Barr, Kingstanding, Birmingham Airport, Selly Oak, Bartley Green, Oldbury and Halesowen. A similar plan two years later showed the Brierley Hill route under construction in 2005 but ten years later it was still a 'might have been'.

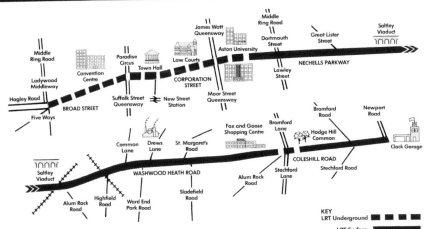

The first line of the West Midlands light rail network as planned in 1985. WMPTE

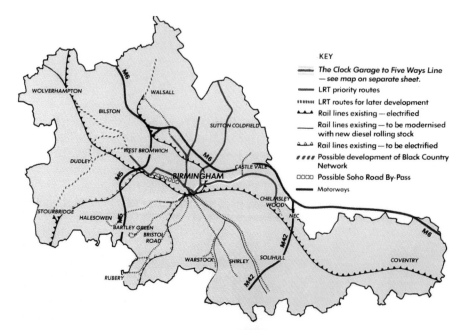

KEY

━━━ The Clock Garage to Five Ways Line
— see map on separate sheet.
━━━ LRT priority routes
▪▪▪▪ LRT routes for later development
◣◣◣ Rail lines existing — electrified
──── Rail lines existing — to be modernised
with new diesel rolling stock
◠◠◠ Rail lines existing — to be electrified
▰▰▰▰ Possible development of Black Country
Network
▢▢▢▢ Possible Soho Road By-Pass
━━━ Motorways

The light rail network for the West Midlands as proposed in 1985. WMPTE

A light rail vehicle on Soho Road, Handsworth as proposed in 1985. WMPTE

By 1989 the artist's impression used the French Grenoble tram as its model with the fleet name 'Midland Metro'. WMPTE

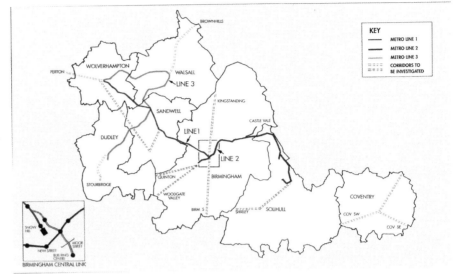

The 20 year strategy produced in 1992 included Coventry and other new corridors. WMPTE

Proposed Midland Metro Network

Existing Metro route
Metro route under construction 2005
Proposed Metro routes
Possible Metro extensions

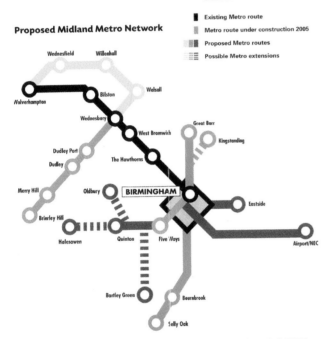

The proposed Midland Metro network in 2004. WMPTE

The extension to New Street, now called Grand Central, opened in 2016 and a further extension, to Centenary Square, opened in 2019. The Westside Metro extension is being opened progressively to Edgbaston and an extension to Wolverhampton railway station is nearing completion. Further extensions to Dudley and Birmingham Eastside are programmed. Other routes are likely to remain *'might have beens'* for the foreseeable future.

Existing and planned Metro extensions in West Midlands in 2002. WMPTE

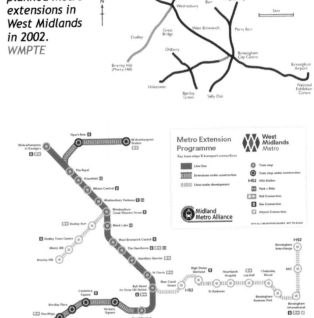

The Midlands Metro extensions, now renamed West Midlands Metro, as planned in 2019. West Midlands Metro

16. London Tramlink (formerly Croydon Tramlink)

Croydon was once on the southern edge of the vast London tramway network. Routes ran south to Purley, west to Sutton and Mitcham, East to Addiscombe and South Norwood and north to Streatham and the Embankment. The last trams ran in 1951 and trolleybuses replaced some routes until 1960 when they too succumbed to the ubiquitous motor bus.

A large new housing estate was developed at New Addington east of Croydon, initially in the 1930s but expanded in the 1960s and 1970s to reach a population of 21,000. The only link into Croydon was a slow bus service. Plans for various automated peoplemover type links in the seventies came to nothing.

As described in Chapter 19, a report in 1986 looked at many possible routes for light rail in London, one of which was to serve New Addington. A three line network was developed using existing or former rail alignments to Wimbledon and Beckenham with a new segregated highway based route to New Addington. Parliamentary powers were obtained in 1994. Construction started towards the end of 1996 and the first trams ran in 2000.

Tramlink has proved very successful and is now an integral part of the local economy. Not surprisingly adjacent authorities are keen to see the tram extended to their towns. Two north-south extensions, Streatham to Purley and Tooting to Sutton would be added to a line from Crystal Palace to Beckenham. While considerable planning on these routes has been undertaken by TfL and the Crystal Palace route was close to being implemented, none have so far been approved.

Detailed planning and consultation was undertaken for the Crystal Palace extension and some work on other extensions but all were cancelled for financial or political reasons.

The Crystal Palace and Sutton routes would use railway alignments, probably replacing existing suburban services. The Purley and Streatham routes would be street tramways, reinstating former tram routes 16 and 18 which were replaced by buses in April 1951. Those routes ran through Streatham and Brixton to the Embankment and Blackfriars. If Cross River Tram had been built, it would have been feasible to connect the Streatham route to CRT at Brixton and reinstate a through tram service to central London.

The London Borough of Merton has been keen to obtain a Tramlink extension into the Borough and prepared a plan showing an extension from Wimbledon station to Mitcham Junction via Colliers Wood and Mitcham under the name of Merton Tramlink. Interchange with the underground would be at Wimbledon to the District line and Colliers Wood to the Northern line. It would re-join the Wimbledon Tramlink line at Mitcham Junction, thus forming a loop.

In 2014 Merton and Sutton Councils undertook a consultation on a route from South Wimbledon to Sutton via St Helier Hospital. Interchange would be available with the Underground, Northern line at South Wimbledon and Morden, Tramlink at Morden Road and National Rail at Sutton. The consultation response was overwhelmingly positive with 84% of people supporting or strongly supporting the tram scheme. In 2017 Mayor of London Sadiq Khan announced that funding for the tram scheme was no longer available. Another potentially beneficial and popular tramway 'might have been'.

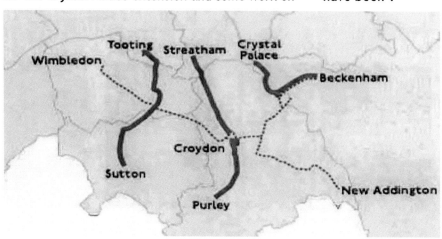

Possible extensions to Croydon Tramlink defined by TfL.

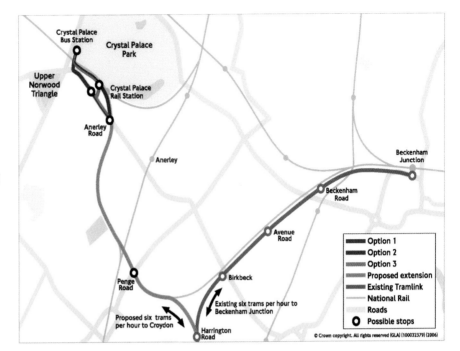

Options for an extension of Croydon Tramlink to serve Crystal Palace. *TfL*

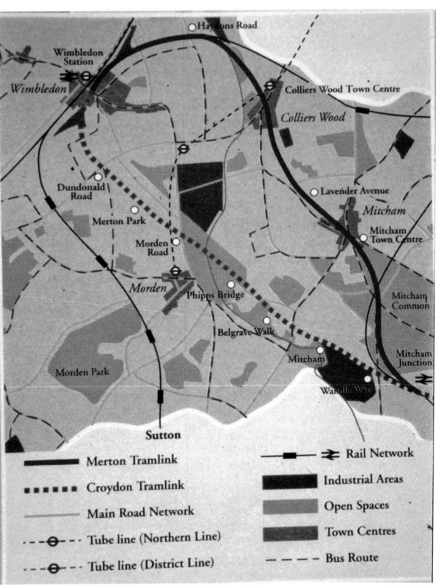

The London Borough of Merton's plan for a Tramlink extension from Wimbledon station to Colliers Wood and Mitcham.

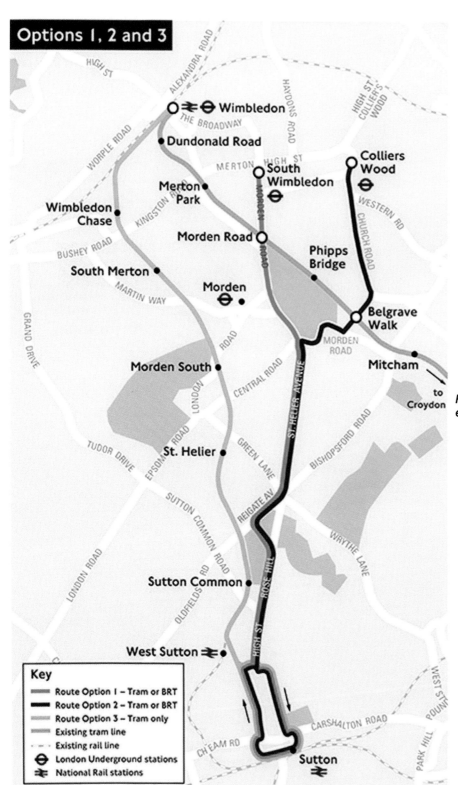

Route options for the Tramlink extension to Sutton. *TfL*

Key
- Route Option 1 – Tram or BRT
- Route Option 2 – Tram or BRT
- Route Option 3 – Tram only
- Existing tram line
- Existing rail line
- London Underground stations
- National Rail stations

Three possible routes for the Tramlink extension to Sutton were the subject of a consultation exercise and in 2020 TfL announced that they would select the option that would connect Sutton with Colliers Wood Northern line underground station. This was not the option favoured by Sutton Council. However TfL did not have the £420m to pay for it. Given that all transport budgets were stretched to breaking point by the pandemic it seemed unlikely that this extension would happen any time soon and in July 2020 the Mayor of London 'paused' the Sutton tram line.

2020 was the 20th anniversary of Croydon Tramlink. It has been widely acknowledged as a huge boost to the local economy, but that has not been enough to justify any extensions. So far they all remain as *'might have beens'*.

17. Nottingham

Most of the new generation tram schemes were developed by PTEs who had the legal powers of the 1968 Transport Act to support their plans. It was more difficult for non-Metropolitan authorities to progress a tram project, but Nottingham succeeded. A client Group of Nottingham City Council, Nottinghamshire County Council and Nottingham Development Enterprise undertook feasibility studies into light rail routes in the late eighties and proposed a network in 1989, see figure below. The Hucknall route was built as the first phase and the Beeston and Toton route part of the second phase. The Gedling route and part of an inner circle remain as *'might have beens'* although they may yet be built at some future date.

Nottingham's first new tram line opened in 2004 from the main railway station to Hucknall in the north west with a spur to a park and ride site near the M1 motorway at Pheonix Park. Extensions to the south west to Toton Lane and Clifton were opened in 2015. The trams have had a major positive impact on the local economy, providing high quality public transport to the major shopping centre, main railway station, universities, major hospital, regeneration areas and many other key passenger objectives.

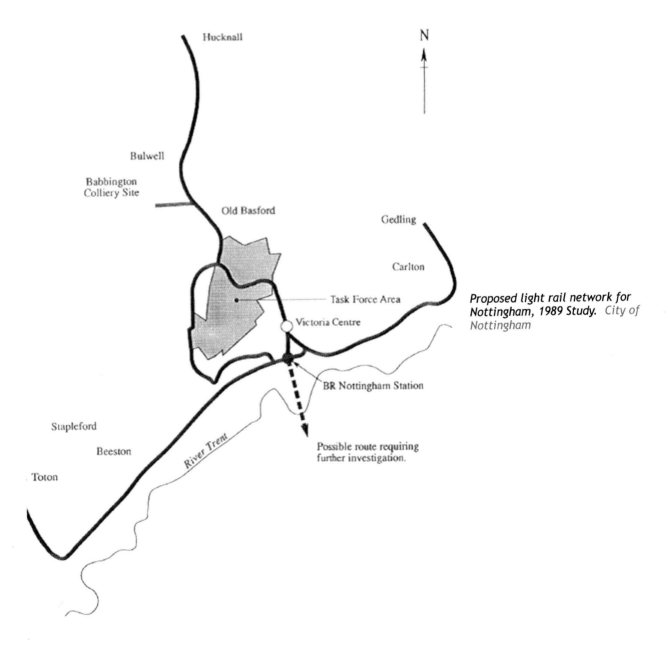

Proposed light rail network for Nottingham, 1989 Study. City of Nottingham

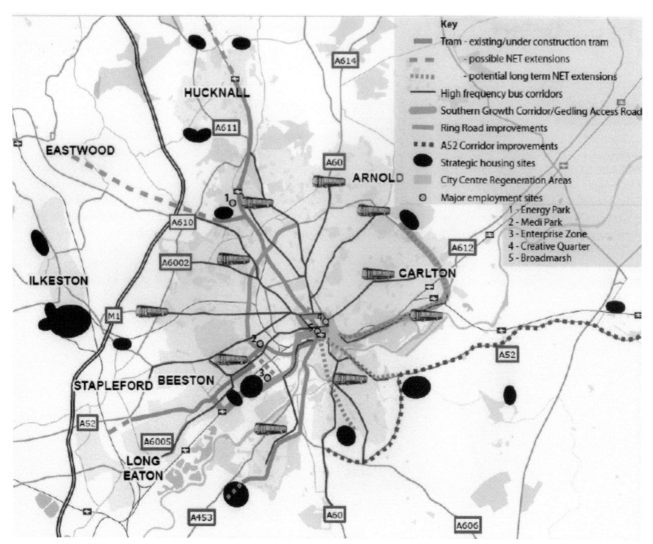

Key
▬▬ Tram - existing/under construction tram
▬ ▬ - possible NET extensions
▪▪▪▪ - potential long term NET extensions
── High frequency bus corridors
▬▬ Southern Growth Corridor/Gedling Access Road
▬▬ Ring Road improvements
▪▪▪▪ A52 Corridor improvements
⬤ Strategic housing sites
▬ City Centre Regeneration Areas
○ Major employment sites
                    1 - Energy Park
                    2 - Medi Park
                    3 - Enterprise Zone
                    4 - Creative Quarter
                    5 - Broadmarsh

Possible extensions to the Nottingham Express Transit system. NET

Not surprisingly there has been strong support
for extensions to the network and a long list of
possible schemes has been drawn up. Four are
extensions to existing lines, six are new lines,
including the original Gedling route, and two are
potential tram-train routes. The most likely is the
extension from the current terminus at Toton Lane
to the HS2 station and possibly continuing to East
Midlands Airport and even into Derby. Given the long
timescales for HS2 it is not likely to be progressed
in the near future. In fact none of the possible
extensions could be considered short term but it
remains to be seen how many turn out to be *'might
have beens'*.

18. Edinburgh

The City of Edinburgh had an extensive tram system serving most parts of the city and beyond. Like Glasgow they were still building new trams into the post war period. The last trams ran in 1956 and nobody dreamt that they would ever return; but trams did once again run along Princes Street in 2014.

The early tram system was cabled hauled, unusual for a British city, being the fourth largest in the world. By 1923 all the cable cars had been replaced by electric trams powered by overhead lines. The electric tramway was expanded until the second world war slowed progress. One potential route was a 'might have been' tramway with a difference. In 1939 tracks were laid and some overhead wires erected along Ferry Road to Crew Toll in the north west of the city. But they were never used. Despite the system having new trams and being in relatively good condition, in 1952 the drastic decision was taken to get rid of all the trams and within only four years the fleet of 350 trams and 46 miles of track had gone.

On the 25th anniversary of the last tram in 1981, Lothian Regional Transport, successor to Edinburgh Corporation Transport, published a celebratory leaflet. They acknowledged that there was still a strong pro-tram lobby and tramways were still suggested as a solution to Edinburgh's traffic congestion problems. The spirit of the tram lived on in Edinburgh and it was very much alive on the continent as any visitor to European systems would know. They commented "if trams ever did return to Edinburgh they would be very different from the stately machines ambling down the middle of the road." That prediction came true in 2014.

Long before trams did return to Edinburgh's streets, a succession of light rail plans were advocated by Lothian Regional Council and others. In 1989 a Public Transport Strategy for Edinburgh was unveiled for consultation after a two year study. Two light rail options were proposed, one with mainly street running routes and the other a light metro line using the abandoned Scotland Street rail tunnel. Both options would have served

LIGHT RAIL

KEY

▭	Built-Up Area
══	On-Street Light Rail Routes
■■■■	Off-Street Light Rail Routes
●●●●	Underground Light Rail Links
– – –	Separate Bus Routes
──	ScotRail Routes
◯	Possible Park-and-Ride Sites
◇	Possible Light Rail/Bus Interchanges

Lothian Regional Transport Light Rail option in January 1989.

LOTHIAN REGIONAL COUNCIL

EDINBURGH METRO

NORTH-SOUTH LINE

St Andrew's Square, Leith, Muirhouse, Liberton and Gilberton.

The preferred strategy comprised the north-south light metro as a first priority and an east-west light metro and improvements to rail and bus services. Public consultation was planned for autumn 1989 and a series of meetings was held around the city between October and December. It took until June 1991 to consider the results of the consultation and refine plans for the north-south metro with a route length of 18.5 km including 4.4 km in tunnel with 36 stops and 31 LRVs and a cost of £300m.

Ten years later in 1998 a private sector company was formed, 'The New Edinburgh Tramways Company' (NETCo), led by academic Professor Lewis Lesley. The proposed route started at Haymarket station and ran along Princes Street and through St Andrew's Square to Leith Walk then via Great Junction Street to the Ocean Terminal and along Lindsay Road to Newhaven. Professor Lesley planned to use his low profile shallow tram rail and the low cost lightweight light rail vehicle he had developed. The City Council were not impressed and in 2002 decided to develop their busway plans instead. But seeds had been sown and much of Lewis Lesley's route between Haymarket and Newhaven became part of Transport Initiatives Edinburgh's Line 1 plan the following year. As is now well known trams did finally run on Edinburgh's streets in 2014 after a long problematic gestation which nearly saw the whole plan cancelled. Despite strong public opposition the project was

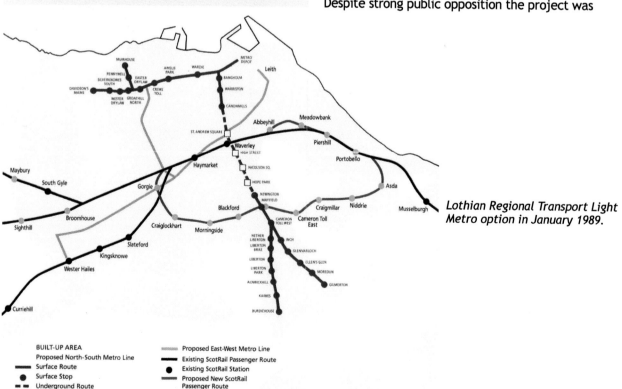

Lothian Regional Transport Light Metro option in January 1989.

BUILT-UP AREA
Proposed North-South Metro Line
— Surface Route
● Surface Stop
- - Underground Route
□ Underground Stop

═══ Proposed East-West Metro Line
— Existing ScotRail Passenger Route
● Existing ScotRail Station
═══ Proposed New ScotRail Passenger Route
● Possible New ScotRail Station

An artist's impression of an
Edinburgh tram for the 1989 plan.

Trams along Leith Walk in
Edinburgh, this route is now being
constructed.

held together with a combination of parts of Line 1
and Line 2 between the Airport, Haymarket and York
Place. The extension down Leith Walk to the Ocean
Terminal had to be cut out to save costs which had
risen way beyond acceptable levels but it is now
back in favour and under construction. So Leith Walk
(where tracks should have been laid in 2009) will
happen but the Line 3 route to Gilmerton remains as a
'might have been'. It is to be hoped with the success
and popularity of Edinburgh trams that they will be
extended further before too long.

Edinburgh is a good example of a tramway project
that transitioned from being almost a point of derision
to demands for extension, once people saw what
the trams were like and had first-hand experience of
them. This is not uncommon with tram schemes.

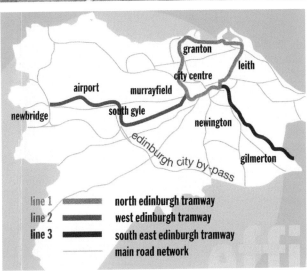

Transport Initiatives Edinburgh three line tram system
proposed in 2003.

19. London

A city the size of London would justify a book on its own of tramway schemes that *'might have been'*. All this chapter can do is give a taste of some of the ideas that could well have been built in the later years of the twentieth century or early twenty first century if politicians or accountants had not stepped in.

London's last first generation tram was sent to the scrap heap in 1952 but memories of the well-loved trams lived on. In official circles they were discarded into the dustbin of history, but not in the minds of many Londoners. It took another three decades before the concept of light rail could be raised in professional circles again. London Transport and British Rail jointly produced a report 'Light rail for London?' in 1986 (Ref.31) which scrutinized forty possible conversions of existing or disused secondary rail routes to light rail. The aim was to increase passenger usage and create new opportunities for travel.

No doubt another objective in BR's mind will have been to reduce operating costs and subsidy levels, as was demonstrated conclusively by Manchester's light rail lines. The Docklands Light Railway had by then been approved and was under construction, but the report laid the foundations for the Croydon tram scheme.

A report entitled 'Street Trams for London' by Chris Wood (Ref.40) was published by CILT in 1994. At that time CILT stood for 'Centre for Independent Transport Research in London' and not the now more familiar 'Chartered Institute of Logistics and Transport'. The report was sponsored by the London Transport Unit for Disabled Passengers and the LRTA. Light rail had already been accepted for Croydon Tramlink and London Regional Transport had obtained Parliamentary Powers to build and operate the three line network in 1994.

Examples of street running trams from around Europe were given together with the newly opened tramways in Manchester and Sheffield. Drawing on existing bus routes with high bus flows, a number of radial and ring routes were identified as potential street running tram routes, as shown in the above plan. Two bus routes, 24 Pimlico to Hampstead Heath and 29 Palmer's Green to Camden Town, were selected to illustrate how conversion to tram operation could be considered, although the difficulties that would be encountered were acknowledged. While perhaps regarded as a bit far-fetched at the time, the report was in fact far-sighted as the Cross-River Tram route developed by Transport for London some years later did include Waterloo to Euston and Kings Cross/St Pancras.

Case studies from the continent were described and a section on level boarding technologies to ensure that any system was fully accessible. The regulatory framework for light rail planning in the UK was outlined. While this report was entirely independent and not 'official ', it is probable that it did reflect developing thinking amongst some very senior managers within London Transport.

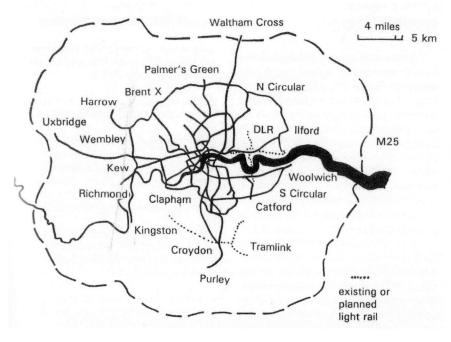

Routes warranting further investigation for a potential tram network for London. Street Trams for London report, 1994.
Chris Wood

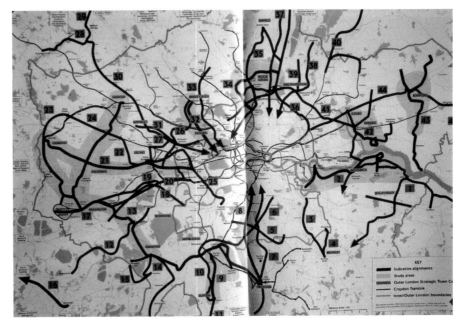

Indicative alignments in outer
London. LT Planning June 1995.
London Transport Planning

Only a year later in 1995 London Transport produced a report 'New ideas for Public Transport in outer London' (Ref.42) which described a range of intermediate modes including guided buses, trolleybuses, tramways and light rail. A detailed comparison of twelve modes included heavy rail and upgraded bus services as well as the tracked options. Advantages and disadvantages of each system were outlined with examples and indicative costs.

Forty five indicative alignments were identified, shown in the plan above. It also showed Croydon Tramlink, which had received Royal Assent in 1994 and was being developed at that time, still the only new generation tram system in London. The plan shows possible extensions to Tramlink and the potential tramway corridors along Uxbridge Road,

through Woolwich and in Barking and Ilford which were later studied by London Transport Planning.

In 2000 Transport for London was created under the Greater London Authority and assumed the functions of London Regional Transport. The first Mayor of London was the controversial left wing Councillor Ken Livingstone who was a keen supporter of tram schemes. By 2003, a number of projects had been defined, as shown on the plan below.

West London tram

The West London Tram project would have re-installed the tramway from Shepherds Bush to Uxbridge, originally built by the London United Tramways Company from 1901, inherited by London

TfL Light Transit Proposals

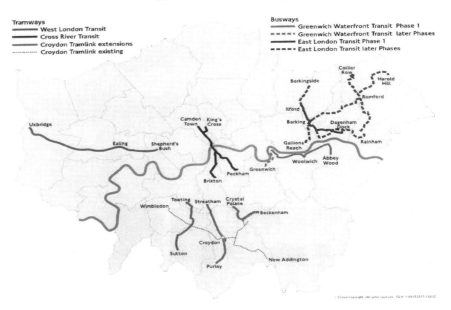

TfL Light Transit Proposals in
London in 2003. TfL

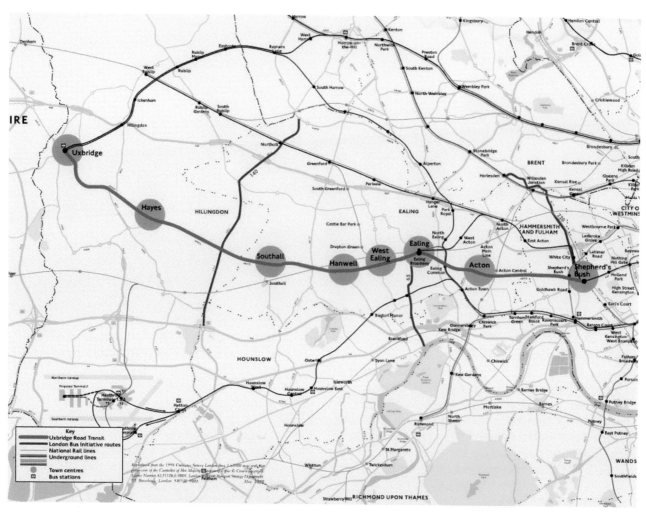

The route of West London Tram from Uxbridge to Shepherds Bush, a classic rapid transit corridor. *TfL*

When the West London Tram project was cancelled, there was a suggestion that trolleybuses could be used instead. Trolleybuses ran on this route from 1936 to 1960. Nothing came of the suggestion and the 207 is still a bus route.

Might Have Been Trams and Tramways

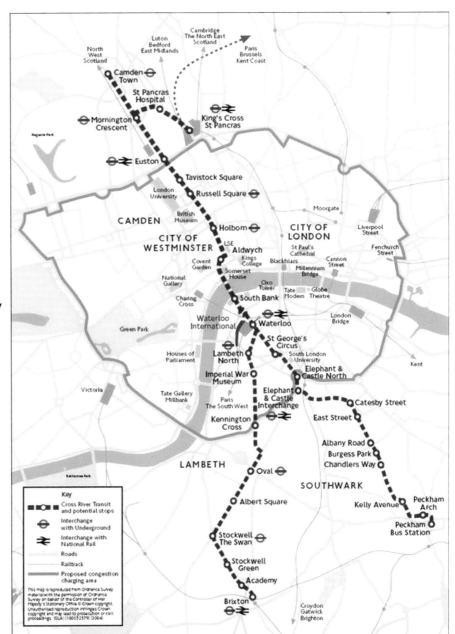

Cross River Tram route planned by TfL linking Waterloo with Euston and King Cross St Pancras. *TfL*

A vivid illustration of a 'might have been' tram, the mock-up of a Cross River Tram after the project had been abandoned. This Citadis 300 type has been acquired by the Crich Tramway Museum for possible future display. *Andrew Waddington*

An artist's impression of a tram at Waterloo Station.

Transport in 1933 and closed in 1936 when it was replaced by trolleybuses. The trolleybuses were themselves replaced by diesel buses in 1960.

Uxbridge Road is one of the few main radial corridors into London which has no rail service. It is crossed by several underground and suburban rail lines, but the main route is the preserve of buses which struggle to carry the loads along this busy congested thoroughfare. It is a 'classic rapid transit corridor' linking the major district centres of Uxbridge, Hillingdon, Hayes End, Southall, Hanwell, Ealing, Acton and Shepherds Bush, as in the plan on page 112. Several major shopping centres, hospitals and universities contribute to heavy demand for public transport which trams would have been able to meet admirably. It would have demanded some imaginative and courageous traffic management, but nothing beyond the scope of similar schemes in France or Spain. Strong opposition in some pockets emerged along the route and Ealing Borough Council turned against the scheme. It was dropped by TfL on the pretext that Crossrail would make it unnecessary. In fact it would have fulfilled a different role from Crossrail and would have been complementary to it. West London Tram was scheduled to open towards the end of 2012 but instead it became a *'might have been'*.

Cross River tram

The desperate need for additional capacity on the Northern Line was a primary reason for Cross River Tram. The north-south route would have linked Camden Town, Euston and Kings Cross/St Pancras in the north over Waterloo Bridge to Waterloo, Elephant and Castle, Peckham and Brixton in the south. The whole route was street running but with a high level of segregation from road traffic and priority at traffic signals.

Planning and design were well advanced with an opening date of 2016 envisaged but in 2008 Boris

Johnson became London Mayor and promptly cancelled all the remaining tram schemes including Cross River Tram, ostensibly on cost grounds but in reality for political reasons. Another *'might have been'* tram project was added to the list, one that would have fulfilled a desperate need and given central London a high profile tramway. While Paris has built ten tram lines in the past 25 years, London has managed none, apart from Croydon Tramlink.

While the route from Euston to Kings Cross via Mornington Crescent might seem somewhat bizarre (perhaps to impress a certain radio programme?) the Cross River Tram scheme as a whole was well conceived and developed and would have been of enormous benefit to central London.

Oxford Street tram

In 2008 Ken Livingstone repeated his idea for replacing the buses on Oxford Street, London's busiest shopping street, with trams. Over 250 buses per hour make the 'buses and taxis only' street congested and bus speeds very slow. Making it pedestrian and tram only would be a massive improvement, not least to air quality. Buses would be phased out gradually and even taxis would have to use parallel streets. But it depended on his re-election as London Mayor and of course that did not happen as Boris Johnson won that election. He soon killed off the idea.

Yet another proprosal for trams along Oxford Street came from Trampower in 2009, an even more ambitious plan to link West London Tram with Cross

☐ Tram Stop   ● Tube Station

An Oxford Street tram route from Shepherd's Bush to Limehouse.
Trampower

River Tram, both of which have been scrapped by Mayor Johnson. It would run the length of Oxford Street, extended at the west end to Shepherd's Bush and at the east end to Bank, Fenchurch Street and Limehouse. It would be part of a network termed 'Southwark Supertram' linking key areas of the city and west end.

Trams on Oxford Street may not be entirely dead yet. The West End Commission which was overseeing the future of the West End revisited the idea in 2012. Its report did not recommend trams, but the concept is still mentioned from time to time by various interests. It is very unlikely to be built unless the Mayor promotes it and that is not going to happen with Mayor Sadiq Kahn. The fares freeze may be laudable but starves TfL of funds for new schemes.

Greenwich Waterfront tram

The light transit proposals in 2003 included a line termed 'Greenwich Waterfront Transit' running from Greenwich town centre via North Greenwich, Charlton, Woolwich and Thamesmead to Abbey Wood. It was intended as a bus based system, but Greenwich Borough and some members of the Greater London Authority would have preferred it to be a tramway. This line, and a similar proposal north of the river termed 'East London Transit', were not considered to have high enough traffic potential to justify tramways but would be designed as busways with the possibility of longer term conversion to tramways.

A TfL report in 2001 examined a range of options for Greenwich Waterfront Transit from bus to tram or trolleybus. As a significant proportion of predicted demand was dependent on new development which was speculative, it was concluded that the higher cost of the tramway option could not be justified initially. A busway could be converted to tramway in the future if patronage levels increased. However the whole project including busways was cancelled by Mayor Boris Johnson in 2008, the year that Mayor Ken Livingstone had planned to open it.

One section between North Greenwich and Charlton was actually constructed as a busway to serve the Millennium Dome. It was intended to be wire guided, rather than the more accepted kerb guidance. The guidance electronics were installed but were not successful and it only operated as an unguided busway. Following a number of accidents the busway was removed in 2019 and replaced by a dual carriageway road for all traffic. Greenwich Waterfront Tramway joined the ranks of *might have beens*.

20. Should have made it tramways

Leeds

The City of Leeds has the unenviable record of the least successful light rail planning in Britain. Its population of over three quarters of a million is claimed to be the largest conurbation in Europe with no tramway, light rail or metro. Its sad history is made worse by the fact that it once had one of the best tram systems in Britain and very nearly became the only one with a modern light rail system based on an established first generation tramway, as outlined in Chapter 8.

The table opposite lists thirty events in the struggle to develop new transit systems for Leeds from the ill-fated 1945 plan to modern times. The prototype single deckers of 1953, the closest any British tram came to the ubiquitous American PCC car, were made redundant before they entered service. Upgraded bus services have been tried several times, and are still seen as the best solution, but have only resulted in further patronage decline.

Trolleybuses were planned in the 1980s and parliamentary powers were obtained to run them on any road in West Yorkshire, but they never got beyond the drawing board. A plan in 1985 showed 'Electrobus' routes in three phases in Leeds and Bradford with longer term plans for light rail on seven routes in Leeds, one of which was to Middleton using the original tramway alignment. In 1988 a Bill was introduced in Parliament for a light rail line to Seacroft and Colton, but political differences ensured it would not get far. The following year, an

automated transit system, copying Leeds' twin city of Lille in northern France, was seen as the future. The line would have been mainly elevated running from Middleton via the city centre to Seacroft, but its enormous cost made it a non-starter.

The next plan was termed 'Metro-line' starting at Leeds Town Hall and extending to Seacroft, Crossgates and Colton, to be in operation by 1993. Future additions would take trams to Headingley, Roundhay, Kirkstall, Holbeck and Middleton, effectively restoring much of the tramway thrown away in the post-war years. It even included an extension from Headingley to Leeds/Bradford Airport, still needed 25 years later.

A brief flirtation with guided buses finally gave way in the early 1990s to a recognition that the most effective system for Leeds would be light rail, forty five years after the original tram subway plans. By 1993 Royal Assent had been received for the first Supertram Act to re-instate the tramway to Middleton and extend it to Tingley. Further authorisation followed in 2001 for lines to Headingley and Lawnswood, and Seacroft making a three line system totalling 28 km including a city centre loop.

Tenders for the construction and operation of Leeds Supertram were invited and a preferred bidder selected. Some preliminary works were carried out in the central area. It was reported that over £40million had already been spent on the project which would see trams running in Leeds again

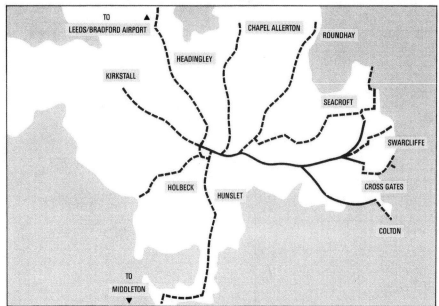

Metro-line was a light rail route in 1987 from Leeds Town Hall to Seacroft and Colton, to be running by 1993. WYPTA

Leeds transit systems 1945 - 2016 (none built)

1945   Tram tunnels under city centre planned by Leeds City Engineer and Transport Manager, excellent project but not implemented.

1953   Three single deck prototype trams for subways enter service, but tram tunnel plans already scrapped.

1959   Last Leeds trams, system abandoned including miles of segregated tracks (later accepted as a huge mistake).

1965   'Fastaway' bus rapid transit introduced. Failed to attract car users and services withdrawn.

1977   'WYTConsult' transportation study suggests light rail for corridors in Leeds, not pursued.

1982   Trolleybus powers for Leeds included in West Yorkshire (Parking and Transport) Act 1982. Authorises WYPTE to construct trolleybus routes on any road in West Yorkshire.

1985   'ElectroBus' trolleybus system planned for Leeds and Bradford by WYPTE. Key objective to reduce air pollution. Stage 1 routes to Roundhay, Moortown, Hunslet, Middleton and Cottingley. Stage 2 to Bradford. Section 56 grant application November 1985 rejected by DoT.

1987   Leeds City Council and West Yorkshire PTE propose tramway along York Road to Seacroft, Cross Gates and Colton (re-instating original abandoned tramways), termed 'MetroLine'.

1988   Bill promoted in Parliament by West Yorkshire PTE for light rail line to Seacroft and Cross Gates but subsequently withdrawn due to opposition from Leeds City Council and residents.

1989   Leeds Advanced Transit (LAT) proposed by Leeds City Council on route from Middleton via city centre to St James's Hospital using automated rubber tyred elevated system (VAL system as in Lille, Leeds' twin city).

c.1990   Leeds Dual Transit (LDT) concept proposed by Yorkshire Rider based on guided bus technology. Partly implemented on York Road, Scott Hall Road and Selby Road.

1991   Leeds Transport Strategy published, decision to proceed with South Leeds LRT line.

1992   Submission of Parliamentary Bill for South Leeds line.

1993   Leeds Supertram Act receives Royal Assent for tram route to Middleton and Tingley.

1994   Leeds Transport Strategy includes light rail lines, busways and highway schemes.

1995   Bids received for South Leeds line.

1996   Full funding bid for South Leeds line, submission of Transport and Works Act Order.

1998   Government embargo on new major schemes.

1999   Scheme dormant.

2000   Government's Ten Year Transport Plan published, qualified funding approval for three lines. Transport and Works Act Order for North and East Leeds lines.

2001   Leeds Supertram (Extension) Order 2001 approved for lines to north and east Leeds. Government funding for Supertram approved.

2002   Tendering for all three lines.

2004   Secretary of State for Transport Alistair Darling cancels Supertram and tells WY to get a bus system.

2007   Metro propose Tram-train route linking Harrogate and Castleford lines, possibly with street running through the city centre.

2007   Metro propose trolleybus system linking Headingley and Stourton with city centre loop.

2010   Government approve funding for Bodington and Stourton routes but not East Leeds or city centre loop.

2012   Programme Entry approval obtained by Metro and Leeds City Council for trolleybus scheme, TWA Order to be sought in Spring 2013.

2014   Public Inquiry held for trolleybus scheme.

2016   After public inquiry Government cancels trolleybus scheme but allows Leeds to retain £173.5m funding.

2016   Proposal for tram-train to Leeds-Bradford Airport. Decision to provide to new station on Harrogate rail line instead with bus link to Airport.

2018   Major review of transport plans fails to mention trams or light rail.

2019   August 2019 Advanced Urban Transit Technologies Market Testing.

2019   2033 Vision: Three line transit network linking Dewsbury, Bradford, Leeds, Thorpe Park, Castleford and University.

by 2007/08. Then in 2004 the Secretary of State for Transport, Alastair Darling, announced that funding was being withheld. This was confirmed in November 2005 and the re-introduction of trams to re-invigorate the local economy was scrapped.

The reason given was unacceptable increase in costs, but as previously mentioned similar levels of cost increases in highway schemes did not result in their cancellation. It is probable that one factor was the Government's insistence on procuring the tram system through the private sector with full risk transfer, ensuring that bidders would place a very high price on the risk. Funding it in the public sector would have been manageable and much cheaper.

It was widely believed that Mr Darling simply did not like trams; he cancelled tram schemes in Liverpool

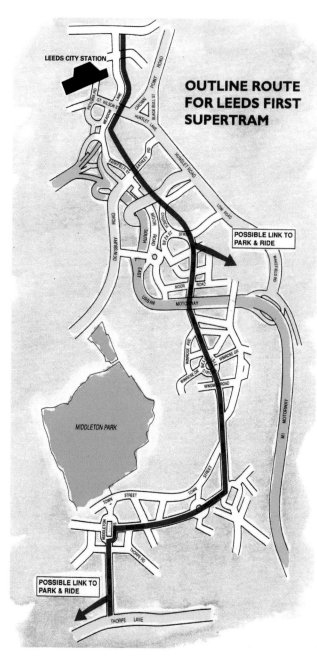

OUTLINE ROUTE
FOR LEEDS FIRST
SUPERTRAM

LEEDS CITY STATION

POSSIBLE LINK TO
PARK & RIDE

MIDDLETON PARK

POSSIBLE LINK TO
PARK & RIDE

The Supertram route to Middleton as planned in 1991. Park and ride sites were at Stourton for M1 and Tingley for M62. Metro

and South Hampshire at the same time, as well as all Manchester's Metrolink tram extensions. But while Leeds and Liverpool simply acquiesced in the cancellation, Manchester refused to accept it and mounted a huge campaign to get the decision reversed. They eventually won and now have a 100 km network which has transformed public transport in the Metropolitan County. It can be little consolation to the citizens of Leeds that having spent the next six years developing a trolleybus system instead of a tramway (although nobody really thought trolleybuses could do the same job), that too was cancelled by the government and Leeds is now left with diesel buses. Leeds is once again relegated to the *'might have beens'*.

In 2019 the West Yorkshire Combined Authority unveiled its latest plan for rapid transit in West Yorkshire. A three line network would link Dewsbury with Bradford, Leeds city centre and Leeds University, Leeds Dock with Thorpe Park via the city centre, St James Hospital and Seacroft and a third line from the University to the south via Leeds Dock to park and ride sites on the M62 and M1 and to Castleford. Some sections have previously formed part of light rail plans and it would appear that significant sections are based on existing rail alignments. Completion would not be until at least 2033. It remains to be seen whether this plan will have any greater chance of success than any of its predecessors.

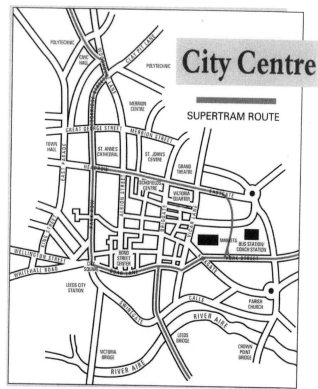

Leeds Supertram would have operated around a loop in the city centre. Metro

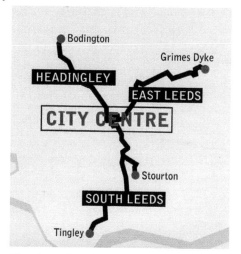

The three line Supertram network. Metro

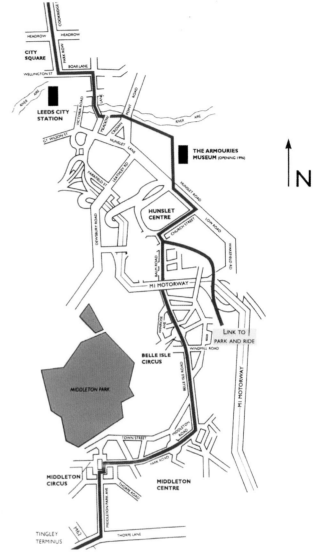

Leeds Supertram route from City Square to Middleton received Royal Assent in 1993. *Metro*

Supertram in Leeds City Square, looking west. *Metro*

An impression of 2001 of Boar Lane with Supertrams. Metro

The Vevey Urbos light rail vehicle proposed for Leeds in 2002. Vevey

2033 Emerging City Region Transit Network with HS2

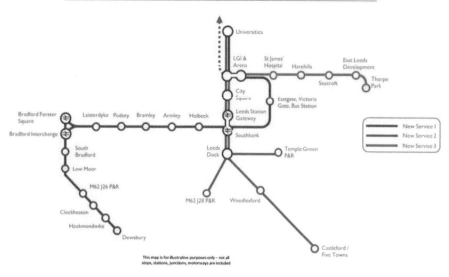

West Yorkshire Combined Authority transit network for 2033. WYCA

Liverpool

Since the early 1990s a string of studies for Merseytravel (the PTE for the Merseyside area) examined transit system options for the city of Liverpool embracing heavy rail, light rail, tramway, trolleybus and busways. Although a tramway seemed a preferable option, an assumption that Liverpool would not attract government funding on the scale of Manchester's resulted in a decision to go for a guided trolleybus, perhaps under the mistaken impression that the Secretary of State for Transport might be more amenable to some new technology.

Under the heading of 'Merseyside Rapid Transit' the line was planned from Albert Dock via the city centre, University, Wavertree Technology Park and Knotty Ash to Page Moss with a possible extension eastwards to Prescot. The route would be mainly on reserved track within the highway and would make extensive use of former tramway reservations along East Prescot Road.

Articulated duobuses would be used, trolleybuses with diesel engines for off-wire operation, and guidance would be electronic using a buried cable rather than the more familiar kerb guidance used in Leeds. This was a high risk strategy as this technology had not been used anywhere except in the Channel Tunnel service tunnel, which is a protected environment with no impact of adverse weather conditions or normal passenger interaction. It was to be used on the Greenwich Millennium busway developed by London Transport in 2000 and was installed but never operated in normal passenger service and was subsequently removed.

The Merseyside trolleybus scheme was taken through the project development stages in 1997 and an application for a Transport and Works Act Order was submitted in 1998. A public inquiry was held towards the end of that year and in 1999 the planning inspector ruled against the project, a recommendation accepted by the Secretary of State for the Environment, Transport and the Regions. Among reasons given were safety concerns for trolleybuses operating through a pedestrian area and that the need for the system had not been proven. One objector commented "the scheme continues to be sold by its promoters as a 'rapid transit' system when it is in truth far from that". The same criticism would not have been made about a tramway.

Merseyside's trolleybus had been planned to start construction in 2000 and begin operating in 2001 but instead was confined to the waste paper basket after seven years expensive work.

Merseytravel lost no time in preparing a replacement Merseytram scheme with three lines using conventional low floor light rail technology:

- Line 1 would run from Kings Waterfront to Kirkby via city centre, West Derby, Utting Avenue East and Croxteth. A city centre loop would link Pier Head, Moorfields, Lime Street, Queen Square, Paradise Street and Albert Dock.
- Line 2 would run from the city centre loop to Prescot via Old Swan and Page Moss, similar to the abandoned trolleybus route.
- Line 3 would run from the city centre loop to Liverpool Airport at Speke via Allerton and Garston or Hunts Cross.

A Merseyside Rapid Transit trolleybus passes Liverpool Roman Catholic Cathedral, project cancelled in 1999. Merseytravel

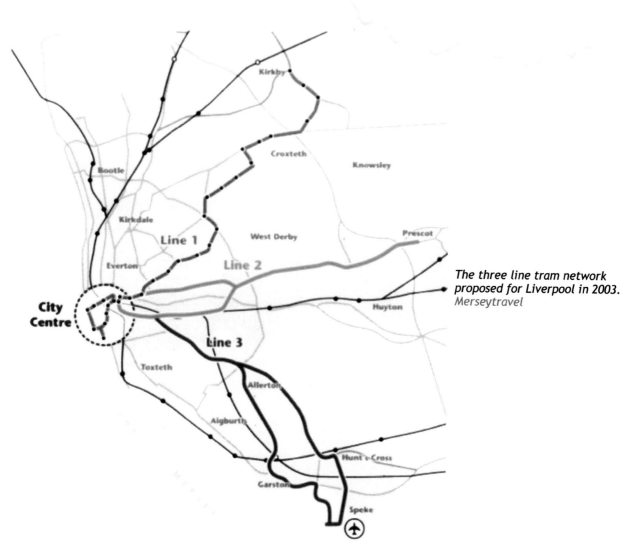

The three line tram network proposed for Liverpool in 2003. *Merseytravel*

All the alignments were highway based with a high level of segregation and extensive use of former tramway reservations, which still exist along many main roads in the city.

In December 2002 Government funding was announced for Line 1 and a public consultation exercise was undertaken to determine support for the scheme. This showed that over 85% of respondents

Merseytram at Port of Liverpool Building, Pier Head. *Merseytravel*

Broadway stop on Utting Avenue East on Merseytram Line 1.
Merseytravel

Merseytram on Lime Street passing St George's Hall.
Merseytravel

Merseytram passes Liverpool Town Hall with European style pavement café, 'might have been'. *Merseytravel*

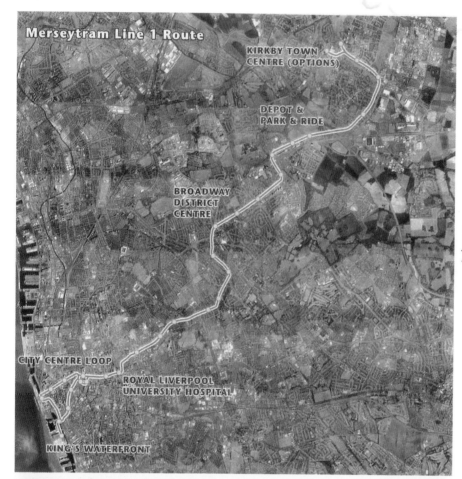

The route of Merseytram Line 1 from King's Waterfront to Kirkby. Merseytravel

Merseytram city centre loop route. Merseytravel

supported or strongly supported the tramway and the city centre loop with negligible opposition.

In 2004 Merseytravel obtained a Transport and Works Act Order for Line 1 with approval from the Secretary of State. Project development was aimed at letting a contract to allow work to start in 2005 and line 1 to open in 2007, in time for Liverpool's European Capital of Culture in 2008. At last it seemed Liverpool was all set to get its trams back. But then in November of 2005 Transport Minister Derek Twigg, Alastair

Darling's sidekick, cancelled the scheme, despite all the previous approvals. Tram rail had already been ordered and delivered and Bombardier were convinced that they only needed the signature on the tram order to begin construction. Cost increases were the inevitable reason given for scrapping the scheme.

Merseytram was still placed as a priority in Merseytravel's Transport Plan for 2006-2011 and further attempts to revive the Line 1 project were made in 2008. In 2009 Transport Minister

The system would have followed standard light rail practice with standard gauge track, 750Vdc overhead power supply and low floor articulated trams. A total of 16 stations would serve the 750,000 population in the area with eleven trams. A public enquiry was held in 1999 with the promoters, Hampshire County Council and Portsmouth City Council. The Transport and Works Act Order was granted in July 2001. Tenders were invited in 2002.

Two contracting consortia were selected with a view to work starting in 2003/04, but in 2003 the Government said costs had risen too high and the project could not proceed. One reason was the

Sadiq Khan (who held office for less than a year) effectively killed off Merseytram with complex financial requirements which Liverpool and Knowlsey Councils and Merseytravel could not meet. In 2013 Merseyside Integrated Transport Authority formally closed the Merseytram project and another promising British tram scheme was confined to the 'might have been' list, even after spending millions of pounds over more than a decade.

South Hampshire

The coastal strip between Southampton, Portsmouth and Havant is rapidly developing, encouraged by the completion of the M27 motorway. Existing public transport is by bus and suburban rail. A particular problem exists between Fareham and Gosport which has only one main road, the mainly single carriageway A32, but has plenty of redundant Ministry of Defence land ripe for redevelopment. Through the centre of the existing housing areas is a former railway alignment which links Fareham and Gosport and could be extended at each end to form a local rapid transit system.

Studies in the late 1980s and early 1990s showed that a 14 km route could start at Fareham bus station in the centre of the town, run on street for a short distance to Fareham railway station and then follow the redundant railway to Gosport, where another short section of street running would take the line to the Ferry Terminal. The keystone of the system would then be a tunnel under Portsmouth Harbour, rising to Portsmouth Harbour railway station and The Hard bus station. A third section of street running would terminate at Portsmouth and Southsea railway station in the city centre. The project was named South Hampshire Rapid Transit (SHRT) Phase 1. Phase 2 would take light rail to Southampton, mainly using existing heavy rail tracks.

The 1995 consultation brochure illustrated the tram tunnel concept. *Hampshire CC*

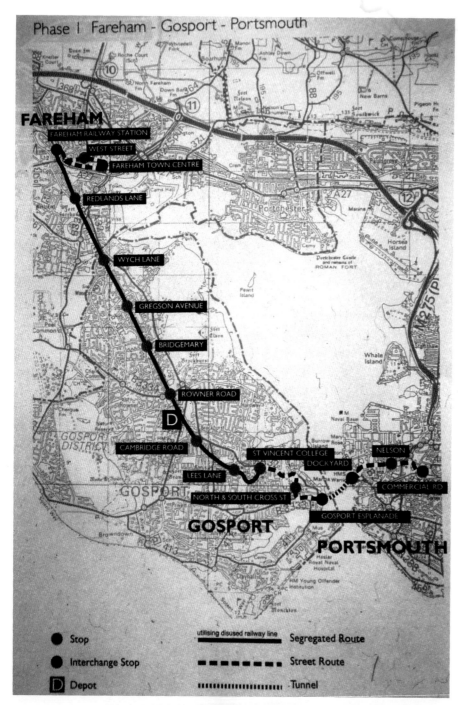

FAREHAM

FAREHAM RAILWAY STATION
WEST STREET
FAREHAM TOWN CENTRE

REDLANDS LANE

WYCH LANE

GREGSON AVENUE

BRIDGEMARY

ROWNER ROAD

D

CAMBRIDGE ROAD

GOSPORT DISTRICT

LEES LANE

GOSPORT

NORTH & SOUTH CROSS ST

ST VINCENT COLLEGE
DOCKYARD

NELSON

COMMERCIAL RD

GOSPORT ESPLANADE

GOSPORT

PORTSMOUTH

● Stop
● Interchange Stop
D Depot

utilising disused railway line ——— Segregated Route
- - - - - - Street Route
.... Tunnel

SHRT Phase 1 would link Fareham with Gosport and Portsmouth with a tunnel under Portsmouth Harbour, avoiding a 14 mile road journey. HCC

Government requirement to lower the tunnel by 2.5m to accommodate the new aircraft carriers which the Royal Navy had decided to purchase, but this was not mentioned at the public enquiry. Hampshire County Council were understandably reluctant to accept the Government's decision and they resubmitted their bid in 2004 keeping to the original £170m grant figure which had been agreed in 2001. However this did not satisfy the Secretary of State, Alistair Darling, and in November 2005 he rejected the plans and withdrew the funding approval.

SHRT cost the Hampshire taxpayer many millions to develop and take through all the planning and approvals stages, obtaining government approvals along the

way. It also cost the contracting companies substantial monies in putting their bids together. Cancelling this project (and Leeds and Liverpool) has not only lost a good worthwhile transport investment which would have transformed the local economy, but it has severely damaged the whole light rail industry. No authority in England has promoted a new tram system since.

An attempt to salvage some benefit from the ruins of the tram project resulted in one section of the former railway being converted to a busway. The current intention is to develop a bus rapid transit network around the Portsmouth harbour area, but it will not include the keystone Gosport tunnel. The strategic plans for Hampshire still show a possible light rail or

SHRT trams would serve
Portsmouth Harbour and The Hard,
with HMS Victory and the Dockyard
Gate in the background. *HCC*

The SHRT tunnel under Portsmouth
Harbour would reach the
surface adjacent to Portsmouth
Harbour railway station and the
bus station. Gosport is in the
background. *HCC*

Computer-generated images of the
proposed LRT scheme

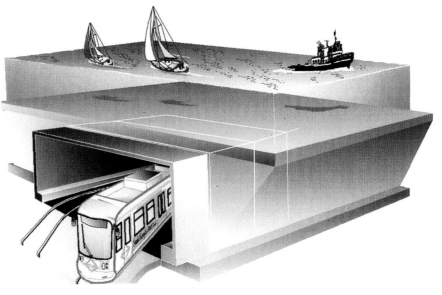

An immersed tube tunnel was
planned, similar to the Medway
road tunnel in Kent. *HCC*

The Gosport Ferry provides a frequent service across the Harbour from Portsmouth. It would have been replaced by the trams although a residual ferry service would probably have been retained. *Tony Young*

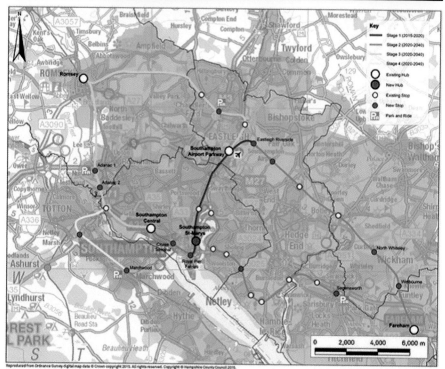

The Solent Local Enterprise Partnership Light Rail Network. *Solent LEP*

tram train link from Fareham to Southampton along the Netley railway, but the chances of this being achieved in the foreseeable future are remote.

The concept of light rail for South Hampshire will not lie down. In 2016 the Solent Local Enterprise Partnership produced a Transport Investment Plan for strategic road and rail routes and a Solent Light Rail Network. It also included bus rapid transit, the airport and ferries. The proposed light rail network is based largely on existing rail lines including the Southampton to London Waterloo main line between Southampton and Eastleigh. It is not clear what evaluation has been undertaken for the operational and engineering feasibility of this concept,

particularly as this section is only double track and is heavily used by intercity trains.

The plan indicates either trams or tram trains could be used, but given the protracted efforts to create a relatively short tram-train route in Sheffield this would appear to be somewhat ambitious. If achieved it would take trams onto the Fareham-Botley-Eastleigh-Southampton route, the Netley line with a new link into Southampton, two routes to Romsey and the line to Marchwood. This plan could well be destined to become another 'might have been'.

21. Not yet made it tramways

While Manchester was approaching initial operation, the first to accept street running tramways, a massive movement towards reintroducing trams was gathering pace across Britain. By the early part of the 21st century it had reached fever pitch. The All Party Parliamentary Light Rail Group discussed many possible schemes. At a meeting in December 2010 a list of towns and cities with the potential for light rail was presented. See Table 21.1 below.

Places in green type are those which had some form of tramway and those in blue had some form of segregated busway. Those in red had developed tram schemes to an advanced state but had then been cancelled by the government. The remainder did not have any form of segregated light rail or busway although a few like Glasgow and Bristol did have heavy rail suburban systems.

While some of these places will perhaps never see any form of tramway, it at least illustrates the perceived need for something better than buses to combat congestion. Others, notably Leeds and Liverpool remain as cities which desperately need fixed track public transport which hopefully will someday be achieved. Some of these are described briefly in the following paragraphs.

Avon, Greater Bristol

When the Metropolitan County Councils were created in 1974 Avon County was also created, but not as a Metropolitan Council, despite having a population of over 1 million. That meant that it did not have a Passenger Transport Authority and Executive like the other Mets either. If it had done, it would almost certainly have had a thriving tram network by now. Bristol must rank with Leeds and Liverpool in the league of great *might have been* tram cities. There can be no doubt that a conurbation the size of Greater Bristol needs strong public transport to combat congestion and pollution.

Over the years there has been no shortage of tramway style plans for Bristol. In 1988 a private consortium under the chairmanship of MEP for Bristol Richard Cottrell, 'Advance Transport for Avon' proposed a phased light rail network to be built and funded privately. It would extend to Bradley Stoke and Yate in the north, Bath in the south east and lines to the south and west. A first phase would include the city centre to Portishead, Yate, Filton via Temple Meads and south Bristol via Bedminster. The first parliamentary Bill would be deposited in 1987 followed by Bills in 1988 and 1989 with the first phase opening in 1991, before Manchester's Metrolink. The whole network would be complete by 2000.

Table 21.1. The potential market for lower cost light rail or trams.

Aberdeen	Edinburgh (u/c)	Newcastle upon Tyne
Barking	Exeter	Norwich
Bedford	Gateshead	Nottingham
Belfast	Glasgow	Oxford
(Birkenhead)	Gloucester	Plymouth
Birmingham	Guildford	Portsmouth/Fareham
Blackpool	Kettering	Preston
Bournemouth	Kingston upon Hull	Reading
Bradford	Kingston upon Thames	Runcorn
Brighton	Lancaster	Sheffield
Bristol	Leeds	Southampton
Cambridge (u/c)	Leicester	Southend
Cardiff	Liverpool	Stoke on Trent
Chatham	Llandudno	Sunderland
Chelmsford	London-Croydon	Swansea
Chester	London - Docklands	Swindon
Cleveland	London - Cross River	Plymouth
Corby	London - West London	Walsall
Coventry	London - Oxford Street	Watford
Crawley	Luton	West Midlands
Dartford	Maidstone	Weymouth
Doncaster	Manchester	Wimbledon
Dundee	Middlesborough	
East Lancashire	Milton Keynes	

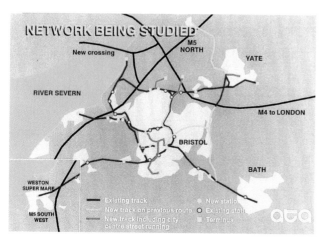

The network studied by ATA for Bristol including city centre street running.

The futuristic styling for ATA's light rail vehicle.

The first Bill did receive Royal Assent, but subsequent Bills were withdrawn. ATA realised that funding the system without any public support was not feasible and a joint approach was adopted with Avon County Council and some District Councils. However, the agreement was terminated in 1992 following ATA

being placed in receivership. On reflection their plans may have had considerable merit but were totally unrealistic. They relied on sharing tracks with heavy rail on some routes with 750 V dc overhead line which would not have been acceptable to British Rail or their successors. But Avon County Council still wanted to pursue a light rail solution.

In 1993 the Rapid Transit Division of Badgerline, then the major local bus operator, proposed a GLT system (Guided Light Transit). Double articulated electrically powered rubber tyred vehicles would run on a concrete guideway, similar to a guided bus. A network of routes was proposed linking Henbury, Cribbs Causeway and Bradley Stoke in the north with Bishopsworth, Withywood and Hartcliffe in the south via Temple Meads and the city centre.

A GLT vehicle was demonstrated in Bristol with manual steering, but the project did not progress any further. The Department of Transport thought that GLT could do the same job as light rail but at lower cost. They required light rail promoters including GMPTE to evaluate GLT as an option even though transport planners knew it was unlikely to be a sensible solution. The only commercial application of GLT opened in Caen, France in 2002 but it was plagued with technical problems and had to be converted to conventional tramway.

Avon made rapid progress picking up the pieces and in July 1994 published plans for a light rail network. These followed the familiar pattern of routes to Bradley Stoke and Yate in the north, Portishead in the west and Withywood and Hartcliffe in the south. More detail was shown for a street running route through the city centre linking Temple Meads station

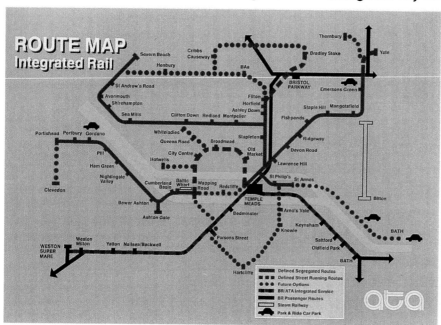

ATA envisaged an integrated rail network covering the conurbation.

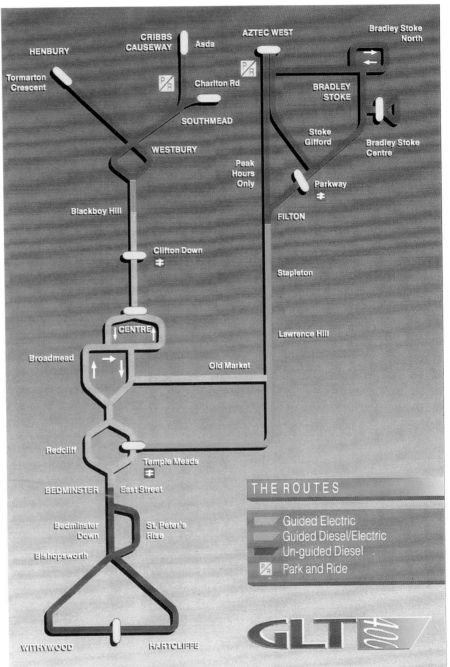

The GLT route network proposed by Badgerline in 1993.

A Belgian double articulated GLT vehicle on test in Bristol in 1992.
Tony Young

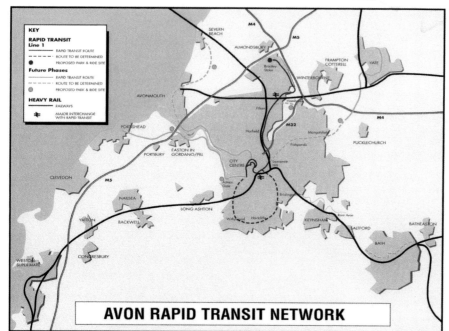

Avon County Council's light rail plans in July 1994. Avon CC

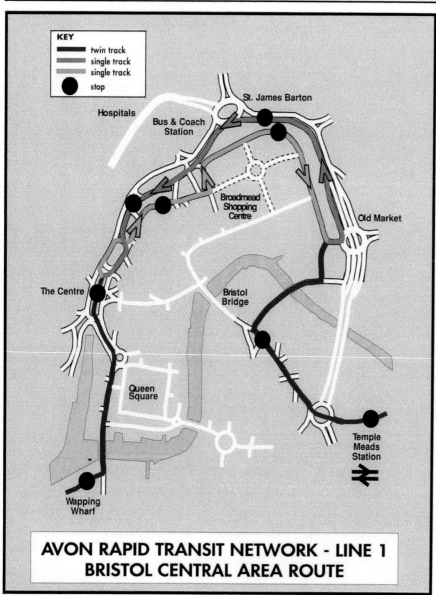

Avon County Council's light rail plans in July 1994. Avon CC

with the shopping and commercial centre. Improving air quality was a major objective, an even more crucial issue twenty years later.

A year later, on the one hundredth anniversary of Bristol's first generation trams, Avon relaunched the rapid transit plan under the name The Westway. The route network remained more or less the same. A Parliamentary Bill would be promoted in 1996 for the first route to Bradley Stoke with 37 stops and a run time of 28 minutes. Private sector funding was again on the agenda, but limited to about 20% of the capital.

Avon set out a detailed timetable for obtaining parliamentary powers, applying for government grants, construction of the first line and operation in 2001/2. But then the death knell was sounded by the government abolishing Avon County Council and replacing it with four district councils, Bristol City Council, South Gloucestershire Council, North Somerset Council and Bath and North East Somerset Council. There was no mechanism to continue the project and it was effectively abandoned.

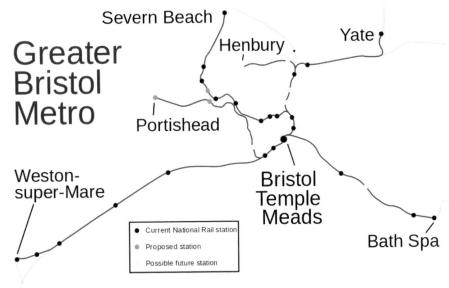

The plan for a Greater Bristol Metro uses existing heavy rail lines.

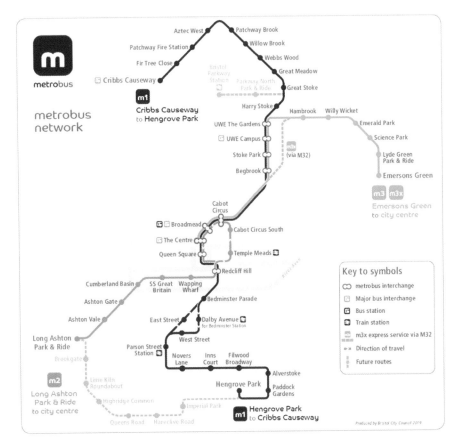

The Bristol Metrobus network which opened in 2018.

In 2001 yet another light rail plan was launched termed 'Bristol Supertram'. The Government's Ten Year Plan 'Transport 2010' published in July 2000 listed twenty five light rail lines to be built in the next ten years including Bristol and South Gloucestershire. Promoted by the two councils a core route was proposed, running from the city centre northwards to Filton, Bradley Stoke and Almondsbury with park and ride at the M4/M5 interchange. A route length of 16.7km would have 17 stops.

In March 2001 the DETR announced that subject to detailed agreement the scheme had passed its economic and technical criteria and should receive funding for the estimated £194m capital cost. Protracted discussions about methods of procurement and route details resulted in South Gloucestershire withdrawing from the project in 2003. More uncertainties resulted in Bristol City Council cancelling the project in 2004 even though it had already spent £1.5 million.

While a long string of light rail and tramway plans over thirty years have so far come to nothing, it seems unlikely the concept of light rail for Bristol will go away entirely. Chronic congestion, air pollution and environmental damage will surely encourage more plans, but latest thinking seems to favour a heavy rail solution, Greater Bristol Metro, using existing railway lines (also known as Metro West). Frequencies proposed are not 'Metro' standard as light rail would have been. For the foreseeable future trams in Bristol will remain *'might have beens'*.

Meanwhile a Metrobus network has been developed with three routes. The first opened in 2018 using biogas powered double deckers with a mixture

of guideway, reserved bus lanes and motorway running. Some parts of the routes were previously proposed for light rail.

Problems due to roadworks and congestion have resulted in criticism from the operators as well as from users. The group advocating trams for Bath are aiming to extend their tramway interests to Bristol and have lobbied the West of England Combined Authority to include trams in their strategic planning. It remains to be seen whether Greater Bristol will remain as another tramway *'might have been'* and will manage to survive with its heavy rail metro and busways.

Cardiff

The original Cardiff tramways had all gone by 1950, replaced by trolleybuses which had themselves been replaced by diesel buses by 1970. If Greater Cardiff had been blessed with a PTE when local government reorganisation was implemented in England, it is highly likely that light rail would have been on their agenda. As it was the municipal bus operator carried on through the seventies and eighties and it was not until the nineties that studies of possible light rail routes were initiated. Cardiff has remained one of the few municipal bus operators, like Nottingham and Edinburgh which both now have popular tram routes.

In 1991 a study of public transport in Cardiff Bay area, although not published, was understood to have recommended the rubber tyred GLT (Guided Light Transit) system, which at the time was favoured by the DoT as a cheaper alternative to light rail.

Various other studies all tended to focus in on the Bute Street branch line from Cardiff Queen Street to Cardiff Bay, often extended into the docklands area to serve new development. Other plans would

p51

A light rail vehicle proposed for Cardiff in the early 21st century.

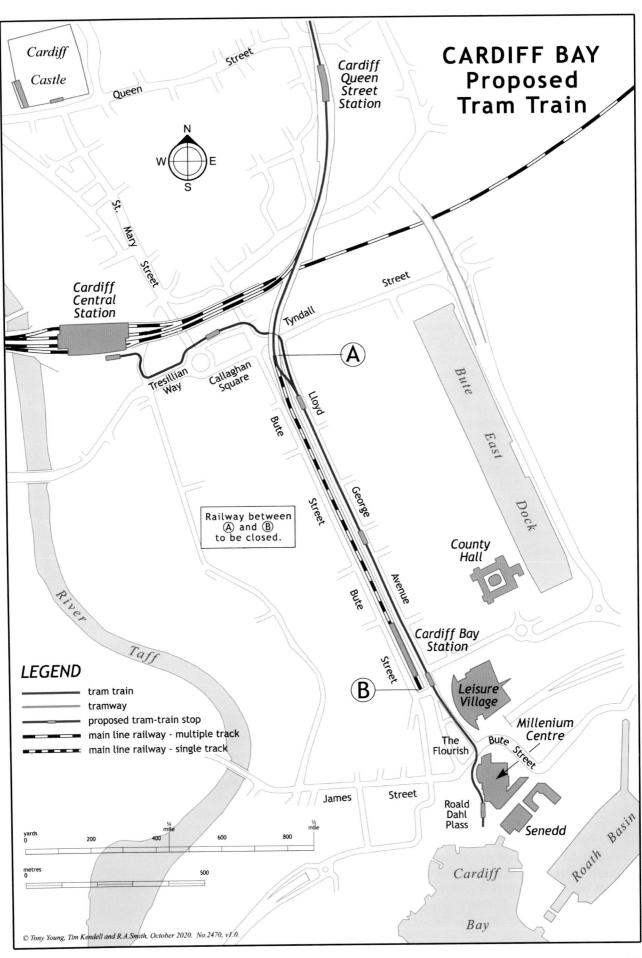

Cardiff Castle

Queen Street

Cardiff Queen Street Station

St. Mary Street

**CARDIFF BAY
Proposed
Tram Train**

N
W E
S

Cardiff Central Station

Tyndall Street

(A)

Tresillian Way

Callaghan Square

Lloyd Street

Bute Street

George Street

Bute East Dock

Railway between
(A) and (B)
to be closed.

River Taff

County Hall

Avenue

Cardiff Bay Station

LEGEND

—— tram train
—— tramway
▭ proposed tram-train stop
▬▬ main line railway - multiple track
▬ main line railway - single track

Bute Street

(B)

Leisure Village

Millenium Centre

The Flourish

Bute Street

James Street

Roald Dahl Plass

Senedd

Roath Basin

yards
0   200   400   600   800
¼ mile   ½ mile

metres
0   500

Cardiff

Bay

© Tony Young, Tim Kendell and R.A.Smith, October 2020. No.2470, v1.0.

A South Wales Metro tram-train for the Cardiff Bay area and Welsh Valley lines.

convert some of the Valley lines to light rail, perhaps starting with Pontypridd. They would be extended on street through the city centre.

Yet another study in 1996 was to examine four possible light rail routes, again including Cardiff Bay and Pontypridd, but with mixed heavy and light rail on the latter. Street running options in the city centre were to be investigated. Six contracting consortia were selected to bid for the construction of Bute Avenue but the inclusion of light rail was not certain. Twenty five years later there is still no sign of the tramway.

Even worse, outrageous plans for a cable car or even a 'Safege' style suspended monorail were being mooted. One ray of hope was that Cardiff Bay Development Corporation were looking to Karlsruhe for inspiration. Their tram-train network has been one of the greatest light rail success stories in Europe.

In 2019 a £1bn South Wales Metro plan was approved, which included purchase of tram-trains and the construction of light rail routes. Keolis-Amey are acquiring Stadler vehicles similar to the Sheffield tram-trains, which will run to Cardiff Bay and on some of the Valley lines. Details of the routes were still being developed. It looks as though trams will at last reach Cardiff city centre and Cardiff Bay after some 30 years of planning so one *'might have been'* will be!

Cleveland

Local government in the Tees valley has a complex history. In 1968 the predominant towns of Stockton-on-Tees and Middlesbrough were absorbed into Teesside County Borough, which only lasted for six years. Cleveland County Council was a non-metropolitan authority created in 1974, formed with parts of County Durham and the North Riding of Yorkshire on both sides of the River Tees. In 1996 it was abolished and replaced by unitary authorities in Stockton-on-Tees, Middlesbrough, Hartlepool and Redcar and Cleveland.

If Teesside had been made a Metropolitan County in 1974, like Tyneside, it would probably have built a light rail system. Now with its fragmented local government that possibility is remote. Its population of half a million would make it a candidate for some form of transit system and several attempts were made.

Even before the new Cleveland authority had taken office, the LRTL (Light Railway Transport League, later the LRTA) produced a report on a possible light rail network for the Cleveland area (see chapter 7).

Cleveland undertook a consultation on light rail in 1992.

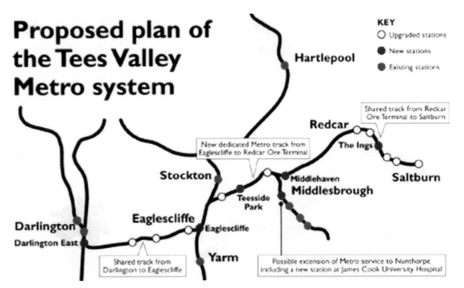

Proposed plan of the Tees Valley Metro system

Proposed Tees Valley Metro

KEY
○ Upgraded stations
● New stations
● Existing stations

Hartlepool

Shared track from Redcar Ore Terminal to Saltburn

Redcar

The Ings

New dedicated Metro track from Eaglescliffe to Redcar Ore Terminal

Stockton

Middlehaven

Saltburn

Middlesbrough

Teesside Park

Darlington

Darlington East

Eaglescliffe

Eaglescliffe

Yarm

Shared track from Darlington to Eaglescliffe

Possible extension of Metro service to Nunthorpe including a new station at James Cook University Hospital

The type of vehicle envisaged for Tees Valley Metro.

Mindful that a few miles north the Tyneside Metro had been approved and construction was about to start, it seemed logical that a similar approach could be made for Teesside.

Nothing more was heard about light rail for Cleveland for the next 25 years. Then in 1991 a public consultation envisaged four light rail route options linking Stockton, Middlesbrough, Saltburn, Ormesby, Coulby Newham and Ingleby Barwick. Alignments were a mixture of existing railways, segregated alignments and street running. A majority of respondents supported the plans but there was significant opposition to the street running sections and some support for busways instead. The plans were dropped.

A study of light rail options was undertaken leading to a public consultation in 1992. Four

possible route options received majority support with only 15% against but a petition against the plans led the Cleveland County Council to commission a further study of light rail and alternatives, published in 1993. The light rail plans were dropped in favour of guided buses and improvements to the local rail services, neither of which have been progressed. A private sector led proposal for re-introducing trams in 2003 was considered by Middlesbrough Council but did not proceed any further.

Termed 'Tees Valley Metro', two upgraded rail lines were proposed, Darlington – Middlesbrough – Saltburn and Hartlepool to Nunthorpe Parkway. An artist's impression of the vehicle looks like a street running tram-train with overhead power supply although refurbished class 158 diesel multiple units were more likely. The only part of the plan to be

Table 21.2. Potential customers for Coventry-style very light rail. WMG.

Potential Customer	Notes
Black Country local authorities	Comprises Dudley, Sandwell, Walsall, Wolverhampton
West of England Combined Authority	Includes Bristol and Bath
Leicester City Council	
Liverpool City Council	
Derby City Council	
Leeds City Council	
Glasgow City Council	Proposed route between the airport and the city centre
Cirencester Town Council	
Isle of Wight Council	
Midlothian Council	Southeast of Edinburgh
HS2 Architects for Toton Station	Proposed route serving Toton HS2 station

The VLR system envisaged for Coventry.

The VLR system envisaged for Coventry.

implemented was a new station at James Cook University Hospital on the Esk Valley line which opened in 2014.

All the local authorities supported the plans and even the Department for Transport indicated their support but funding was not forthcoming so the project was abandoned. Nothing more has been heard of any tramway plans, another *'might have been'* case.

Coventry - very light rail (VLR)

For many years it has been argued that light rail and tramways would be more widely used if capital costs could be reduced, especially rolling stock, track and power supply. A project aiming to prove the

concept is termed 'Very Light Rail' and was initiated in Coventry in 2016 by the Warwick Manufacturing Group (WMG) at Warwick University. Funding has been supported by West Midlands Combined Authority, the Coventry and Warwickshire Local Enterprise Partnership and the Government's Local Growth Fund.

A first phase route is envisaged by Coventry City Council from Coventry railway station to the University Hospital via the city centre for completion in 2024, although an initial stage to the city centre could be open in 2021. Next would be a line from the station to Warwick University leading to a four line network connecting major residential, industrial and commercial areas across the city, and a direct connection to the HS2 Birmingham Interchange station.

Vehicles would be battery powered with no need for overhead lines, running on a lightweight steel track and would eventually be autonomous. Passenger capacity would be between 50 and 70. A prototype model is planned for 2021. The plan does not appear to include fully segregated tracks so the feasibility of autonomous operation is questionable.

Interest in smaller tramways has been around for over half a century, particularly in the UK, USA and Japan, often under names like 'minitram', 'autotram' or 'cabtrack'. Most had small capacity vehicles of about 20 passengers although 'cabtrack' only used 4 to 6 seaters. Some have been investigated by the Transport and Road Research Laboratory in Crowthorne but very few have ever reached prototype stage and most never got beyond the drawing board. Some proposals were made for such systems in Sheffield and Leeds but never developed. Warwick University has a long history of research into small tram schemes, see for example the paper in 1973 by I.G.Black et al (Ref.27). It will therefore be extremely interesting if the latest proposal actually comes to fruition.

The VLR promoters have listed a number of authorities that they consider could be potential customers for a VLR system, see table opposite. There can be little doubt that the possible applications for VLR could be many and varied, given the level of interest in light rail from authorities and promoters throughout Britain who would love to have a tram system but consider it way out of their reach. It would be great to think that this time it will not become just another *'might have been'*.

Glasgow tram

Glasgow once had the largest tram network in Britain apart from London, with over 1,000 trams and more than 200 miles of track. It was still building new trams after the second world war when most cities were scrapping theirs. The trams were extremely popular and when the last one ran in 1962 a quarter of a million people braved torrential rain to say goodbye.

By the early 1990s transport planners were searching for ways to bring trams back to the city, realising that a huge mistake had been made. In August 1994 Strathclyde Regional Council unveiled its plans for trams in Glasgow, part of the integrated transport strategy developed by Strathclyde PTE, successor to Greater Glasgow PTE. Line 1 would run 12 miles from Maryhill in the north west to Easterhouse in the east via the city centre. Original tram reservations would be used, but over half the route would be street running, including the whole of the city centre route.

Alternative routes in the central area used either St Vincent Street in both directions or St Vincent Street and Bath Street as a one way pair, both options serving George Square, which once had trams on three sides. Extensions would extend to Drumchapel in the north west, Balornock in the north and Tollcross in the south east.

In Scotland the legal process for promoting a tramway was quite different from that in England and still is. An application for a Provisional Order has to be submitted under the Private Legislation Procedure (Scotland) Act 1936. Strathclyde submitted their order in March 1995, with a three month public inquiry the following year. At the end of the inquiry the proposal was rejected by the Commissioners after only 24 hours deliberation, hardly long enough to evaluate the mass of technical information presented. There was no right of appeal. More than £2 million was spent on developing the scheme but the Commissioners, who did not include any expertise on tram systems or even integrated transport planning, were not required to give any explanation or reason for their decision. It may be pure speculation, but the recently privatised bus operators were vehemently opposed to trams.

Strathclyde Tram would run along Kelvin Way past the Gilbert Scott Building of Glasgow University. A tunnel option was rejected. SPTE

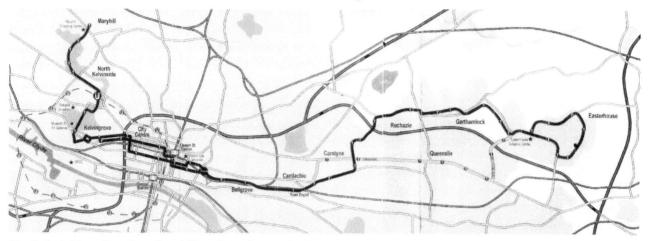

Strathclyde Tram Line One, Maryhill to Easterhouse via City Centre. SPTE

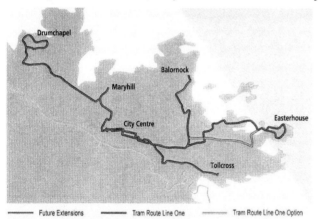

Strathclyde Tram proposed extensions in 1995. SPTE

SPTA's chairman, Councillor Charlie Gordon, said Glasgow had "missed out on the chance of a twenty-first century mode of transport which had the overwhelming and enthusiastic support of the public."

The idea of trams coming back to Glasgow is still around. In 2014 the City of Glasgow and SPT commissioned a study for a tram route from the city centre to the new Glasgow Harbour, across the River Clyde to the Southern General Hospital, through Govan and then back over the river to the city centre. Extensions could serve Braehead shopping centre and possibly Glasgow Airport or even further.

SPT decided that this route would not see trams running along it, but rather an "ultra-modern" bus service termed "Clyde Fastlink" would operate part of the route, running from the city centre to the Glasgow Harbour area. However SPT stated that they were leaving open the option of laying tram lines on this route and replacing the buses with a light rail system. Until then it remains a *'might have been'* tramway.

In November 2016 plans were unveiled for a tram-train link between Glasgow Airport and the city centre at a cost of £144m. The route would run from Glasgow Central Station to Paisley Gilmour Street on existing rail tracks and then on street to the Airport. An alternative plan for a separate light rail line from the city centre to the airport via Paisley would have been cheaper at £102m but was not selected. Tram-train construction could begin in 2022 with completion and operation in 2025. Journey time would be 16½ minutes with four trains per hour. Earlier plans for a heavy rail link to the airport had been scrapped in 2009.

Council leaders in Glasgow and Renfrewshire approved the plans in December 2016. It looked as though, after many *'might have been'* projects for light rail in Glasgow, this one would actually happen. However after another three years of delay, the project was rejected in 2019 for financial reasons. Now a completely new city wide Metro system is being proposed which will presumably cost a great deal more than the tram-train. One line would serve the airport. Light rail yet again seems to have fallen by the wayside. Glasgow is littered with *'might have been'* tramways.

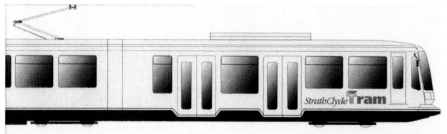

The illustration used on Strathclyde Tram publicity was instantly recognisable as the Sheffield tram which entered service in that city in 1994. SPTE

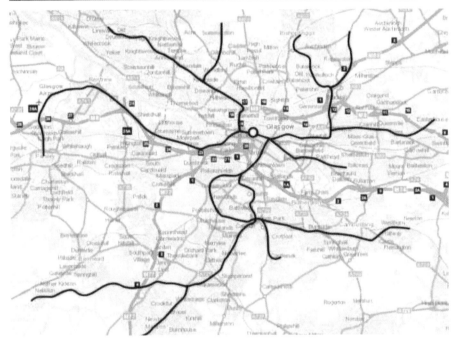

An artist's impression of a tram-train arriving at Glasgow Airport.

Proposed Metro tram plan for Glasgow 2019.

An artist's impression of the proposed Glasgow Metro.

Glasgow metro

Yet another attempt to bring trams back to Glasgow was launched in 2019 by the Glasgow Connectivity Commission, chaired by Professor David Begg. They claim the plan is feasible and necessary. A comprehensive Metro system serving as much of the city as possible would link the rail networks around Central and Queen Street stations using a new tunnel. Eleven branches would extend into the suburbs in the north, south, east and west, making use of some former tram reservations and using some existing or former rail alignments. The first leg of the Metro would be from Paisley Gilmour Street Station to Glasgow Airport and then continue through Renfrew along the south side of the Clyde to the city centre. No timescales have been specified.

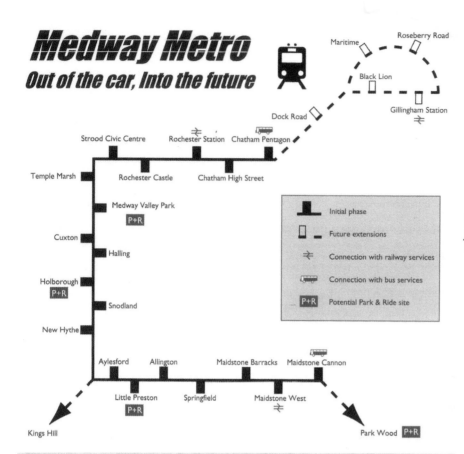

Medway Metro
Out of the car, Into the future

Legend:
- Initial phase
- Future extensions
- Connection with railway services
- Connection with bus services
- P+R Potential Park & Ride site

The proposed Medway Metro route from Chatham to Maidstone in 1995. Kent CC

Stations shown on route: Maritime, Roseberry Road, Black Lion, Gillingham Station, Dock Road, Strood Civic Centre, Rochester Station, Chatham Pentagon, Temple Marsh, Rochester Castle, Chatham High Street, Medway Valley Park P+R, Cuxton, Halling, Holborough P+R, Snodland, New Hythe, Aylesford, Allington, Maidstone Barracks, Maidstone Cannon, Little Preston P+R, Springfield, Maidstone West, Kings Hill, Park Wood P+R

The Medway Metro brochure and light rail vehicle, clearly based on a contemporary Grenoble design. Kent CC

Medway Metro

In the 1990s Kent County Council undertook a number of studies of light rapid transit. One of the more significant was for the Medway valley embracing Gillingham, Chatham, Rochester, Strood and Maidstone. The impetus came from increasing congestion, as traffic had doubled in twenty years and was forecast to double again, and from an increasing concern for the environment. Just building more roads would not solve the problem.

The Medway towns may not seem an obvious location for light rail but the population of the

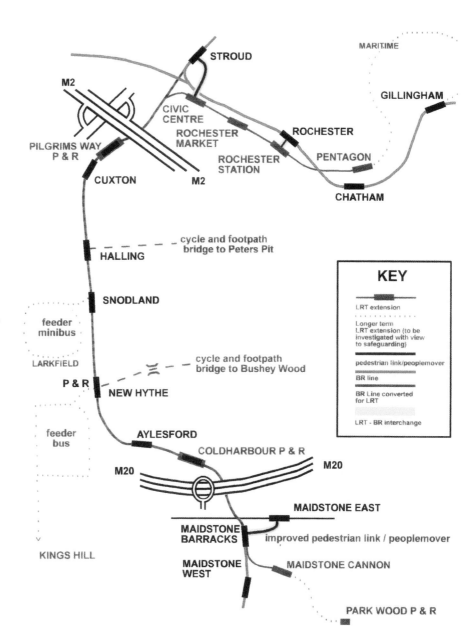

MARITIME

STROUD

M2

GILLINGHAM

PILGRIMS WAY
P & R

CIVIC
CENTRE

ROCHESTER
MARKET

ROCHESTER

ROCHESTER
STATION

PENTAGON

CUXTON

M2

CHATHAM

cycle and footpath
bridge to Peters Pit

HALLING

SNODLAND

*The Medway Valley LRT package
proposed in 1994.* Kent CC

feeder
minibus

LARKFIELD

cycle and footpath
bridge to Bushey Wood

P & R

NEW HYTHE

KEY

LRT extension

Longer term
LRT extension (to be
investigated with view
to safeguarding)

pedestrian link/peoplemover

BR line

BR Line converted
for LRT

LRT - BR interchange

feeder
bus

AYLESFORD

COLDHARBOUR P & R

M20

M20

MAIDSTONE EAST

MAIDSTONE
BARRACKS

improved pedestrian link / peoplemover

KINGS HILL

MAIDSTONE
WEST

MAIDSTONE CANNON

PARK WOOD P & R

Medway towns themselves is 250,000 and if you add in Maidstone and Malling reaches 400,000. The underused British Rail line between Maidstone and Strood, the Medway Valley Line formed the basis for the study. If it was converted to light rail it could be extended at each end to give much improved access to town centres and increase its catchment area. Adding 4 km of new track to the 18 km railway was estimated to increase passenger numbers six fold. Freight services would be maintained.

Street running would allow light rail vehicles to leave the railway at Maidstone Barracks or Maidstone West to reach a terminus at Maidstone Cannon. After leaving the railway near Strood the line would run on street through Rochester to terminate at Chatham Pentagon. A future extension could continue the line to Gillingham. Park and ride car parks would be located close to the M2 and M20

motorways. Interchange with bus services would be provided at Maidstone Cannon and Chatham Pentagon and with existing rail services at Maidstone West, Rochester and in the longer term Gillingham.

In 1995 the project was named 'Medway Metro' and discussions were progressing with District Councils, Railtrack and South Eastern Trains. Potential depot sites were identified and work commissioned to examine issues with low floor trams and third rail power supply. British Rail research at Derby had already undertaken some studies.

After spending several years developing plans for the Medway Metro, Kent County Council decided not to progress the project any further. More studies for the Chatham area could possibly include a tramway but it seems more likely that light rail for the Medway will remain another *'might have been'*.

In 1998 local government reorganisation saw the creation of unitary authority, Medway Council, which inherited responsibility for Rochester, Chatham and Gillingham from Kent County Council. The new Medway authority still considered that a new rapid transit system was needed to serve the Riverside area, where substantial new development was planned. A further study was undertaken in 2002 which proposed two light rail routes, west-east from Strood to Gillingham Business Park via Rochester, Chatham, Brompton and Gilllingham and a north-south route from St. Mary's Island towards Rochester Airport via Chatham. The two lines would share an alignment for a short distance into the centre of Chatham. Further studies were recommended to develop the system but no further work was undertaken and the concept does not appear in more recent plans for Medway.

Preston

The city of Preston is the administrative centre for the County of Lancashire, with a population of 115,000. For thirty years until 1934 it had a six line standard gauge municipal tramway. For the next three quarters of a century local transport was dependent on buses.

A transportation study undertaken in house in 1992 by Lancashire County Council recommended bus priority measures and park and ride. It also identified a disused rail alignment from Bamber Bridge area in the south east to the city centre for conversion to a busway with the potential in the longer term for introducing light rail. It includes a bridge over the River Ribble. Another disused alignment to the north east of the city, the former railway to Longridge, could be added in to make a cross city guided bus or light rail route. Further studies the following year concluded that the

benefits would not justify the capital costs.

Like many similar towns, congestion has continued to be a major problem and some park and ride sites have been introduced with small buses. A private company, Preston Trampower Limited, has developed plans for a 6.5 km tram line using part of the former Preston to Longridge railway alignment to link Preston railway station with Deepdale and a park and ride site at Bluebell Way, close to the M6 motorway. It would also serve Deepdale Retail Park, Preston North End football ground and the East Preston Business Park.

The vehicle proposed for Preston is the 'City Tram' developed by Professor Lewis Lesley using automotive products to reduce costs. It was demonstrated on the Wirral Tramway in Birkenhead in 2005 and on the Blackpool Tramway two years later. It was subsequently upgraded but has not operated for several of years and was understood to be in store in the Preston area. Use would also be made of low cost track and overhead line equipment developed by Professor Lesley over a number of years.

It is intended to obtain authority to construct and operate the tramway using planning powers rather than the Transport and Works Act powers normally used. Planning approval was granted by Preston City Council in 2016 for the pilot line and depot and further approvals were being sought in 2017. Initial operation was anticipated in 2018 but was not forthcoming. Professor Lesley has previously proposed tramways in a number of other cities including Liverpool, Edinburgh, Middlesbrough and Galway none of which have been realised.

The 'City class' tram prototype was returned to Blackpool in 2020 after several years stored in

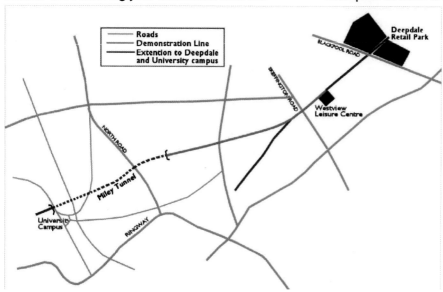

The Preston Guild Line tramway showing the initial demonstration line. Preston Trampower

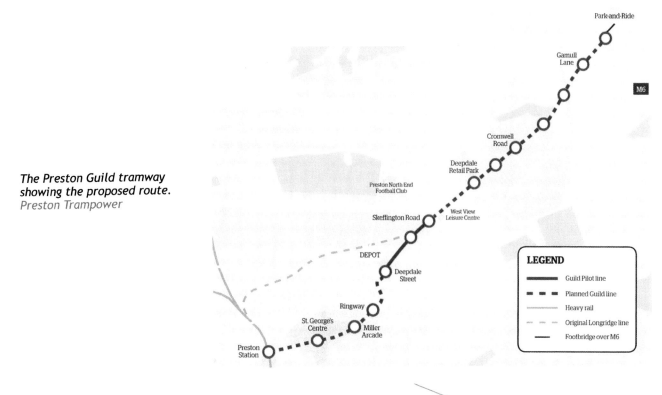

The Preston Guild tramway showing the proposed route. Preston Trampower

LEGEND

Guild Pilot line
Planned Guild line
Heavy rail
Original Longridge line
Footbridge over M6

Visuals of the proposed tram for Preston. Preston Trampower

Visuals of the proposed tram for Preston. Preston Trampower

the open at a Preston marina. It's future seems uncertain. If the Preston project could be achieved it would open a way forward for many other medium sized cities which would otherwise remain '*might have beens*'.

The prototype tram developed by Professor Lewis Lesley operated on demonstration on the Birkenhead tramway in 2005. Tony Young

The upgraded 'City Tram' proposed for Preston. Tony Young

An impression of a Preston Guild tram crossing a main road junction in Deepdale. Preston Trampower

An impression of a Preston Trampower tram on Fishergate. Preston Trampower

22. Historic cities

Congestion and pollution are particularly intrusive in historic cities with narrow streets, many ancient buildings and large tourist numbers. Perhaps not surprisingly, some have looked to the tramway as a potential saviour, able to bring large numbers of people into the city centre with minimum disruption or intrusion. Some such cities did once have electric tramways, even passing through medieval gateways, as in York or Chester. Short-sightedly they were long ago replaced by diesel buses, which themselves are now being banished from streets given over to pedestrians. Some examples are described below. During the past thirty years, most of these cities have commissioned studies of possible tramways but none have yet been built.

Bath

The ancient city of Bath in Somerset lies 11 miles south east of Bristol. Famed for its Roman baths, which are still a popular tourist destination, it also has a fine medieval abbey, the Georgian Royal Crescent and a modern university. The River Avon runs through the city surrounding the central area on three sides. The population of 90,000 would be considered too small to support a tramway today, but for thirty five years from 1904 Bath had its own electric tramway.

A fleet of 40 trams operated over six routes radiating from the centre, including steep hills up Lansdown Road to the north and up Wells Road to the south. In the city centre an anti-clockwise, mainly single track, loop wound its way round the narrow city streets, passing the Abbey, Guildhall, Great Western railway station and other historic buildings. The last tram ran in May 1939, not long before the outbreak of the second world war.

As in other congested historic cities, pressures to come up with a different solution to traffic problems prompted the local council, Bath and North East Somerset (BANES), to consider more radical ideas. In the late 1990s a series of rapid transit studies had looked at various options, mainly bus based, although a study by JMP for the City of Bath and Avon County Council in 1995 did include a possible tramway. A local group, The Bath Tram Re-Introduction Group (BTRIG), also known as 'Bathtrams', proposed an extensive tram network for Bath, much of which would have recreated the original tram system of 1904.

In 2000 BANES commissioned another study to examine a possible tram network and to review the Bathtrams proposal, this time undertaken by

Like many historic cities Bath once had a tramway network. Bath Reference Library

An artist's impression of a double deck tram for Bath. M.L.Lane

Hyder Consulting with the Transportation Planning Partnership. It concluded that while a tramway would meet many policy objectives of national and local government, most of the routes proposed were unlikely to generate enough patronage and would be better served by buses. It would be difficult to create segregated alignments. Two routes, Western Riverside and Newbridge and to Lambridge could be linked to park and ride sites and could potentially be segregated, at least in part.

Nothing further was heard of these plans and a Bath tramway looked like another '*might have been*'. But good ideas will not lie down and in June 2017 BANES announced that it was again

The Bathtrams proposed tram network for Bath in 2000.
https://bathtrams.uk/proposal

The Bath Trams Group have organised meetings and conferences in Bath to promote trams for the city. *Bath Trams Group.*

funding a study into the feasibility of bringing back trams to Bath. The cabinet member for transport, said: "The idea of introducing some sort of a light-rail system in Bath has clearly caught the imagination of a number of people in the city and we feel this idea warrants further investigation."

Yet another study was undertaken in 2017 by Atkins. This examined a range of issues including

road widths and gradients, existing traffic and commuter flows, design factors, track and power supply, depot, environmental constraints, corridor assessments and total costs. A new group was set up with an impressive array of expertise to progress a tram network for Bath and possibly extending to Bristol. A number of public meetings and conferences were held and the group is still very active. It remains to be seen whether this group will succeed.

The Bathtrams proposed network diagram showing the original Bath Electric Tramways network. *Bath Trams Group.*

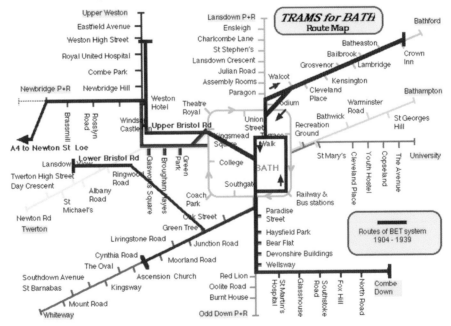

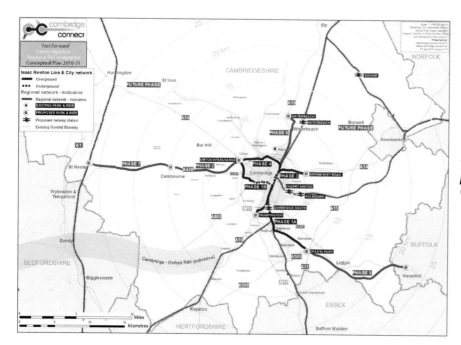

The 'Cambridge Connect' light rail plan for Cambridge. Cambridge Connect

Cambridge

Like Oxford, Cambridge once had horse drawn trams but never had electric trams. Plans for a 10 km light rail line between Trumpington on the south side of the city and Oakington to the north via the city centre were made in 1991. They would have used some former rail alignments, with street running through the city centre. The plans were dropped in 1992 when the guided bus plan was adopted instead, which was built and opened in 2011. This covers a much longer route to St Ives via a former railway alignment.

The concept of building a tramway resurfaced in the 21st century, but in a rather different form, with tunnels under the city centre. Various research projects have examined the feasibility of tunnelling under Cambridge city centre and the ground conditions are suitable. The current proposal, termed 'Cambridge Connect' has an initial route called 'the Isaac Newton' line which would be the first of seven phases.

Phase 1 would link Girton Interchange in the north west on the A14 with Granta Park to the south east and Trumpington park and ride in the south. The central section would be in tunnel with interchange with heavy rail services at several Cambridge stations and with bus services. Park and ride would be provided at eight locations and later phases would include conversion of the guided busway to light rail.

The total cost of this ambitious plan could be in the region of £2bn which for any provincial public transport scheme might be regarded as far too expensive; but when one highway scheme, the A14 upgrade, has cost £1.5bn it should not seem unrealistic. The benefits to the local economy of Cambridge would be enormous, not to mention environmental improvements. Will it become just another '*might have been*'?

A rival scheme has proposed using Chinese 'trackless tram' rubber tyred articulated vehicles optically guided. This uses technology developed in France some twenty-five years ago and used in Rouen in Northern France since 2001. It is not reliable (it does not work if it snows or the paint wears out) and even in Rouen is only applied through junctions and for stop docking. The vehicles are standard rubber tyred buses and therefore create pollution from brake and tyre wear. It is to be hoped that this option dies a natural death.

Chester

A Roman city with a proud history, Chester has a population of just over 80,000 and is the county town for West Cheshire. It is only a stone's throw from the Welsh border. It was an early convert to pedestrianisation, initially with buses allowed access to the main shopping streets. Congestion of the city centre streets is a common problem and the railway station is a long walk from the centre.

A traffic study in 1990 proposed a tramway from Chester Zoo, a popular tourist attraction, to the city centre via Chester railway station. Two park and ride sites would be located at the Zoo and near the link road from the M53 motorway.

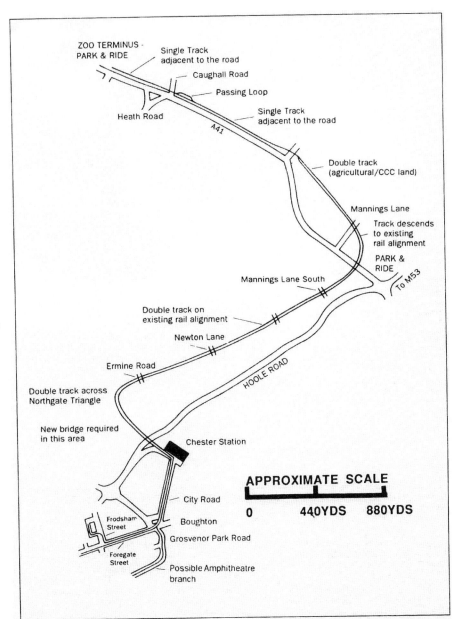

The Zoo tramway line proposed in 1990. TAUT

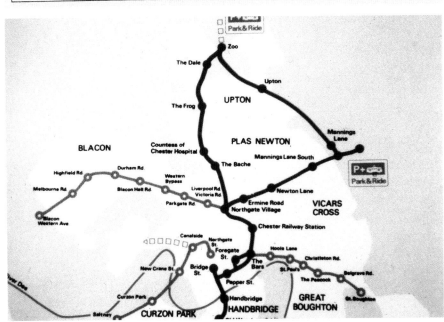

A plan of possible tram routes for Chester in 1993.

An artist's impression of a tram for Chester termed 'Trac21'. It was based on contemporary Genever trams, the first low floor cars in Europe.

A Chester tram at Chester Railway Station where it would have provided a quick link into the city centre.

Proving that trams can co-exist with ancient buildings in a historic city, even running through a city wall gate. Narrow gauge trams ran in Chester from 1903 to 1930.

CHESTER
AT THE CROSSROADS
A Light Rail System for the City

A leaflet describing the proposed light rail system for Chester. Authorities were still wary of using the term 'tram' in case it gave an old-fashioned image.

In 1991 an expanded plan included the Zoo line and others including the redundant Mickle Trafford rail line. Perhaps encouraged by the rapidly developing light rail system in nearby Greater Manchester, Cheshire County Council was keen to progress a scheme, but Chester City Council had reservations and wanted to see the structure plan and local plans completed first. The tramway scheme was briefly revived in 1995 in a Millennium Fund bid but was replaced with a busway plan. Powers to build a busway were obtained in 2002 but the offer of government funding was turned down by Cheshire County Council. The scheme has yet to be built. Chester's tramway has joined the ranks of *'might have beens'*.

Lancaster

Lancaster had a small 3 mile first generation electric tramway which opened in 1903 and lasted until 1930, with just twelve trams. There was also a private horse tramway which ran the four miles to Morecambe and survived until 1921, one of the last horse tramways in Britain. The two systems were never connected.

Lancashire County Council carried out a transportation study in 1993 to examine public transport solutions for the congested city centre. Bus priority measures and a park and ride route were proposed but trams were not considered.

Lancaster once had electric trams.

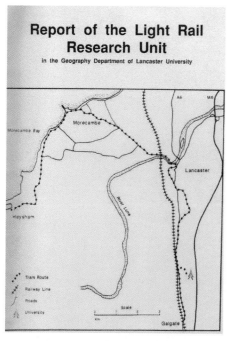

Report of the Light Rail Research Unit
in the Geography Department of Lancaster University

The Lancaster University Light Rail Report in 1992. *Lancaster University*

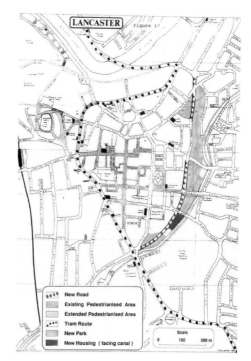

The proposed tram route through Lancaster city centre. *Lancaster University Report*

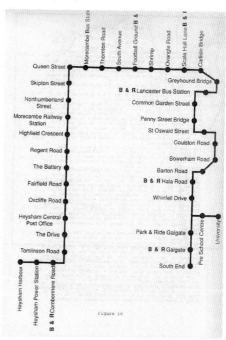

The proposed tram route from Lancaster to Morecambe and Heysham, 1992. *Lancaster University Report.*

The previous year a group at Lancaster University produced a report on a possible tramway to link the University with Lancaster, Morecambe and the port of Heysham. Familiar problems of congestion and increasing traffic levels brought air and noise pollution which could only get worse. Solutions to traffic problems were researched in Europe and beyond, but particularly in Germany, for towns of above 100,000 population. Lancaster's population is only 52,000, but if the adjacent urban area of Morecambe and Heysham is included the total population is well over 100,000. The University adds another 14,000.

Trams supported by a dense network of buses and park and ride emerged as best solution to support the local economy and offer fully accessible clean and quiet transport.

Comparisons were given for car, bus and tram for capacity, space requirements, energy consumption and noise pollution. Specific emissions and primary energy consumption data was given for each mode. Traffic count and bus passenger data were given along the proposed tram route, shown on the report cover and route diagram (opposite). In the city centre an extended pedestrianised area and new road and canalside park were part of the plan.

The route was described in detail, including the traffic management measures needed to allow priority for trams. It was accepted that some restrictions on car movements would be necessary to create the tram route and improvements for cyclists and pedestrians. A ten minute tram service was planned dropping to every twenty minutes in the evenings.

Their estimated cost for the whole 22km tramway was £49m. No doubt this would have proved to be somewhat optimistic, but compared to the Heysham to M6 Link road which opened in 2016 at a cost of £128m, which some believe will do little to relieve congestion in Lancaster, it could have been good value. Perhaps if VLR succeeds in Coventry, it could be an option for Lancaster. Otherwise it will remain a *'might have been'*.

Norwich

Norwich is an important city with a cathedral and castle and many historic buildings and is the county town of Norfolk. Its population of over 200,000 and potential catchment area double that puts it firmly in the realms of a possible fixed track system. Like other historic cities, Norwich had an extensive first generation tramway with ten routes, opening in 1900. Unlike most cities the trams were never municipally owned and succumbed to bus competition in 1935. They were recalled with great affection by those old enough to remember them.

As described in Chapter 7, a report in 1970 by the LRTL proposed a modern tram system for Norwich. It was well received but was not taken any further at that time. Twenty years later two possible networks were evaluated as part of the Norwich Area Transportation Study, linked to park and ride sites adjacent to the outer ring road. In 1996 an updated proposal by the LRTA was considered for a light rail line through the city centre from Harford in the south via Ipswich Road and Castle Meadow

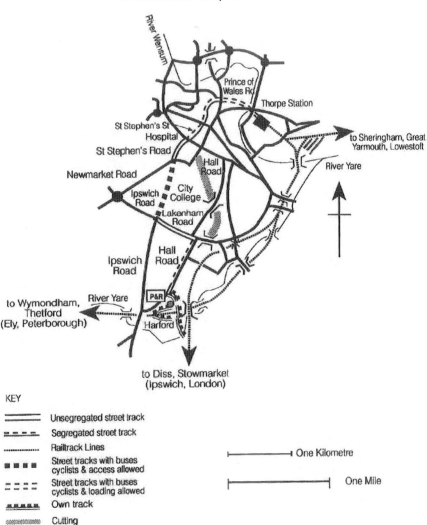

A light rail route through Norwich, LRTA report in 1996.
Chris Wood, LRTA

KEY

———	Unsegregated street track
– – –	Segregated street track
············	Railtrack Lines
▪ ▪ ▪ ▪	Street tracks with buses cyclists & access allowed
= = = =	Street tracks with buses cyclists & loading allowed
▫▫▫▫▫	Own track
▨▨▨▨▨	Cutting

├———————┤ One Kilometre

├———————————┤ One Mile

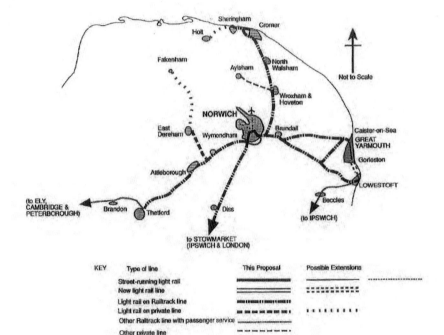

The LRTA plan for light rail in Norwich and Waveney in 1996.
Chris Wood, LRTA

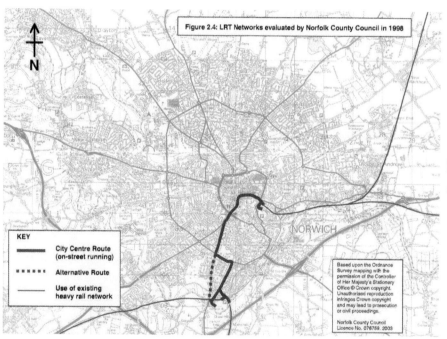

Proposed light rail route to Tuckswood for Norwich in 1998.
Norfolk County Council

to Norwich Thorpe station. Through running onto the railway network could take light rail vehicles to Sheringham, Great Yarmouth and Lowestoft. This could have been an early example of tram-train, before the term became accepted, but this plan was to replace the local trains with trams.

In 1998 a possible light rail route was considered by Norfolk County Council from Norwich station and city centre to Tuckswood to the south, close to the outer ring road with a park and ride site. This was a similar route to the LRTA proposal. Two years later in 2000 a study was carried out by consultants for local bus operator FirstGroup and recommended a light rail line linking the main railway station

through the city centre to the university and the new hospital.

There was a good commercial reason for this route. The new Norfolk and Norwich University Hospital had been built close to the Norwich southern by-pass, to the west of the River Yare valley, and west of the university campus. FirstGroup buses ran a frequent service to the university from the city centre which could have been easily extended to serve the new hospital. But the only link across the river was a narrow private bridge unsuitable for buses. A new bridge for buses was not considered acceptable by planners in the quality environment of the river area, but a tram bridge could have been different, hence the interest of a bus

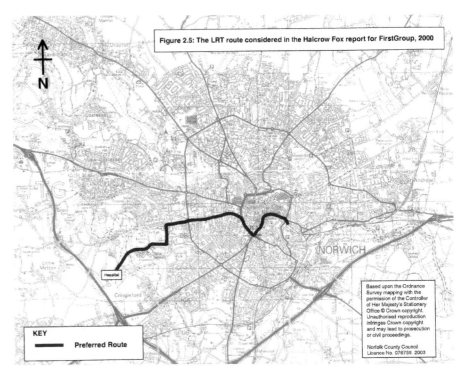

Figure 2.5: The LRT route considered in the Halcrow Fox report for FirstGroup, 2000

Proposed light rail route from city to Hospital in 2000. Norfolk County Council

KEY
Preferred Route

Based upon the Ordnance Survey mapping with the permission of the Controller of Her Majesty's Stationery Office © Crown copyright. Unauthorised reproduction infringes Crown copyright and may lead to prosecution or civil proceedings.

Norfolk County Council Licence No. 076759. 2003

company in a possible tramway. The only other way of buses reaching the hospital was a long way round with consequent increases in operating costs.

In 2003 Norfolk County Council commissioned a Light Rapid Transit Study as part of the Norwich Area Transportation Strategy Review. This was a more detailed study of options including the various plans produced over the previous few years. A set of route options for appraisal included the university and hospital route, extended to a park and ride site at Cringleford adjacent to the A11/A47 interchange, and routes to Thorpe St Andrew and Postwick using existing rail tracks. Possible extensions to serve local plan new

housing sites would serve Bowthorpe, Costessey and Sprowston. Further options could include tram-trains to Sheringham, Great Yarmouth and Lowestoft, as envisaged in the LRTA Report nearly ten years earlier.

After many studies and reports over nearly half a century, Norwich does not seem any nearer to getting trams back. If they did ever return, they would look very different to the open top trams of the previous generation and they probably would not go past the market. The idea has not gone away and the Norwich Society recently encouraged the council to consider trams again. But for the foreseeable future they will remain *'might have beens'*.

Light rail route options for appraisal, 2003 study. Norfolk County Council

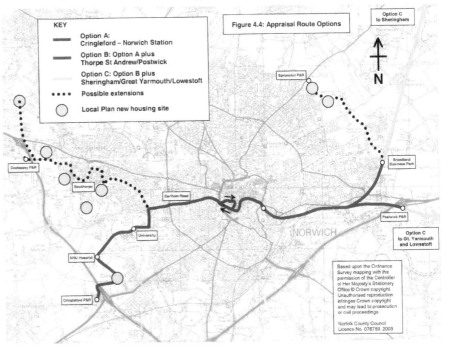

KEY
Option A:
Cringleford – Norwich Station

Option B: Option A plus
Thorpe St Andrew/Postwick

Option C: Option B plus
Sheringham/Great Yarmouth/Lowestoft

Possible extensions

Local Plan new housing site

Figure 4.4: Appraisal Route Options

Based upon the Ordnance Survey mapping with the permission of the Controller of Her Majesty's Stationery Office © Crown copyright. Unauthorised reproduction infringes Crown copyright and may lead to prosecution or civil proceedings.

Norfolk County Council Licence No. 076759. 2003

Open top trams once served the market and city centre.

Oxford

In April 2014 the radical concept of trams for Oxford was reported by the BBC following Oxfordshire County Council initiating a debate on ways of coping with expected population growth by 2031. Termed the 'Oxford Metro', two or three routes are envisaged, coupled with improvements to the existing rail network. The following year a report 'Trams for Oxford' was prepared by leading transport experts from both Oxford universities, which argues that modern light rail transit could be the saviour of historic cities such as Oxford. Oxford City Council commenting on the report said that it believed "a tram network would attract a wider range of users than a bus-based solution". The debate is ongoing but no positive decisions have been made.

A car-free "boulevard piazza" with trams is suggested for St Giles in Oxford. OCC

Grenoble in France is Oxford's twin city with a similar population of just over 150,000. The first tram line opened in Grenoble in 1987 and grew incrementally to five lines totalling 28 route miles of tramway, forming the backbone of the public transport network. It preserves Grenoble's attractiveness as a historic university city and tourist destination, while supporting its success as a major economic centre. Trams could do the same for Oxford.

Perhaps inevitably there are those who do not think trams could ever work in a city the size of Oxford and believe buses are the only answer for public transport. Another destined to be a '*might have been*'?

Salisbury

Although a city the size of Salisbury could clearly not justify a conventional tramway and never had a first generation tramway, it could perhaps be a candidate for a smaller scale light tramway. Like most historic cities it has congestion problems with the familiar environmental consequences. In 1996 an initial feasibility study was commissioned to consider options to improve central area distribution and provide links to park and ride car parks.

A central area alignment would link the major traffic objectives, namely the railway station, coach station, bus station, central car parks, shopping and commercial centre (Market Square) and cathedral. It

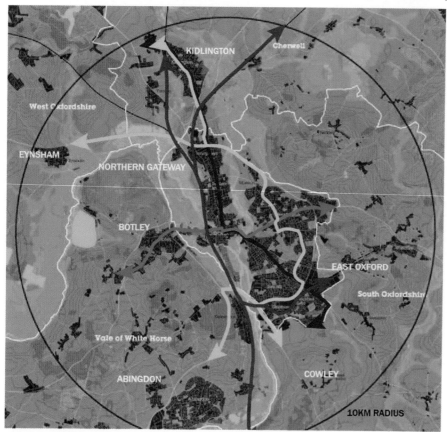

Four possible Metro lines for Oxford. URBED

Oxford's twin city of Grenoble, similar in size to Oxford, started their tram system in 1987 and now have five lines. Tony Young

could also include the new Waitrose development to the north and possibly existing and proposed leisure facilities in this locality. Various possible alignments were described with their pros and cons, running from the railway station to the Market Square and terminating in a pedestrianised High Street. Most of the route would be segregated from road traffic and be single track with passing places.

Possible light tramway routes to the Petersfinger and Beehive park and ride sites were described but as extensive traffic management and highway modifications would be necessary to achieve a satisfactory degree of segregation, neither would be likely to be justified. No surprise then if it is a *'might have been'*.

York

Like other historic cities, York had its own first generation tramway. Horse trams began in 1879 but were replaced by electric trams in 1910, somewhat later than other cities. The network extended along most main radial routes to the Rowntree's chocolate factory in the north, to the racecourse, South Bank and Fulford village in the south, Acomb in the west and Walmgate in the east. From 1920 York also had a trolleybus route from the city centre to Heworth in the north east. Both trams and trolleybuses closed in 1935, since when York has been entirely bus served.

In 2002 City of York Council commissioned the York Mass Transit Study to assist in trying to keep road traffic to 1990 levels. A technical appraisal of all mass transit and hybrid systems commercially available was required to identify those which could

potentially be suitable for York. Systems would need to serve York Central (a proposed major new development on former railway land to the west of York station), York Station, York University and Science Park and the park and ride sites, together with other major developments.

A wide range of systems was considered, but those recommended for further study were guided bus, ultra-light transit and light rail or tramway. Two basic routes were identified, shown in the figure overleaf. A north-south route would link Haxby in the north with Askham Bar in the south and could have branches to Monks Cross and Clifton Moor or Rawcliffe. An east-west route would link the University and Science City in the east with park and ride sites on the outer ring road on the west and serve Acomb and the National Railway Museum. Both routes would serve the railway station and a bus and tram spine through the city centre. The yellow sites on the plan are planned development sites.

While the 2002 study was not taken any further, the idea of trams for York is still around. In 2014 a former York councillor, Christian Vassie, put forward a plan for a modern electric tramway after visiting Brest and Dijon in France which had both opened tram systems in 2012. They had kept their costs down by joint procurement of rolling stock and other equipment.

Mr Vassie suggested one line from Copmanthorpe to the city centre via Dringhouses, Acomb and Holgate to the railway station then northwards to Clifton, Huntington, Haxby and Strensall. A second line would run from Skelton and Rawcliffe through the city centre to Fulford and the University, Grimston Bar and Dunnington.

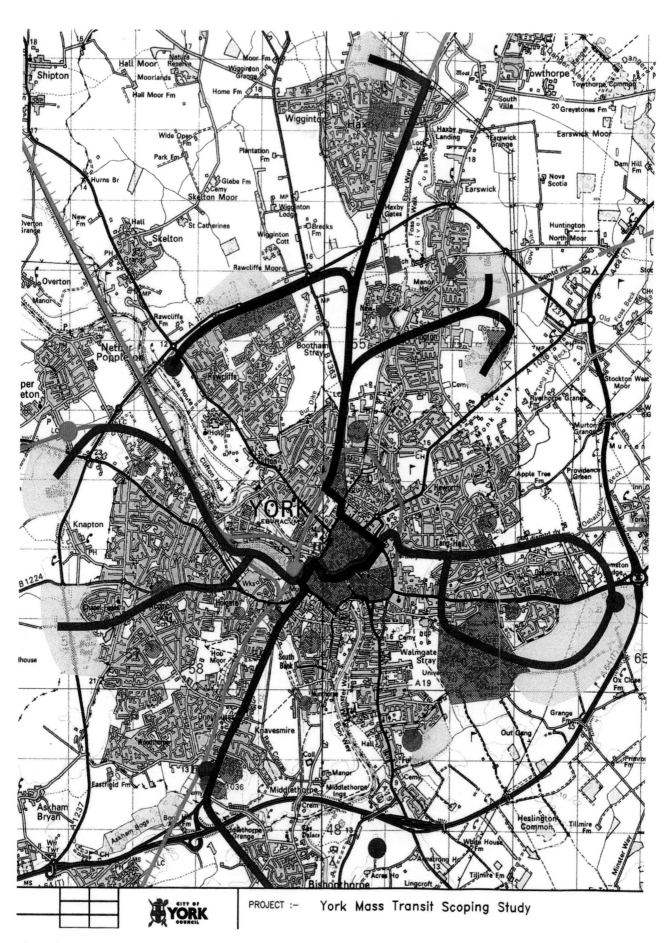

The York Mass Transit Scoping Study route plan in 2002. York City Council

Electric trams served York until 1935. They ran along streets like Museum Street in the shadow of The Minster, and Gillygate, Rougier Street, Coppergate and Walmgate. They could do so again.

York is often considered too small to support a tram system but interestingly its population of over 200,000 is considerably larger than Brest with 145,000 or Dijon with 152,000. Perhaps some day York will escape the category of a *'might have been'* tramway.

23. False starts and wasted plans

In France most urban tramways were abandoned, as they were in Britain, in the thirties to fifties. But in 1973 the French government realised the error of their ways and instituted a new funding mechanism to encourage local authorities to build new transit systems. Initially just in Paris, it quickly spread to all other urban areas throughout France. The principle was simple, a payroll tax on all employers of more than 11 employees was ring-fenced for capital or revenue spending on public transport systems, bus, tram, trolleybus or automated transit. Each authority could decide.

The result over the past fifty years has been a dramatic growth, particularly in new tramways, in towns and cities right across France. The policy has been maintained consistently over the years, not changed every year or two as happens in Britain. Decisions are made at local municipal level, not concentrated in central government. The contrast is stark, Britain lags way behind in the number of new tramway systems built in the past thirty years.

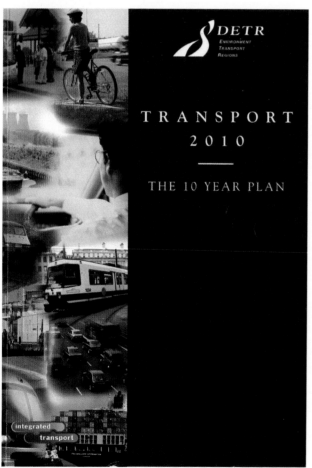

The Government's Ten Year Transport Plan, 2000.

The Ten Year Plan

There have been glimmers of hope. The Ten Year Transport Plan 'Transport 2010' published by the Department of Environment, Transport and the Regions in July 2000 (Ref.48) envisaged up to 25 new light rail lines in major cities and conurbations. This included extensions already planned to Manchester Metrolink, Docklands Light Railway, Tyne and Wear Metro and Nottingham Express Transit. It also included new systems in Liverpool, Leeds, Bristol and South Hampshire, all of which were cancelled or not approved by the same government within a few years.

The Ten Year Plan stated: "There is growing evidence that light rail can be successful in attracting people out of their cars. On Manchester Metrolink for example around 20% of passengers previously used a car for the same journey." The Plan went on to say "We will fund a substantial increase in the role of light rail in our larger cities and conurbations over the next ten years." It never happened.

A target was to at least double light rail passenger journeys by 2010, an admirable objective. If 25 lines *had* been built it would easily have been met. But only a handful were actually built and consequently the increase in patronage was barely 60 per cent. By 2020 the total had been exceeded but it had taken two decades instead of one and many of the hoped for systems had not been built. The increase had been mainly from the four big systems, Tyne and Wear, DLR, Croydon and Manchester (two of which are not tramways).

Affordable Mass Transit

Recognising that the 25 light rail schemes envisaged in the Ten Year Plan had not materialised, the Commission for Integrated Transport produced a Guidance Report under the title of 'Affordable mass Transit' in 2005 (Ref.53). Commission Chairman Peter Hendy went on to become Commissioner for Transport for London and later Chairman of Network Rail.

The Report was in effect a thinly disguised attempt to justify Alistair Darling's cancellation the previous year of three of the tram schemes that were the closest to being fulfilled, on the grounds of cost escalation: Liverpool, Leeds and South Hampshire. Darling had also tried to cancel all the Greater Manchester Metrolink tram extensions, but this created a massive

Affordable Mass Transit, Commission for Integrated Transport.

reaction from politicians, press and public which eventually forced him to change his mind. All those extensions have now been built, but the other three have remained '*might have beens*'.

Given the Government's overriding philosophy, it is perhaps not surprising that the report had a strong emphasis on affordability. In places this resulted in an apparent preference for bus based systems rather than light rail, although the authors would no doubt dispute that. It did contain a large amount of data on capital and operating costs including data on all the light rail schemes then in operation, and a comprehensive list of references. Its primary intention was to assist local authorities in developing high quality mass transit systems. In the ensuing fifteen years only one new tram system was built, Edinburgh (which Darling would also have cancelled given the chance), and no more are yet on the horizon.

Green light for light rail

Some ten years later and a different shade of government produced an encouraging report purporting to herald a new era for light rail, 'Green light for light rail'. (Ref.57) It should perhaps have been called 'amber light for light rail' as it did not open any floodgates, as some would have wished.

It did highlight other variants including Ultra-Light Rail (ULR, sometimes called VLR, Very Light Rail) and Tram-trains and included a useful chapter on reducing the barriers to further investment in light rail.

The Report was well received and Norman Baker MP, Parliamentary Under-Secretary of State for Transport, was credited with taking the subject forward in a way that had not really happened before. It was followed up by a Light Rail Summit with leading figures from the industry to give the whole process a boost. It even mentioned devolving funding to local authorities, as has happened in other countries for years. Another ten years later and devolution of funding was still being more talked about than implemented on the ground.

House of Commons Committee Reports

From time to time Reports are commissioned by the Transport Select Committee of the House of Commons on a wide range of transport topics. These include light rail and tramways. The Transport Committee Fourth Report, Urban Public Transport: The Light Rail Option was published in April 1991 (Ref.35), before the first new generation street running light rail system had opened in Manchester. The Committee consisted of eleven cross party members of parliament under the very able chairmanship of David Marshall MP (Chairman 1987-92).

The Eighth Report of the Environment, Transport and Regional Affairs Committee on Light Rapid Transit Systems (Ref.47) was published in May 2000 and the Tenth Report of Session 2004-05 of the House of Commons Transport Committee on Integrated Transport: the Future of Light Rail and Modern Trams in the United Kingdom (Ref.52) was published in April 2005. By then the Committee was chaired by the late Gwyneth Dunwoody MP (2002-08).

The format is to invite submission of evidence from organisations and individuals on a list of topics which included costs and benefits of light rail, what they need to be successful, how they can be integrated with other transport systems, barriers to development and financing arrangements.

Written evidence is usually submitted by about a hundred organisations and individuals representing promoters, passenger transport executives, local authorities, manufacturers, operators, academics, consultants, user groups and the Department for Transport. Sometimes they were way ahead of their time, for example the 1991 Report which advocated tram trains, but it was nearly thirty years before they started carrying passengers in Sheffield and Rotherham.

The three *'might have been'* tram schemes killed off by Alistair Darling each submitted evidence to the 2004-05 Inquiry: South Hampshire Rapid Transit, Merseytravel and West Yorkshire PTE, but it did not change anything for any of them.

The Committee reached some positive conclusions and clearly would like to have seen more light rail schemes promoted but was realistic about the barriers to success. The Report was very critical of the Department for Transport and made a number of recommendations to improve their input, one of which was to build up its own expertise on light rail. The Department is regrettably still not supported by anyone with light rail experience, thirty years later. The Transport Select Committee also advocated giving more power to local authorities to control their bus services, as a prerequisite to integration.

As so often seems to happen, the Committee undertook another thorough analysis of the issues and produced a valuable report which has not produced a single new light rail project. The *'might have beens'* are alive and well.

DfT Call for evidence on light rail

Another decade and another promising development came in 2019 when the Department for Transport issued its 'Call for Evidence *Light Rail (and other rapid transit solutions)'* seeking to identify opportunities available to introduce new light rail and other rapid transit solutions into towns and cities in England. It did seem to signal a change of attitude in the DfT, almost looking as though they actually wanted to see more tram schemes. Perhaps the realities of climate change were beginning to strike a chord.

Why they should need more evidence when the Department shelves must be weighed down with light rail and tram reports from the last thirty years is beyond belief.

Responses to the 'Call for Evidence' were submitted by a wide range of organisations including local authorities and professional bodies. To date the DfT has been silent on the results, perhaps too bound up with Brexit, a General Election and then the Coronavirus Covid-19. A top level event with the Minister for Transport in Manchester in February 2020 covered trains, buses and cycling but failed to make any mention of trams.

The House of Commons Transport Select Committee visited the Manchester Metrolink mock-up tram body in 1990 on a rare visit away from Westminster. The Chairman, David Marshall MP (first on left) had been a Glasgow tram conductor. (Author Tony Young is on far right.)

24. Never to make it tramways?

Many of the tram projects developed in the latter years of the 20th century have already been described. In this section some of the lesser known ones are outlined. It is unlikely that any of them will ever get built.

Aberdeen

The city of Aberdeen once had a fine tram network with some of the most modern trams in Britain. Twenty new streamlined double deck bogie trams were purchased in 1949 but only ran for less than a third of their life, being scrapped in 1958 when the system closed. It must rank as one of the worst examples of throwing away valuable electric passenger vehicles in British transport history.

Studies in 1989 initiated by Grampian Regional Council reviewed the option for a light rail system but concluded that no worthwhile scheme could be devised and the future lay with bus services.

In 2013 trams were suggested by Aberdeen City Council for two routes, one linking Dyce with the Airport and the other from the harbour to Cove. Strong political opposition was immediate, referring to the disastrous experience with the Edinburgh

tram scheme. If the debate was re-run after the success of Edinburgh trams, perhaps the result would be different.

Belfast

While Dublin has raced ahead since 2004 building its highly successful light rail network, LUAS, Belfast has followed the British tradition of looking at possible tram schemes but failing to make any positive decisions. Northern Ireland Railways first suggested a light rail line in the early 90s using a disused rail alignment from County Down into the city centre and on to Bangor. The study included the discredited rubber tyred GLT as an option. A second scheme was reported in 1991, for a city centre distributor linking car parks, shopping centres and railway stations, possibly with a line to Aldergrove Airport.

In 2003 it was announced that a light rail line was to be built from the city centre to East Belfast. Five years later options were still being tossed around, this time for a light rail line to the Titanic Quarter. A 5 km scheme would run from Great Victoria Street, over the Queens Bridge to the shipyard and then on to Belfast City Airport. This scheme had strong support including from the city's Lord Mayor, but it still didn't happen.

Aberdeen had some of the most luxurious trams in Britain but scrapped them in 1958, years before the end of their lives. Martin Dibbs

Another study had found that bus-based rapid transit produced a positive economic result, while light rail would not. A bus based system could be upgraded to light rail in the longer term future if the demand increased. Approval was given to the bus project, named 'Glider' in 2008 and it finally got under construction in 2014 and opened in 2018. The route runs for 24 km east-west through the city centre.

A tramway would have been segregated throughout, albeit with some street running, but the busway uses conventional bus lanes which do not provide the same level of priority as a tramway. The bus lanes were already used by ordinary service buses as they were completed before the Glider service began. Major problems arose at the Titanic Quarter requiring changes to the bus lane layouts. Target journey times have reportedly not been met but patronage is reported to be growing and additional routes being contemplated. Imagine what Belfast would be like if it had trams like Dublin instead of fancy buses. It 'might have been'.

Brighton

Like most similarly sized towns, Brighton had its own first generation tramway but it was replaced by trolleybuses in 1939, which were themselves replaced by motor buses in 1961. With a population of nearly 300,000, the urban area could well be a candidate for a tram system and studies were undertaken in the 1990s as part of the Brighton Borough Plan. Trams also featured in a consultant's study for East Sussex County Council which also considered trolleybuses and guided buses, trolleybuses being well suited to Brighton's hills (which they demonstrated admirably before being scrapped in 1961).

Nothing came of the studies except more bus priorities, no doubt much needed on the congested streets. Thoughts of rapid transit returned with a demonstration of the Parry Peoplemover in 1994. Two lines were proposed, one extending the Volk's Electric Railway from the Marina to the town centre

A Parry Peoplemover tram in New Road Brighton in 1994.
Royal Pavilion and Museums Brighton and Hove

Volk's Electric Railway in Brighton, the oldest operating electric railway in the world, opened in 1883. Tony Young

Should we be seeing these around Brighton? asked the Brighton Journal in 2016. A tram on the new tramway in Zaragoza, Spain.
Brighton Journal

and the other linking the town centre with the railway station, 7km in total.

It should be recalled that Volk's Electric Railway is the oldest electric railway in the world that is still operating. It was opened in 1883, two years before Blackpool's pioneering tramway but it is not a street-running tramway.

The idea of a tramway for Brighton has been raised more recently in 2016 with support from readers of the Brighton Journal, who stressed the environmental benefits and assumed that the local member of Parliament, Caroline Lucas, would support it, being the only Green Party MP.

Eastbourne

The south coast town of Eastbourne was the first in the world to have a municipal bus service, started in 1903. But it was one of the few towns in England which never had a first generation electric tramway. Many years later it did have a tramway, as described in Chapter 7, a short narrow gauge line along part of the seafront constructed by Modern Electric Tramways Ltd by the late Claude Lane. It ran for almost a mile between Princes Park and Crumbles on a two foot gauge track. The entire operation including the trams were moved to Seaton in Devon where it has been greatly expanded over a three mile riverside route and is very successful.

Like Brighton Council, Eastbourne and East Sussex Councils considered a Parry Peoplemover system in 1995 but this did not result in any firm plans. Perhaps if Eastbourne Council had been more sympathetic in 1969 they might have had an extensive local tramway now.

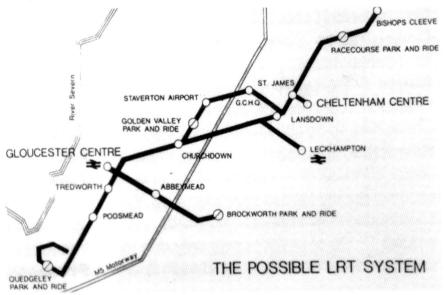

An LRT network for Gloucester and Cheltenham, 1990.

Gloucester

A 24km route for light rail was considered in 1990 to link Gloucester city centre with Cheltenham and park and ride sites. Further studies over the next three or four years included light rail and guided bus options, but no funding was available. The Severn Vale Passenger Transport Initiative was set up with public and private sector representation, initially chaired by Lord Marsh, a former Minister of Transport and Chairman of British Rail for five years. It continued until 1997 but it was accepted that the low density of development and high capital costs made light rail an unlikely candidate for the area. Guided buses remained a possibility.

The light rail concept resurfaced in 2005 and again in 2014, still based on a Gloucester to Cheltenham route, connecting the town centre, racecourse, Bishop's Cleave and possibly Honeybourne. Its population of just over 100,000 makes it an unlikely candidate for any fixed track mode in Britain. In France that would not rule it out.

Hertfordshire

The 10½ km Abbey rail line runs between Watford Junction and St Alban's and is electrified at 25 Kv ac, operated by electric multiple units. In 2009 a plan was unveiled to convert the line to light rail so that the service frequency could be increased. The heavy rail service was limited by the single track and absence of a passing loop and 'one engine in steam' signalling. Future extensions could take trams into Watford High Street and St. Albans city centre which would no doubt have a dramatic impact on patronage. The light rail option was investigated by Hertfordshire County Council with the DfT in 2013, but it was decided not to progress the plan.

The light rail option was still on the cards in a strategy document for Hertfordshire County Council in 2015, although a guided busway was given as a further option. Neither scheme has been progressed, but a more ambitious plan was suggested by Reg Harman the following year called 'Herts Orbital Transit' for a light rail line linking St. Albans with Watford, Hatfield, Welwyn Garden City, Hertford and Broxbourne, a total of 50km. The population of this densely built up area north of London is over 300,000 and could support a tram system. Extensive use could be made of existing and former rail rights of way with short street running sections into town centres. The fragmentation of responsible authorities and absence of potential funding sources make this attractive investment opportunity unlikely to reach fruition. Another excellent concept confined to a *'might have been'* tramway.

Humberside

The City of Hull Tramways once covered much of the city, with over 180 double deck trams and some sections of central reservation on main roads. They were replaced by trolleybuses and the last tram ran in 1945. One is preserved in the city's Streetlife Museum. Hull had some of the most advanced trolleybuses in Britain but they too were scrapped by 1964, leaving the city with no electric traction after 65 years.

A transportation study carried out by consultants in the early 1990s recommended a guided bus network for Hull. The Council adopted the recommended strategy and a first stage 8 km route was defined from the city centre to the Midmeredales development area on the north side of the city at an estimated cost of £15m. A bid for government funding in 1994/95 was unsuccessful and subsequent bids produced no better result. Nothing happended.

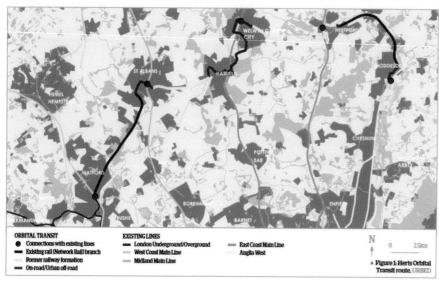

The 'Herts Orbital Transit' light rail route proposed by Reg Harman. LRTA

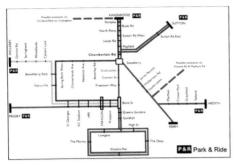

A light rail network for Hull suggested in
2008. *BBC Humberside*

A few years later the BBC Radio Humberside team
proposed a light rail network using mainly redundant
rail alignments around Hull, of which there are many.
Where former rail tracks were not available, central
reservations of main roads could be used, some of
which were former tram reservations. Four routes

were proposed all of which would have park and ride
sites at the outer termini, see diagram on left.

The plans attracted much comment, a majority
favourable but with some criticism of the feasibility,
cost and adverse impacts on traffic and scepticism that
any plan could be achieved. Some even suggested that
monorails would be a better solution! Sadly, a positive
attempt at easing Hull's traffic congestion has become
another *'might have been'* idea.

Kent Thameside

When the Blue Circle quarries in north Kent were
earmarked for a major shopping complex, a pre-
feasibility study was commissioned in 1991 to
consider rapid transit options. Further studies in
1995 proposed a light rail system to link the new
development to Ebbsfleet and the various towns

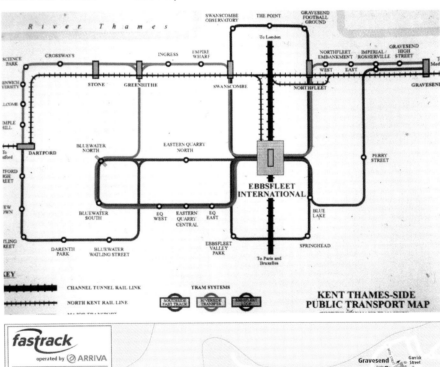

The Kent Thames-side three line
tram network planned in 1995.

The two route Fastrack busway
in Kent Thames-side which might
have been a tramway.

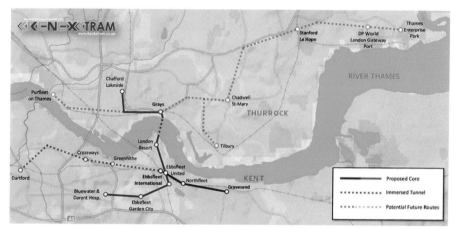

The Kenextram tram network planned by Thames Gateway Tramlink with an immersed tube Thames tunnel.

in north west Kent. A three line tramway would connect Ebsfleet with the Bluewater Regional Shopping complex, Dartford and Gravesend.

The plan was being coordinated by the Kent Thames-side Development Agency, a consortium of local authorities including Kent County Council. A report at the time envisaged that 51% of the route would be on segregated alignment, 45% would be on highway reservation and only 4% street running.

With changes to local government and financial constraints the concept of a tramway disappeared from the agenda to be replaced by a busway following similar routes. Two routes termed 'Fastrack' link Dartford, Gravesend and Ebbsfleet to Bluewater.

Perhaps as loadings increase the possibility of converting it to tramway will again be considered. Until then it remains a *'might have been'*.

One development which could bring trams to at least part of this part of Kent is the private sector proposal known as 'Kenextram', proposed by Thames Gateway Tramlink Ltd. The aim is to provide a 'net zero' emissions transport link across the Thames. A 30km two route tramway with a 1.2km immersed tube tunnel under the Thames would link Grays and Chafford on the north side with Ebbsfleet, Gravesend and Bluewater on the south side.

The Dartford Tunnel opened in 1963 and the Queen Elizabeth Bridge on the M25 in 1991. Both these routes which together form a dual carriageway are heavily congested resulting in serious air pollution in the area. Kennextram would provide a transport solution for local people who have no access to a car, cannot drive or who prefer to use a sustainable means of transport. For most journeys across the Thames a car is essential. The tunnel would be for trams only; if cars were allowed it would defeat the object. It is claimed that demand and an outline business case have been established. Local councils and businesses are strongly in support but no timescales or planning horizons have been specified.

Leicester

The city of Leicester has a population of 350,000, similar in scale to its fellow East Midlands city of Nottingham. But while Nottingham has a successful expanding second generation tram system, Leicester has none. It did have an extensive first generation tramway, running along most of the main radial roads but the last tram ran in 1949.

In 1990 Leicestershire County Council considered a north-south route using part of the former Great Central Railway with street running in the city centre. The benefits were great enough to qualify for government grant under the Section 56 rules of the Transport Act 1968. They did not however believe there would be any realistic chance of funding the project and decided to concentrate on buses and trains instead.

In 1993 the City Council decided to study a possible long term light rail system for the city, perhaps with a central area distributor in the short term. A Parry Peoplemover had been demonstrated in the city in 1992, but low emission minibuses were preferred. Six corridors were

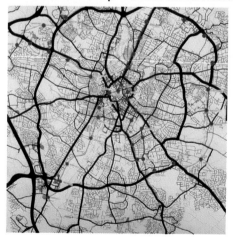

The proposal for a tram network for Leicester in 2019 (red spots indicate potential tram stops). Leicester Conservative Party

considered potential light rail routes for longer term implementation and would generate enough revenue to cover operating costs and create wider economic and user benefits, but not enough to generate the non-user benefits to qualify for government grants. Leicester was added to the 'might have beens'.

A quarter of a century later in March 2019, the local Conservative party proposed a £500m 40 stop tram plan for Leicester. A nine mile route is envisaged as a first phase, partly on highway and partly on reservation. A 'West' phase with 14 stops would begin at the Enderby park and ride and go under Soar Valley Way to Fosse Park then head up to the east of Narborough Road, along the Great Central Way to the De Montfort University campus. It would then run up towards St Nicholas' Circle and up the old Leicester to Swannington railway towards Glenfield where it would join the A50 Groby Road and carry on to stops at the Glenfield Hospital and County Hall before swinging east to a terminal at Beaumont Leys shopping centre.

A second phase of the tram network could serve the city centre and the eastern side of Leicester. There would be a terminal at Jubilee Square in the city centre and from there the tram could run down High Street to a stop by The Clock Tower. Trams would serve Leicester Station and the University. The plans were described as 'conceptual rather than definitive' at this stage.

Sadly the Leicester city Labour Mayor rubbished the idea and claimed it would not be feasible. This was unfortunate because any new tram scheme needs the support of the whole community, across party political or district boundaries. The moment a plan becomes a political football it is lost. Some of the worst first generation tramway abandonments resulted from political clashes, sometimes with a slim majority or even a casting vote. It seems then that Leicester is destined to remain a 'might have been'.

Margate

The seaside town of Margate once had an electric tramway linking it to the adjacent towns of Broadstairs and Ramsgate. The Isle of Thanet Tramways closed in 1937 and since then there have only been buses, and the electric trains which still link the three towns.

In the early 1990s thoughts of providing a railway of some description along the promenade were discussed to attract tourists and support the local economy which, like many seaside resorts, was struggling. The option of a narrow gauge steam railway was not favoured and Thanet District Council produced a report in 1994 for a metre gauge diesel tramway with a motor car and trailer.

The following year a study was commissioned by Kent County Council to investigate the feasibility of a heritage tramway from St Mildred's Bay in the west via Margate railway station to Old Aquarium in the east with a possible extension to Palm Bay, a

A heritage tram on the Seaton Tramway in Devon. Tony Young

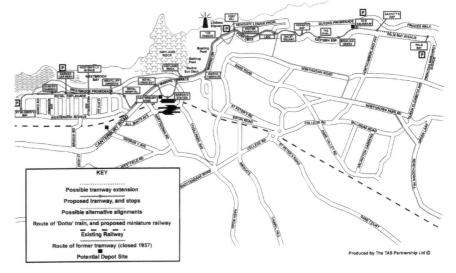

The route for a proposed electric tramway in Margate in 1995. TAS Partnership

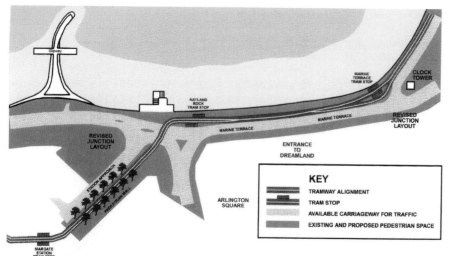

An illustrative alignment for a Heritage Tramway from Margate Station to the Clock Tower. *TAS Partnership*

KEY

	TRAMWAY ALIGNMENT
	TRAM STOP
	AVAILABLE CARRIAGEWAY FOR TRAFFIC
	EXISTING AND PROPOSED PEDESTRIAN SPACE

A Parry Peoplemover heritage tram, a possible option for Margate. PPM

total of 6 km. A metre gauge electric tramway was proposed with twenty stops running along Westbrook Promenade, Marine Terrace and Eastern Esplanade, mainly double track. Many visitor attractions along the seafront would be served including beaches and gardens, amusement parks, the harbour and pier area, the Winter Gardens, tennis courts, putting green, lido and shopping areas.

Much of the route would be on reserved track adjacent to the highway or on some sections within the highway where there was adequate carriageway width. An illustrative alignment was shown along Marine Terrace. Heritage style trams were suggested, about 20m long, articulated and with narrow 2.2m wide bodies. Example tramways which could be a model for Margate were described, the Seaton Tramway in Devon, the Birkenhead tramway and the Parry Peoplemover, which had been demonstrated in a number of towns including Brighton and Folkestone.

Nothing seems to have happened and the Margate tramway ideas have vanished without trace. A *'might have been'* with a slight difference.

Reading

A study in 1989 proposed a two route mainly street running light rail system over 13 km of routes. An east-west route would follow the A4 Bath Road corridor and a north-south route the A33 Basingstoke Road corridor. Both had been first generation tram routes and until 1967/68 were trolleybus routes, extended further out than the tram routes.

A futuristic plan by a group called Reading UK 2050 in 2016 proposed a Central Berkshire and South Oxfordshire Super-Tram network. Four lines would extend to Caversham, Henley on Thames, Twyford, Bracknell, Wokingham, Burghfield and Theale. Interchange with heavy rail and plenty of park and ride sites would be included. It would serve the University and Royal Berkshire Hospital and major shopping centres.

Such a plan may be considered fanciful in Britain but it is comparable with tram and light rail networks in Karlsruhe and Zurich with similar populations.

Sheerness

Sheerness once had a 3ft 6in gauge three route system which opened in 1903. It closed in 1917 earning it the dubious honour of being Britain's first electric tramway closure. It would not be a serious contender for a second generation tramway.

In 1995 a Kent County Council study considered the possibility of converting the existing railway from Sittingbourne to Sheerness to light rail to permit a more frequent service with additional stops. There were several development proposals on the Isle of Sheppey and the access by road or rail was very limited. A light rail line could potentially be extended eastwards from Sheerness to serve more of the island. Perhaps inevitably this became another *'might have been'*.

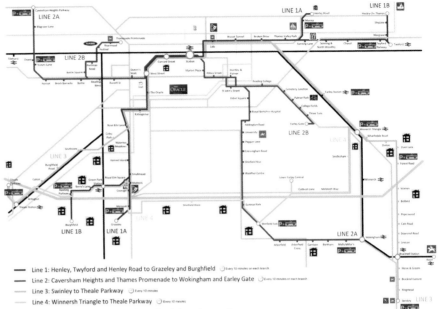

Central Berkshire and South Oxfordshire Super-Tram network.

— Line 1: Henley, Twyford and Henley Road to Grazeley and Burghfield ⏱ Every 10 minutes on each branch
— Line 2: Caversham Heights and Thames Promenade to Wokingham and Earley Gate ⏱ Every 10 minutes on each branch
— Line 3: Swinley to Theale Parkway ⏱ Every 10 minutes
— Line 4: Winnersh Triangle to Theale Parkway ⏱ Every 10 minutes

Central Berkshire and South Oxfordshire Super-Tram

The Briway transit system prototype on the test track in Baynards Park, Surrey in 1991.
Tony Young

Stoke-on-Trent

In 1989 studies began into a light rail system for the Potteries looking at the towns of Tunstall, Burslem, Stoke-on-Trent, Hanley, and Newcastle-under-Lyme. Also considered was the Bri-way rubber tyred minitram system developed by aircraft and helicopter magnate Alan Bristow on his country estate in Surrey. Running on a concrete track it was intended to be fully automatic, similar to the French VAL system, but it never progressed beyond prototype stage. It would not have offered Stoke any benefits over conventional light rail but Mr Bristow was an enthusiastic salesman. (He also tried to sell it to Manchester Airport and failed).

Six corridors were identified which could potentially justify a fixed track system. They would have served Hanley, Stoke, Endon, Etruria and Adderley Green.

In 2000-01 the North Staffordshire LRT Pre-Feasibility Study was carried out for the City of Stoke-on-Trent Council. Some site exploration and basic demographic analysis produced outline route feasibility, mainly for north-south alignments linking the five towns. No firm plans emerged.

In 2018 the local press announced that Stoke-on-Trent City Council was drawing up proposals for a new tram network to link Stoke Station, the city centre and Etruria Valley. The aim was to boost connectivity and cut congestion. Council chiefs were also looking at new light rail services from Stoke to Stockton Brook along the disused Leekbrook railway line and on the Derby line to Blythe Bridge. The authority had been shortlisted for a share of the multimillion 'Transforming Cities Fund' from the government. Nothing more has emerged so it will probably remain as a *'might have been'*.

Swansea

The very first 'tramway' in Britain was the Swansea and Mumbles Railway, opened in 1804 in Swansea running from the town centre to Mumbles Bay at Oystermouth. It was technically a railway as it did not operate on streets and was electrified in 1929 with the largest electric tramcars ever built in Britain. These 106 seater double deckers were the only ones that could operate in coupled trains.

Despite widespread objections the line was closed and replaced by buses in 1960, but various attempts to recreate it have so far failed. In 1990 the Swansea City Council and Wales Tourist Board commissioned a study into re-opening the 4.5 mile line which established that it would be viable. But it remains a *'might have been'*.

Swindon

A consultant's study in 1989, before the first trams had run in Manchester, concluded that a part segregated, part on-street light rail system would be feasible. The first phase would run from Westlea via Wooton Bassett Road to the town centre, continuing northwards via Gorse Hill to Penhill. Extensions would take trams to a park and ride site on the M4, to Walcot, Covingham and Dorcan. The County decided not to progress the scheme, preferring to rely on buses.

Ten years later, seventy years after Swindon's last trams ran, officers at Swindon Council were again thinking about a modern tramway, similar to Manchester, Sheffield or Croydon, to link the town centre, Old Town and the Great Western Designer Outlet Village. The government had earmarked £5bn for tram schemes in Bristol, Leeds, Portsmouth and Merseyside, so perhaps Swindon could be next. Some councillors supported the idea, but others did not see any tram scheme being a viable proposition. In fact none of the other cities they mentioned have yet obtained their system either.

Another ten years later the idea of trams was raised again in 2019, encouraged by the escalating congestion, delays and pollution in the town centre. This time the concept was a tram route linking park and ride sites east and west of the town centre with quick access from the M4 motorway. A hop-on hop-off tram system would make it easy for people to get around the town without having to jump back in their cars to make the journey. It would serve the new Snowasis development as well as the town centre.

With a population of nearly 200,000, if Swindon was in France it would probably have a tram system by now. As it is it will remain a *'might have been'*.

Truro

Like many smaller historic cities, Truro has congestion and parking problems and needed to encourage people to use public transport. A Cornish resident with a knowledge of tram systems, Bob Manders, suggested a possible route in 2003, in discussion with Truro Chamber of Commerce. It would make use of part of an abandoned railway alignment with some new construction and link a Park and Ride site at Threemilestone in the west with the city centre. Stops would serve Treliske Hospital, the College, Newham and Lemon Quay for the shopping centre and bus station.

A low cost low tech solution could use second hand trams from Europe, possibly on metre gauge track. Another option would be to use trams similar to those on the Seaton Tramway. Nothing more was heard of the plan, but a successful park and ride bus service runs from Langarth Park in the West to Tregurra in the East, both with park and ride car parks. This effectively serves the same purpose in the west as a tramway would, the main difference being that the tramway would have been mainly on reserved track and not affected by any congestion.

Windermere

A classic example of an overrun tourist hot spot is the Lake District and its focal point at Windermere. The predominance of car traffic endangers the very peace and environmental quality that visitors clamour for. Professor Paul Salveson, railway advocate extraordinaire, has always dreamt of a Lake District light rail network from Windermere up to Keswick and across to Penrith and Whitehaven. Feeder bus routes would serve places like Coniston with quality park and ride somewhere between Kendal and Windermere for those who want to bring their cars. "The Lakes really needs radical traffic restraint with major investment in the rail and bus services, all operated by the socially-owned Furness Railway, Steamer and Omnibus Co. Perhaps one day he muses". More likely a *'might have been'*.

In Switzerland or Austria such light rail lines would be part of the scenery.

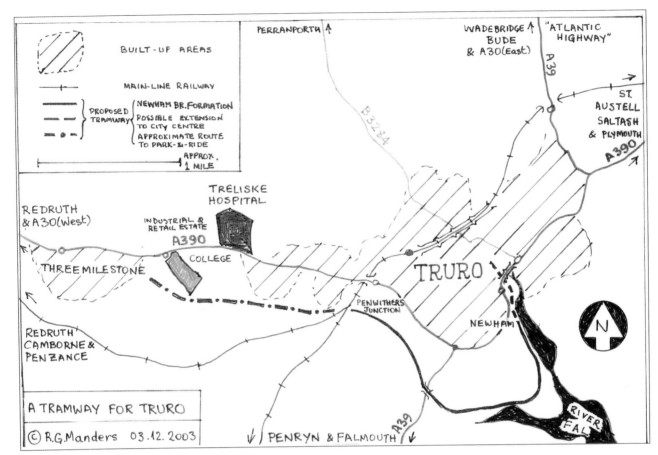

A possible Truro tramway. *Bob Manders 2003*

25. Epilogue

The story of the tramway and of tramcars in Britain is a mixture of huge success and abject failure. While countries like the Netherlands, Belgium, Germany and Switzerland have religiously maintained their tramways from earliest horse drawn days to today's highly efficient environmentally positive networks, Britain has ricocheted from rapid investment to premature abandonment and back to reinstalling light rail systems. France and Spain made Britain's mistake of scrapping most of their first generation trams but realised their mistake and have reversed their policies to create many new tramways.

The wasted investment in first generation lines being built then abandoned and modern trams being launched and then scrapped must run into millions. The cost of putting trams back in the guise of modern light rail networks is many times greater than the cost of their predecessors. But the missed opportunities of building lines or extensions that could have provided a much needed boost to the local economy and environment are worth incalculable sums.

At the beginning of 2021, a report was published by Alstom, 'THE UK'S NEW GREEN AGE A step change in transport decarbonisation' (Ref.63). It shows a large number of towns and cities in Britain where 'opportunities for levelling up the UK's green transport gaps exist' and shows the populations of the areas listed (see map 3 below).
Many of these places are listed in this book, many are 'might have beens'. It is encouraging to see a tram manufacturer (a French one at that) examining the potential market in such detail. None of the reports put out by the Government in the past twenty five years have included anything like this. If they are serious in wanting to know what potential level of interest there is in trams in UK cities, they need only to scrutinise this map.

This book has aimed to show many of the tramways and tramcar designs that could have benefited British towns and cities and contributed greatly to their economic, social and environmental benefits. It is not an exhaustive study, more to give an indication of what we have all missed. To cover all the examples, and bring it fully up to date, would require several more volumes.

The people of Manchester, Nottingham and Croydon now know what a modern tramway can do for their cities. The people of Liverpool, Leeds and Bristol have yet to find out. Will they ever find out?

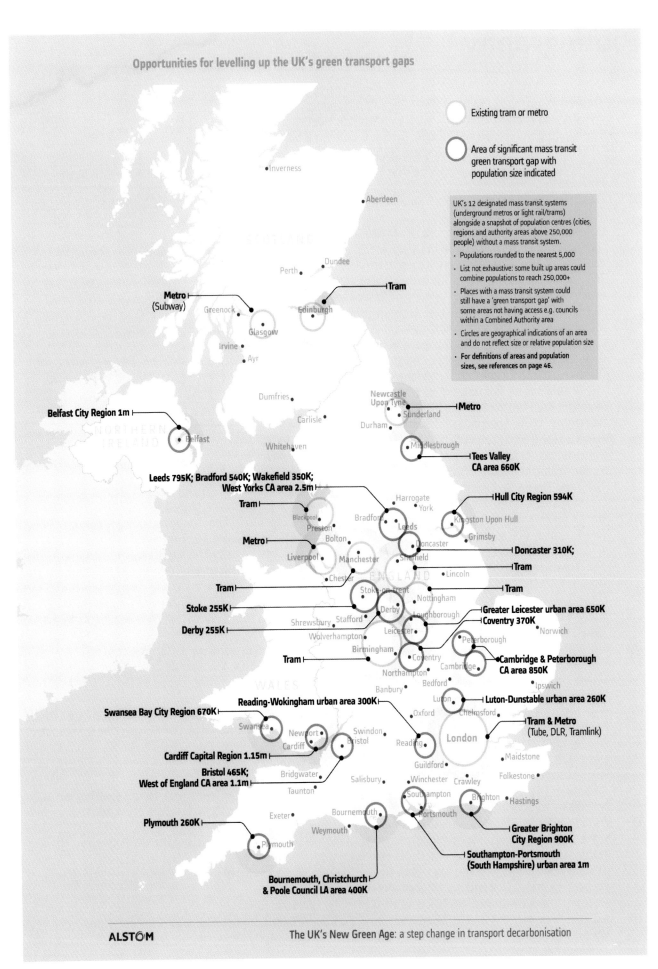

Opportunities for levelling up the UK's green transport gaps

Existing tram or metro

Area of significant mass transit green transport gap with population size indicated

UK's 12 designated mass transit systems (underground metros or light rail/trams) alongside a snapshot of population centres (cities, regions and authority areas above 250,000 people) without a mass transit system.

· Populations rounded to the nearest 5,000

· List not exhaustive: some built up areas could combine populations to reach 250,000+

· Places with a mass transit system could still have a 'green transport gap' with some areas not having access e.g. councils within a Combined Authority area

· Circles are geographical indications of an area and do not reflect size or relative population size

· For definitions of areas and population sizes, see references on page 46.

Metro (Subway)

Tram

Belfast City Region 1m

Metro

Tees Valley CA area 660K

Leeds 795K; Bradford 540K; Wakefield 350K; West Yorks CA area 2.5m

Hull City Region 594K

Tram

Metro

Doncaster 310K;

Tram

Tram

Tram

Stoke 255K

Greater Leicester urban area 650K

Coventry 370K

Derby 255K

Tram

Cambridge & Peterborough CA area 850K

Swansea Bay City Region 670K

Reading-Wokingham urban area 300K

Luton-Dunstable urban area 260K

Cardiff Capital Region 1.15m

Tram & Metro (Tube, DLR, Tramlink)

Bristol 465K; West of England CA area 1.1m

Plymouth 260K

Greater Brighton City Region 900K

Southampton-Portsmouth (South Hampshire) urban area 1m

Bournemouth, Christchurch & Poole Council LA area 400K

ALSTOM

The UK's New Green Age: a step change in transport decarbonisation

Might Have Been Trams and Tramways 177

Bibliography

1. Tramways Act 1870 (33 & 34 Vict. Cap. 78). London. 1870.
2. A History of Canvey Island. A.A.Daly. Frederick Hester. 1902.
3. The Royal Commission on London Traffic. Sir David Barbour (Ch.) (8 volumes). London. 1905.
4. 'Where to go by Car.' John Lingard. 1908.
5. 'Where to go by Tram'. John Lingard. 1924. (Re-printed by Manchester Transport Historical Collection. Rochdale. c.1966).
6. Royal Commission on Transport Report of 1929 "The Control of Traffic on Roads". H.M.S.O. London. July 1929.
7. Passenger Transport Journal. Vol.91 No.2301. August 11 1944.
8. 'Design & Layout of Roads in Built-up Areas', Report of the Departmental Committee set up by the Minister of War Transport. HMSO. London. 1946.
9. Towards Ideal Transport. C.R.Bizeray. Light railway Transport League. Cricklewood. London. 1947.
10. Report on the Future Development of Passenger Transport in Glasgow. E.R.L.Fitzpayne. Glasgow Municipal Transport Committee. Glasgow. May 1948.
11. The Future of Glasgow's Tramways a Fresh Approach to an Old Problem. Light Railway Transport League (Scottish Section). Glasgow. July 1958.
12. Great British Tramway Networks, Fourth edition. Wingate H. Bett and John C.Gillham. LRTL. London. 1962.
13. Tramways of the City of Carlisle. George S. Hearse. George S. Hearse. Corbridge, Northumberland. 1962.
14. The Tramways of Sunderland. S. A. Staddon. Advertiser Press. Huddersfield. 1964.
15. Monorail Application to Rapid Transit in Manchester Preliminary Report. Taylor Woodrow/Safege. November 1965. Southall, Middlesex.
16. Manchester Rapid Transit Study. Report of the Working Party. Ministry of Transport, Manchester Corporation, British Railways. Manchester. September 1967.
17. Public Transport and Traffic. Ministry of Transport. HMSO. London. December 1967.
18. The New Tramway. Peter J Walker. Light Railway Transport League. Cardiff. April 1969.
19. Crossing the Ribble. A.Winstan Bond. Modern Tramway. Vol.32 No.379. July 1969.
20. Transit for Norwich, A Feasibility Study. Peter J Walker et al. Light Railway Transport League. London. 1970.
21. The Tramways of Jarrow and South Shields. George S. Hearse. George S. Hearse. Corbridge. 1971.
22. Transit for Cleveland – a transport study. P J Walker et al. Light Railway Transport League. London. 1972.
23. The Tramways of Halesowen. T Barker. Birmingham Transport Historical Group. BTHG Paper No.4. October 1971.
24. South Lancashire Tramways. E.K.Stretch. Manchester Transport Museum Society. Manchester. 1972.
25. Light Rapid Transit. Some Aspects of Medium-Capacity Urban Rail Systems. P J Walker. Light Railway Transport League. London. 1973.
26. Lifeline 2000. Public transport plan for the future. SELNEC PTE. January 1973. Manchester.
27. Working Paper 21 Advanced urban Transport. I.G.Black, R.F.Gillie, C.J.Longley, T.H.Thomas. Warwick University/Lanchester Polytechnic Urban Transport Research Group. December 1973.
28. London's Tram Subway. C.S.Dunbar. LRTL. London. 1975.
29. A Rail Strategy for Greater Manchester, The Options. Greater Manchester Council. Manchester. April 1983.
30. Rapid Transit for the West Midlands – Introducing the Transport System of the Future. West Midlands PTE. Birmingham. June 1984.
31. Light Rail for London? Report of the BR/LRT Liaison Group. London Regional Transport and British Rail. Autumn 1986.
32. A Study in the decline of the British street tramway industry in the twentieth century with special reference to South Yorkshire. Richard Buckley. (PhD thesis). University of Hull. August 1987.
33. London's Trams. J.Joyce. Ian Allan. Shepperton. 1990.
34. Light Transit systems. Proceedings of symposium in Nottingham. Institution of Civil Engineers. Thomas Telford. London. 1990.
35. Urban Public Transport The Light Rail Option. House of Commons Transport Committee Fourth Report. Volume 1. H.M.S.O. London. 18 April 1991.
36. Transport and Works Act, 1992 Chapter 42. HMSO. London. 1992.
37. A Clean Environment and a Sound Economy: European Transport Solutions for Lancaster and Morecambe. Report of the Light Rail Research Unit, Geography Department, University of Lancaster. A. Redecker, J Whitelegg. Lancaster. 1992.

38. Tramways Remembered East Anglia, East Midlands & Lincolnshire. Leslie Oppitz. Countryside Books. Newbury. 1992.
39. Tramway London, Background to the abandonment of London's trams 1931-1952.Martin Higginson (Ed.). LRTA. Broxbourne. 1993.
40. Street Trams for London. Chris Wood. Centre for Independent Transport Research in London. London. September 1994.
41. A Guide to Kingsway Tramway. London County Council Tramways. Adam Gordon Reprint. Chetwode. 1994. (Original c.1931)
42. New ideas for Public Transport in outer London. London Transport Planning. London. June 1995.
43. A Tramway for Margate A Study for Kent County Council. June 1995. TAS Partnership.
44. A Railway Revolution. Chris Wood. LRTA. Norwich. 1996.
45. The Directory of British Tramways. Keith Turner. PSL.1996.
46. Tramlink Official Handbook. Michael Steward, John Gent and Colin Stannard. Capital Transport. Harrow Weald. 2000.
47. Light Rapid Transit Systems. Eighth Report of the Environment Transport and Regional Affairs Committee. House of Commons. HMSO London. 2000.
48. Transport 2010 The 10 Year Plan. Department for the Environment, Transport and the Regions (DETR). London. July 2000.
49. Norwich Area Transportation Strategy Review. Light Rapid Transit Study. Mott MacDonald. Norfolk County Council. October 2003.
50. Leeds Transport, Volume 3 1932 – 1953. J Soper. Leeds Transport Historical Society. York. 2003.
51. Improving public transport in England through light rail. Eleventh Report of Session 2004-05. House of Commons Committee of Public Accounts. HMSO. London. April   2005.
52. Integrated Transport: The Future of Light Rail and Modern Trams in the United Kingdom. Tenth Report of Session 2004-05. House of Commons Transport Committee. London. HMSO. August 2005.
53. Affordable Mass Transit Guidance. Commission for Integrated Transport. September 2005. London.
54. Leeds Transport Volume, 4 1953 to 1974. J Soper. Leeds Transport Historical Society. York. 2007.
55. Southport in the age of the tram. James Dean and Cedric Greenwood. The Nostalgia Collection. Silver Link. Kettering. 2008.
56. Low cost affordable trams. Tony Young. All Party Parliamentary Light Rail Group. London. December 2010.
57. Green light for light rail. Department for Transport. London. 2011.
58. London Tram Subways – the bigger picture. Ed Humphreys. Tramfare 272, 273, 274. March – October 2013. TLRS.
59. Next Stop Seaton! 60 years of Modern Electric Tramways Limited. David Jay and David Voice. Adam Gordon. Brora. 2014.
60. Lord Ashfield's Trams. Robert J. Harley. Capital Transport. 2014.
61. Trams for Oxford. URBED. The Building Centre. London. 2015.
62. The potential introduction of trams to Bath. Atkins. October 2017.
63. The UK's New Green Age – a step change in transport decarbonisation. Alstom. January 2021.

Also:
Transit Systems reviews (TAS Reports etc.)
Parliamentary Select Committee reports.
Tramway Review magazines.
Modern Tramway magazines.
Tramways and Urban Transit magazines.

Abbreviations

APPLRG	All Party Parliamentary Light Rail Group.
BET	British Electric Traction Company Limited.
BR	British Rail.
BREL	British Rail Engineering Limited.
CC	County Council.
CILT	Chartered Institute of Logistics and Transport.
CRT	Cross River Tram.
DETR	Department for the Environment, Transport and the Regions.
DfT	Department for Transport.
DLR	Docklands Light Railway.
GCT	Glasgow Corporation Tramways.
GEC	General Electric Company Ltd.
GLT	Guided Light Transit.
GMC	Greater Manchester Council.
GMPTE	Greater Manchester Passenger Transport Executive.
GMPTA	Greater Manchester Passenger Transport Authority.
HCC	Hampshire County Council.
ICE	Institution of Civil Engineers.
IMechE	Institution of Mechanical Engineers.
LB	London Borough.
LCCTT	London County Council Tramways Trust.
LRTA	Light Rail Transit Association.
LRTL	Light Railway Transport League.
LRT	Light Rail Transit.
LRV	Light Rail vehicle.
LT	London Transport.
LTHS	Leeds Transport Historical Society.
LUL	London Underground Limited.
LUT	London United Tramways .
MET	Metropolitan Electric Tramways.
MOSI	Manchester Museum of Science and Industry.
MoT	Ministry of Transport.
MTMS	Manchester Tramway Museum Society.
NETCo	New Edinburgh Tramway Company.
PCC	Presidents Conference Car (1930s standard American street tram).
PTA	Passenger Transport Authority.
PTE	Passenger Transport Executive.
PTEG	Passenger Transport Executive Group.
RIA	Railway Industries Association.
SELNEC	South East Lancashire North East Cheshire.
SHRT	South Hampshire Rapid Transit.
SPT	Strathclyde Passenger Transport.
SPTA	Strathclyde Passenger Transport Authority.
SPTE	Strathclyde Passenger Transport Executive.
TfGM	Transport for Greater Manchester.
TfL	Transport for London.
TIE	Transport Initiatives Edinburgh.
TMS	Tramway Museum Society.
ULR	Ultra-Light Rail.
VLR	Very Light Rail.
WMG	Warwick Manufacturing Group.
WMPTE	West Midlands Passenger Transport Executive.

Index

The Light Rail Transit Association

Advocating modern tramways and light rail systems

The LRTA is an international organisation dedicated to campaigning for better fixed-track public transport, in particular tramways and light rail. The Association celebrated its 80th anniversary on 30 June 2017.

Membership of the LRTA is open equally to professional organisations, transport planners and individuals with a particular interest in the subject. Members receive free of charge by post *Tramways & Urban Transit*, the Association's all-colour monthly magazine, as part of their subscription. With tramway and light rail systems being adopted not only in Europe but world-wide, this high-quality journal features topical articles and extensive in-depth news coverage as well as trade news and readers' letters. Details of local meetings in the British Isles are also included.

The LRTA also publishes *Tramway Review* – a quarterly journal devoted to historical material.

Officers of the Association – many with transport industry experience – form part of an extensive network of light rail and tramway information sources, which includes the comprehensive LRTA library.

For more information visit our website: **lrta.org**

To become a member of the LRTA go to: **lrta.info/shop** or e-mail **membership@lrta.org**
Postal address: **LRTA Membership, 38 Wolseley Road, SALE, M33 7AU**

For general enquiries contact: **secretary@lrta.org**
Postal address: **LRTA Secretary, 8 Berwick Pace, Welwyn Garden City, Al7 4TU**

To order copies of our wide range of books go to: **lrta.info/shop**
Orders may be sent by post to: **LRTA Publications, 38 Wolseley Road, SALE, M33 7AU**

Books due to be published by the LRTA over the next eighteen months include:

Modern Trams - Volume 1

Traditional Tramway Architecture

The Tramways of Portugal

Upper Silesia Tramway Guide

Tramways in Milan

Rail Based Public Transport in Canada

Potential authors of books on subjects relevant to the Association's interests are invited to contact the Publications Director of the LRTA at:
24 Heath Farm Road, FERNDOWN, BH22 8JW

Notes

Notes

Notes

Might Have Been Trams and Tramways